MacPerl

Power and Ease

Vicki Brown and Chris Nandor

Edited by Rich Morin

Foreword by Matthias Neeracher

Published by Prime Time Freeware

MacPerl: Power and Ease

Vicki Brown and Chris Nandor
ISBN 1-881957-32-2

Prime Time Freeware   info@ptf.com
370 Altair Way, #150   www.ptf.com
Sunnyvale, CA   +1 408 433-9662
94086 USA   +1 408 433-0727 (fax)

9 8 7 6 5 4 3 2 1

Contents

Part I - Preparation

Part II - Learning The Language

Part III - Advanced Topics

Part IV - Reference

Dedications

To Jennifer

My inspiration in all things
                - *Chris*

We know what we are, but know not what we may be.
Shakespeare, *Hamlet*, 4.5.42

To Dr. Rita R. Colwell

with gratitude and thanks
                - *Vicki*

- *First And Foremost ...*
- *Technical Assistance ...*
- *And Review ...*
- *Ancillary Materials ...*
- *Publicity And Documentation ...*
- *Last But Not Least ...*

Acknowledgements

When you start community-building,
what you need to be able to present is a plausible promise.
Your program doesn't have to work particularly well.
It can be crude, buggy, incomplete, and poorly documented.
What it must not fail to do is convince potential co-developers
that it can be evolved into something really neat
in the foreseeable future.

– Eric Raymond, *The Cathedral and the Bazaar*

This book would have been possible, but not nearly as good or as much fun to create, without the input, assistance, and support of many people. We apologize to anyone we have missed in our acknowledgements below – please understand that any failure to mention your name is a result of our faulty memories, not a comment on your contribution!

First And Foremost ...

First and foremost, our sincere thanks go to Larry Wall, the creator of Perl, and to Matthias Neeracher for deciding that an implementation of Mac-Perl would make a good "weekend project", as well as for his continuing help and support throughout this project! Your work has been our inspiration; we hope we have met your expectations. Without you, there would have been no Perl, no MacPerl, no book.

We also wish to acknowledge Eric Raymond, whose seminal paper "The Cathedral and the Bazaar" inspired us to put our developing chapters up on our web site, accept readers' comments and criticism gratefully, and end up with a much finer product than we could otherwise have achieved.

We're very pleased with our cover art. We hope you find it as inspirational as we do, and we wish to acknowledge and thank the artist, Delight Prescott, for allowing us this opportunity to use her work in our book.

The book wouldn't have been the same without the editorial and publishing skills of Rich Morin. We also have Rich to thank for some of the text, including Chapters 1-3, which allow reader to first peek, then dip, and finally step boldly into what may well be a new world. These chapters, we hope, have made our book accessible to a wider audience!

Vicki and Rich wish to extend special thanks to Chris Nandor for his expertise, his unflagging energy, his sense of humor, and his partnership in this project. Without Chris, this would have been a very different book.

Technical Assistance ...

We wish to thank various friends and relatives of the authors and the publisher for their forbearance, their help in reviewing chapters-in-progress, and their good-humored willingness to be cast in examples. We'd especially like to thank – Banjo, Bill Page, Don Wallace, Doug McNutt, Ed Morin, Erik Fair, Fester, Jennifer Nandor, Joyce Uggla, June Brown, Marilyn Krieger, Rachel Morin, Rick Auricchio, Rick Beveridge, Shira Zucker, Tom Brown, and Valerie Wingfield.

We received some invaluable assistance and ideas along the way from several employees of Apple Computer, Inc. In particular, our thanks go to Carl De Cordova, Chuq Von Rospach, and Colin McMaster.

For technical assistance on the fine points of Perl and MacPerl programming, the Macintosh Toolbox, Apple Events, and MPW Perl, we wish to thank – Alan Fry, Charles Albrecht, David Blank-Edelman, Doug McNutt, Eric Zelenka, John Saxton, Matthias Neeracher, and Randy Ray.

For computer science lore and anthropological insights, technical assistance on points of programming in general, and for sundry discussions, comments, and ideas, we wish to thank – Dick Karpinski, Eric Raymond, and Gene Dronek.

And Review ...

The MacPerl email list and the MacPerl Pages (www.ptf.com/macperl) have each served as a great source of inspiration, examples, reviewers, and assistance. Through these, we reached our first-line audience. We received a wealth of insightful and helpful comments on our draft chapters. The book would not have been the same without this input and feedback.

Our thanks go to – Alan Lanning, Alex MacAuley, Alex Satrapa, Andreas Marcel Riechert, Andrew McKenzie, Ben Cranston, Ben Ko, Bob Taylor, Craig Patchett, David Beck, David Schooley, Elton Hughes, Eric Petersen, Eve Edelson, Frederick Hirsch, George Michel, Graham Barr, Greg Hanek, Hans Mulder, Isaac Wingfield, Jim Burton, John Baxter, and John Canning.

Also to – Jon Bjornstad, Joseph DiVerdi, Karsten Meier, Ken Arnold, Malcolm Ross, Mark Gordon, Mark J. Lilback, Mark Manning, Mark Rauterkus, Mason Thomas, Nils Dahl, Packy Anderson, Paul Schinder, Peter Furmonavicius, Peter Gradwell, Peter Prymmer, Renay Miller, Rich Pavonarius, Richard Lewis, Richard Warren, Scott Bilow, Sean Mahony, Will Merrill, and Xah Lee.

And, for cool code submissions, examples, and/or submissions of stories ("How I use MacPerl"), our thanks to – Alan Fry, Alex Satrapa, Angus McIntyre, Ben Wilkes, Dave Belcher, Darin Morley, Georg Bauer, Hai Ng, James Meehan, Josh Gemmell, Ken Tanaka, Lindsay Davies, Mike Pasini, Paul Schaap, Paul Steinkamp, Philip L. Robare, Sean M. Burke, Tom Cloney, and Tomas Garcia Ferrari.

Ancillary Materials ...

This product would not have been quite the same without the inclusion of the ancillary software on the CD-ROM. For this, we must acknowledge the many tireless authors and maintainers of the CPAN, as well as Jon Orwant and David Fickes (Advice Press) for their assistance in helping us put a CPAN snapshot on the disc.

Many thanks to the Freeware, Shareware, and Commercial application authors who have allowed us to distribute their work, including – David Schooley (AETE Converter), RavenWare Tools (AETracker), Peter Keleher (Alpha), Peter Lewis (Stairways Software: Anarchie, Internet Config, Netpresenz, ...), Bare Bones Software (BBEdit), Brad Hanson (BBEdit Perl Plug-Ins), Lindsey Davies (BBEdit Perl palette), and Rolf Braun (Better Telnet).

Also – John Norstad (Disinfectant), Dartmouth College (Fetch), Simon Brown (FontView), David Catmull (Icon Machine), José Gutiérrez (MacGzip), KlepHacks Shareware (Netbots), PreFab Software (PreFab Player),

Gregory Dow (Progress Bar), Aladdin Systems (StuffIt Expander), Sauro Speranza (Suntar), and Chris Hawk (Quid Pro Quo).

Thanks to Apple Computer for MPW and other materials, to Jon Howell for the FAQ-O-Matic (used on the MacPerl Pages), to MetroWerks for the copy of CodeWarrior (used in Chapter 23, *Building MacPerl and Extensions*), and to MindVision Software for Developer Vise (used in the MacPerl Installer).

Publicity and Documentation ...

Perl in general and MacPerl in particular are seeing more press these days. Our hats are off to the folks who are writing about Perl and MacPerl, and to the publishers who are helping to get the stories out. In particular, thanks to – Charles Cave, Dale Dougherty, Doug Pryor, Eric Gundrum, Jon Orwant, and Neal Ticktin.

The Internet makes all manner of communication possible; we can all be publishers on the World Wide Web. Thanks to Sandra Silcot for the original mailing list archive and for the *MacPerl Primer*; to Bob Dagliesh, Bob Wilkinson, and Hal Wine for the *MacPerl FAQ*; and to David Turley for the MacPerl mailing list archive. For MacPerl and Perl Web pages of all sorts, thanks to – Adam Weisser, Brad Cox, Chuck Houpt, Craig Patchett, Michiko Nozu, Paul Schinder, and Peter Chen.

Last But Not Least ...

The authors wish to thank their families for their support and interest (even if they probably won't need a copy of the book, they'll gladly accept one and ask to have it autographed :-). Our thanks to the Browns, the Nandor and Nobles clans, and the Morins, Pages, and Zuckers.

The authors also wish to thank their co-workers and technically-minded programmer friends for various mind-bending discussions and for putting up with a lot of MacPerl evangelism; the members of the MacPerl mailing list, the Perl/MacPerl IRC chats, and the USENET Perl newsgroups for questions, answers, and occasional debate; the authors of our excellent Perl reference books; and the Perl 5 Porters for their commitment to a better Perl.

Finally, we'd like to thank you, the reader, for buying this book and helping to give MacPerl a wider audience. This is for you. Happy programming!

- *Typography*
- *Terminology*
- *Personal Pronouns (he, she, or it?)*
- *Style*
- *Footnotes*
- *URLs*

Conventions

> *There is nothing sacred about convention:*
> *there is nothing sacred about primitive passions or whims;*
> *but the fact that a convention exists*
> *indicates that a way of living has been devised*
> *capable of maintaining itself.*

– George Santayana, *Persons and Places: The Middle Span*

Computer programming languages are not the only means we have of encoding information. To aid us in our explanations, we use the following conventions throughout this book:

Typography

We use different fonts and type faces to convey information about the items we are discussing:

Bold font is used the first time a **keyword** or important term is used, or when we wish to emphasize a term that you should recognize. Many of the words you find in bold can also be found in the Index.

Italic font is used for chapter titles, section names, and titles of recommended reference works. It may also be used when we want to emphasize a point. If you see something in italic font, *pay attention*.

Geneva font is used for "Macintosh computer voice". This includes much of what you might see on your screen, such as the names of files and folders, window titles, dialog box items, and menus. You may see **bold Geneva** used if we are referring to something important, such as a menu item you should remember.

Fixed width font is used for "Perl computer voice". When we ask you to type some code on the keyboard, or show you a response that Perl provides, we'll use a fixed width font such as `Courier`. Fixed width font is also used for "MPW voice".

Terminology

If you are new to programming languages, you may find that some of our terminology is new as well.

Scripts and Other Programs

We will refer throughout the book to the terms **script** and **program**. Programs are sets of executable code which tells the computer to do something. A script is a type of program, usually **interpreted**, as compared to a **binary** or **compiled** program. Scripts are often shorter, or perhaps simpler than compiled programs; however, the distinction between scripts and other types of programs is somewhat arbitrary. For now, consider that all scripts are programs, but not all programs are scripts.

Characters

The following are new names for some familiar characters:

Quotation marks: ", ', and `

You may be more familiar with these as "quotes", 'apostrophes', and `what are those?`. We call them "**double quotes**", '**single quotes**', and `**backquotes**`. Occasionally, you will see references to the single quote as a 'forward quote', to further distinguish it from the also single but back-angled backquote.[1] Colloquially, quote marks may be referred to as **tick marks** or ticks.

Slash marks: / and \

The **slash**, /, may be familiar to you from other contexts. You may not be as familiar with the **backslash**, \. Both are used throughout Perl. The backslash is sometimes referred to as the **escape character**.

---

[1] Some, but not all, fonts show this quote as "leaning forward", ´.

Brackets and Braces: [ ], { }, < >

Technically, these characters are all termed **brackets**, specifically, [**square brackets**], {**curly brackets**}, and <**angle brackets**>.[2] A more specific and less verbose name for the curly brackets is **braces**. Left and right angle brackets may be referred to separately in certain contexts as **less than** and **greater than** signs or as **left arrow** and **right arrow**.

Personal Pronouns (he, she, or it?)

Throughout this book, we occasionally refer to the reader, or to the MacPerl user, in the third person. When we do so, we use the word "he" in its traditional English grammatical sense as a gender-neutral singular pronoun. We considered several possible "politically correct" alternatives, but settled on traditional grammar as the form which best met our personal tastes. If you prefer some other pronoun, feel free to substitute it in your mind as you read.

Style

Indentation

Computer programs in general, and Perl programs in particular, tend to have a "**block structure**" which can (and should!) be emphasized by indentation. Here, for instance, is some example code without indentation:

```
while (...) {
if (...) {
...
}
}
```

Here is the same code, indented by two spaces per level (the standard followed in this book and preferred by some programmers):

```
while (...) {
  if (...) {
    ...
  }
}
```

---

[2] Parentheses, ( ), are sometimes called "round brackets", but you are unlikely to find this usage in this book.

Here is the same code, indented by four spaces per level (the standard recommended by Larry Wall and followed by many Perl programmers):

```
while (...) {
    if (...) {
        ...
    }
}
```

Our choice of a two-space indentation has more to do with the constraints of book publishing than with any preference on our part. We use four spaces in our own coding, but acknowledge that the two-space style is perfectly readable, if a bit cramped for our taste.

Neither of us, by the way, likes the "eight-space" indentation style. It strikes us as hard to read and also uses up a lot of valuable space on each line. On the other hand, TMTOWTDI (the Perl motto: There's More Than One Way To Do It). The important thing, in any case, is consistency!

Punctuation

In computer programming, precise syntax is necessary to ensure that the computer does what the programmer expected. Authors who program computers frequently require similar precision in their English prose.

Quoted punctuation is a particular example of this. In Perl, there is a world of difference between the command

```
print 'hello';
```

and the command

```
print 'hello;'
```

In writing this book, we subscribe to the convention that punctuation is placed within the closing quote marks only if the punctuation itself is part of the quoted material.[3]

Parentheses

Many computer programming languages are quite strict about syntax rules, such as using parentheses to enclose the parameters of function calls (and

---

[3] Doubting readers are referred to *Webster's Standard American Style Manual*, Merriam-Webster, Inc.

other places).[4] Perl, however, takes a more liberal approach. Parentheses are generally neither required nor forbidden – as the programmer, it's often your call. Parentheses can be used to improve the clarity of the code. At other times, they may just be a nuisance.

For this book, we've taken the approach that parentheses are more helpful than not, so you will see a lot of parentheses in our examples. As you become familiar with Perl, you can decide when to omit parentheses from your code.

> **Note:** There are certain times (e.g., when creating lists or in certain control flow statements) when parentheses may be required to make the expression unambiguous. If you have been omitting parentheses and you get a seemingly inexplicable syntax error, try adding parentheses to see if that solves the problem.

One common place where parentheses are frequently left out is the `print` statement. As you saw above, we wrote

```
print 'hello';
```

We could just as easily have written

```
print('hello');
```

Neither approach is wrong, but the unparenthesized version is somewhat more common.

Our goal for this book is to teach you Perl. Our secondary goal is to teach you how to write clear, maintainable, easy to understand code. Throughout the book, we will make recommendations for what we regard as proper syntax, and we'll usually take a fairly conservative approach. Whether you decide to take our advice is your decision. The important thing is that your programs work and (preferably) that other people can understand them!

Footnotes

Throughout the book, we have used footnotes to set off interesting[5] bits of information which are related to, but not required by, the main text. We use footnotes to point out some of the more esoteric aspects of Perl, to put things

---

[4] If you don't know what a function is, don't worry. We'll explain in the next few chapters.

[5] At least, we think they are interesting!

into historical context, to make comparisons to other languages, or just to make a side comment.

Don't worry if the information presented in the footnotes seems advanced or even a bit strange. That's why we've set it off in a footnote!

URLs

We have omitted the leading "`http://`" from most of the World Wide Web **URLs** (**Uniform Resource Locators**) listed in the book. If a site needs to be accessed by some other means (e.g., FTP), we will say so explicitly.

Foreword:

MacPerl Escapes From The Laboratory

*I also record those events which led, by insensible steps,
to my after tale of misery, for when I would account to myself
for the birth of that passion which afterwards ruled my destiny
I find it arise, like a mountain river,
from ignoble and almost forgotten sources;
but, swelling as it proceeded, it became the torrent which,
in its course, has swept away all my hopes and joys.*

– All quotes from Mary Shelley, *Frankenstein*

In summer 1991, I was called by the Swiss army to do my compulsory 17 weeks of military basic training. Soon, I had settled into a reasonably comfortable office job and arranged myself with the funny habits and dress code expected from me. However, I experienced severe withdrawal from my programming habits, and started looking for a programming project to do on weekends. Since I had ported Gawk (GNU Awk) to the Macintosh the preceding winter, and recently had become aquainted with Perl on UNIX machines, I decided to attempt a port of Perl.

*It was on a dreary night of November
that I beheld the accomplishment of my toils.
With an anxiety that almost amounted to agony,
I collected the instruments of life around me,
that I might infuse a spark of being
into the lifeless thing that lay at my feet.*

The port proceeded quickly, and in August 1991, I was able to report the first partial successes. Tim Endres saw one of my USENET postings and started getting involved in cleaning up my initial attempts. When my military service ended in November, I had a little more spare time for the port. In January, we announced the first release of MacPerl, 4.0.2, to the public.

The first release was written for the Macintosh Programmer's Workshop (MPW), a command line oriented programming environment. MPW provides a natural habitat for tools like perl, and I had assumed that my target audience would have MPW anyway. The release consisted mainly of an MPW tool looking very similar to the way it looks today, supporting perl 4.019, which back then was the latest and greatest release of Perl.

As a gesture to the Macintosh Human Interface, there were the commands "ask", "answer", and "pick", which would put up simple dialog boxes. Almost as an afterthought, I also created a very primitive standalone application, so people could run a script on a machine where they didn't have MPW installed.

The favorable reception of our efforts encouraged me to do further work on library functions, and during 1992, I added first DBM support and then, in December, socket support. By that time, it had become clear that I wouldn't get rid of MacPerl-related email anytime soon, so in January 1993, I created a mailing list to support it.

> *I had gazed on him while unfinished; he was ugly then,*
> *but when those muscles and joints were rendered capable of motion,*
> *it became a thing such as even Dante could not have conceived.*

The original Macintosh port of Perl was written for the Macintosh Programmer's Workshop (MPW), a command line oriented programming environment. MPW provides a natural habitat for tools like Perl, and I had assumed that my target audience would have MPW anyway. User feedback, however, quickly proved that the primitive standalone application I had included in the first release as a last-minute thought was more popular than the MPW-based version, and users urged me to make the standalone version friendlier.

1993 turned out to be an eventful year for MacPerl. In Spring, Apple asked for permission to put MacPerl on their E • T • O (Essentials • Tools • Objects) CD-ROM series. I was thrilled to see my work immortalized in this way and looked forward to seeing it spread to a wider audience.

The wider audience, however, also meant new users who no longer agreed with my original view of what MacPerl was about. User feedback increasingly proved that the primitive standalone application was more popular than the MPW-based version, and users urged me to make the standalone version friendlier.

In summer 1993, I was finally ready to address the requests for an implementation of Perl in a real Macintosh application with better online help. By fall 1993, the MacPerl user interface had a look that it has kept (with minor adjustments) until today. In October 1993, I released version 4.1.0, the first version with a true Macintosh human interface.

> *For the first time, also, I felt what the duties*
> *of a creator towards his creature were,*
> *and that I ought to render him happy*
> *before I complained of his wickedness.*

The next three years, I focused on keeping MacPerl up to date with the big external changes that occurred: I spent most of 1994 getting MacPerl to run natively on Apple's new PowerPC architecture (and borrowing PowerPC machines for my development and debugging work). By the time I released MacPerl 4.1.4, the first PowerPC native version, in December 1994, Perl 5 had come out, so I spent most of 1995 porting Perl 5 and reexamining all my old code in the process. The MacPerl user base had grown a lot by then, and new users kept finding new bugs and shortcomings, so 1996 was a year for various bug fixes and user interface tweaks.

Once the basic porting work for Perl 5 was done, I finally was able to pursue another project which I had wanted to try for a long time, and in 1997, I could finally start creating MacPerl interfaces for the Macintosh Toolbox, in order to make it possible to tackle a wider range of tasks with MacPerl and to use it for creating prototypes of Macintosh applications This project is still a work in progress (I just did the Sound Manager interfaces a few weeks ago).

Although 1998 will bring great changes to my professional and personal life, I suppose there will always remain some room in it for MacPerl, and always something to be improved: New OS versions, new versions of Perl, maybe even a new, improved, user interface for MacPerl itself. Who knows?

> *What do you demand from your captain?*
> *Are you, then, so easily turned from your design?*
> *Did you not call this a glorious expedition?*
> *And wherefore was it glorious?*
> *Not because the way was smooth*
> *and placid like a southern sea,*

> *but because it was full of dangers and terror,*
> *because at every new incident your fortitude*
> *was to be called forth and your courage exhibited,*
> *because danger and death surrounded it,*
> *and these you were to brave and overcome.*

Now, in early 1998, a little more than six years after the initial release of MacPerl, I'm happy and proud to be invited to write a foreword for this book, the first ever book to be devoted entirely to MacPerl.

With the publication of *MacPerl: Power and Ease*, MacPerl has escaped from the laboratory for good: With a book and a CD-ROM to its name, it has now undoubtedly become a *bona fide* product, and with Vicki Brown's and Chris Nandor's excellent presentation, I'm confident that it is now accessible to a much wider range of users than ever before.

All that remains for me to do is to exhort you to go forth, put MacPerl to use, and, above all, never to forget to have fun!

Matthias Neeracher, April 1998

Part I

Preparation

Never believe on faith,
See for yourself!
What you yourself don't learn
you don't know.

– Bertolt Brecht, *The Mother*, 1932

Each traveler should know what he has to see,
and what properly belongs to him,
on a journey.

– Goethe, quoted in Johan Peter Eckermann's
Conversations with Goethe, 1823

Chapter 0:

Introduction

Humans like history,
like to know why things start and end,
like to have reasons for it...

– James Herndon, *How to Survive in Your Native Land*

For many people, programming is a fearsome and formidable thing. Programmers are the wizards of this modern technological world, considered by many to have powers beyond those of ordinary "users". The Macintosh, with its user-friendly interface, ease of use, and dearth of accessible programming tools, has, we're sorry to say, perpetuated this belief.

On many computer systems, programming languages are just an extension of the normal **command language** that makes the computer work. The Macintosh's mouse-oriented interface, although comfortable to use, insulates its users from both command and programming languages.

The purpose of this book is to show you that programming is within your grasp. Like the rider on our cover, you can harness the power of the programming dragon. Our Perlescent dragon is formidable, and extremely powerful, but the rider has him firmly in hand. Together, they can work wonders of great power, going places they never dreamed possible, all through the "magic" of programming.

What Is Perl?

Perl (and, by extension, **MacPerl**) is a convenient and powerful language for administrative programming, CGI scripting on the World Wide Web, data analysis and filtering (e.g., error checking and reformatting), network programming, and more. In short, Perl can be used for almost any programming project you may have in mind.

> **Note:** Perl is either the "Practical Extraction and Report Language" or, less formally, the "Pathologically Eclectic Rubbish Lister". Really.

Perl is an **interpreted**[1] language with a substantial support library. Because most Perl code is distributed in source (human-readable) form and because the library code has been **ported** to many operating systems, Perl code can be quite portable. Whether a piece of code actually *is* portable depends, as always, on the programming techniques chosen by the code's author(s).

On Unix systems, Perl is well on its way toward taking over all substantial scripting functions, supplanting traditional Unix tools such as sh ("Bourne shell"), awk, and sed. On Macintosh systems, Perl can be used just as readily (with the added attraction that there is nothing to "unlearn").

Perl was created in 1987 when its author, Larry Wall, decided that existing scripting languages were insufficiently powerful for the distributed bug reporting project he was working on. Seeing the potential in his new tool, Larry was gracious enough to release Perl as **freeware** (freely redistributable software).

Other programmers picked it up, tried it, liked what they saw, and suggested enhancements and modifications. In only a few years, Perl grew substantially, both in capabilities and in adherents, and was soon well on its way to becoming one of the most powerful and popular computer languages in use today. Although Perl was originally written for the Unix operating system, it has since been ported to (made to work with) many different systems.

The recent rise in popularity of the World Wide Web has assured the popularity of Perl for some time to come. Perl is not a "strongly-hyped language" like **Java**, but it has shown itself to be an indispensible tool for creating and maintaining Web sites. Perl is used for **CGI scripting**, site management, and many other duties.

---

[1] To be precise, Perl code is not interpreted directly. The code is first "compiled" into a more executable form (i.e., *syntax trees*) within the Perl process. This modified form of the code is then interpreted. A "real" compiler (i.e., one which generates machine codes) is also under development, for those who care strongly about either execution speed or the ability to distribute binary (hence, relatively private) programs. (We don't!)

MacPerl has also been in existence for several years (the first version was released in 1991), but its popularity has not increased at the same rate, and certainly not to the level we feel it deserves. The Macintosh is a friendly, easy to use, and very popular computer system. MacPerl is an elegant and friendly Macintosh adaptation of an extraordinarily powerful (and popular) programming language. Why, we wonder, hasn't it taken off?

We believe that the lack of clear, printed documentation and formal distribution methods has been a large part of the problem. With no introductory or printed reference material, and no Macintosh-oriented distribution CD-ROM, many prospective MacPerl users might well feel apprehensive about getting involved.

And, because very few Mac-related magazines cover programming issues, many potential MacPerl users may not even know that a Macintosh version of Perl exists! It is our hope that this product will resolve most of these issues, helping the MacPerl community to grow substantially.

What About AppleScript?

The Macintosh is a wonderful, easy-to-use, and powerful system. It is also inherently interactive. To perform a task, the user must (usually) move the mouse, select an icon, click a button, and otherwise interact with the computer. Sometimes, it would be nice to automate these interactions so they can take place without the user's presence, intervention, and possible mistakes!

AppleScript is Apple's answer to this need. AppleScript is a **scripting** language for the Macintosh. The **scripts** send **Apple Events** (request and notification messages) to **scriptable applications** (applications that have been designed to accept these events). Using AppleScript, any Macintosh user can write or run a simple program to automate many of the ordinarily interactive aspects of using the Mac.

For example, one could use a script to tell the Finder to open an application or to empty the Trash. AppleScript can tell applications to do things as well; you might use a script to tell your email program to connect to the mail server and download any new messages. Thus, if you have used AppleScript, you may be asking yourself what MacPerl can do for you that AppleScript cannot. The answer is: plenty!

AppleScript was designed to "talk to" Macintosh applications, automating steps that users would otherwise perform interactively (using the mouse and menus). Perl, in contrast, was designed to work primarily with data.

A typical Macintosh system holds a large number of data files: spreadsheet and data base files, word processor documents, and more. In fact, to the Finder, every document (and folder!) is a form of data. Where AppleScript excels at working with programs, Perl excels at working with data – performing extractions, calculations, or transformations at your command.

Using MacPerl, you can have the best of both worlds. MacPerl is able to send AppleScript commands and Apple Events from inside of your MacPerl program. Thus, you can use the interaction automation features of AppleScript in conjunction with the powerful data transformation features of Perl, all in one powerful program. This feature of MacPerl is so important that we've devoted an entire chapter (in Part III of this book) to AppleScript and Apple Event programming with MacPerl.

What About Other Languages?

Although the Macintosh was designed to be usable without requiring its users to program, programming languages for the Macintosh have been in existence and readily available for many years. These have ranged in complexity and cost from simple and inexpensive (e.g., **HyperCard**) to complex and often expensive (e.g., commercial **C/C++** code development packages).

With the advent of Apple Events, several new languages have become available which comply with Apple's **Open Scripting Architecture** (**OSA**). We covered AppleScript in the previous section. Userland **Frontier** is a very popular freeware OSA compliant language with a more **algebraic syntax**.

Many application programs, such as spreadsheets and data bases, contain specialized internal scripting languages (e.g., **Visual Basic**). Freeware and shareware implementations of common languages, such as **Tcl** and **Python**, are available for downloading from many servers. Why, then, should you be learning MacPerl?

First, it's not just because we think Perl is better than all of these other languages.[2] Perl is a very popular and well-used language. When you start

---

[2] We actually do think so, but we'd probably get into an argument with some people if we said so, and that's not what we're here for!

learning Perl, you'll be able to find many books on the subject (including this one!). You'll also be able to find many people (e.g., on the USENET) who can help answer your questions if you get stuck.

Fundamentally, however, most popular computer languages are good for something; if they weren't, they would no longer be popular. When choosing a language for a project, you should use a combination of criteria:

• Are you already competent in a language that can do the job?

• What special features would you like (i.e., help to make a language particularly well suited to the problem you need to solve)?

• Are there books, tools, user groups, and libraries of examples and support code to help you get started in using the language?

• Will the language you choose be applicable to other problems in the future? That is, can you **leverage** your programming skills?

Perl is an excellent, flexible language that can be used for many different types of projects. Perl's large and active user community has provided many examples, resources, and tools. We think you'll like Perl, once you've tried it. Rather obviously, that's why we wrote this book!

Even if you've already been programming on the Macintosh in another language, give MacPerl a try. You don't have to give up on other languages, but you are quite likely to be very impressed by the things MacPerl can do.

If, after trying MacPerl, you don't find that it fits your needs, feel free to give this book to a friend. The choice of language is also a personal one, after all the technical reasons have been satisfied. The most important criterion is that you be able to solve the problems you encounter with the language you choose.

Scope

This book has a very large charter. It starts with introductory computer programming concepts, moves on to actual syntax (using MacPerl), then proceeds to increasingly complex and specific topics, including binary file manipulation, CGI scripts, network programming, and more. In order to meet these goals, we have made some carefully-considered compromises.

Specifically, this book omits or abbreviates coverage of some advanced Perl constructs. These are well covered by other books (in particular, the O'Reilly offerings) and would have made this book unreasonably large. Because in Perl **"There's More Than One Way To Do It"** (**TMTOWTDI**), we have been able to demonstrate all of the critical MacPerl concepts without resorting to the more esoteric Perl programming idioms.

You will be able to make very good use of MacPerl without venturing into Perl's more arcane constructs. Consequently, this book can function as a self-contained reference for the essential parts of the language.

We recommend, however, that you go on to investigate the larger world of Perl programming. Perl is a very big and powerful language; a proper under-standing of it will introduce you to a substantial amount of computer science!

Audiences

Wherever there are beginners and experts, old and young,
there is some kind of learning going on,
and some kind of teaching.
We are all pupils and we are all teachers.

Gilbert Highet, *The Art of Teaching*, 1950

The prospective audience for this book, like the Macintosh community, is extremely diverse. Some readers will be experienced programmers; others will have no knowledge of programming at all. In addition, the readers' motivations will vary, spanning curiosity, business or educational needs, and more; no one description could possibly cover every possible reader!

Some things, however, are clear. Although you do not need to have any particular knowledge about programming, you should be comfortable with Mac OS and interested in learning how to make better use of your machine.

As an experienced Macintosh user, you should know how to launch applications, use menus, edit text, and so forth. In addition, you should recognize and be familiar with the most common menus – File, Edit, Help – and their standard items – New, Open, Close, Save, Quit, Copy, Cut, Paste, Undo.

You should also have an interest in learning new things. Specifically, you should be interested in learning how to program your Macintosh! Although we are willing to take on students who merely *need* to learn programming, our real motivation comes from those who really *want* to learn about it!

It is not necessary, however, that you already know how to program computers. Some programming knowledge (in whatever language) is certainly a plus, but this book can teach you programming from scratch, if need be. At some point, you will want to peruse the generic Perl reference material, but the book provides enough background material to make that leap possible.

This book also addresses the needs of experienced programmers who wish to learn about MacPerl in particular. It covers many issues that are specific to the Mac environment: Apple Events and AppleScript, droplets, line termination, MacPerl runtimes, MPW, resource forks, text editors, and more.

Here are some profiles of prospective MacPerl users, listed in alphabetical order.[3] See if you recognize yourself (or a friend) …

Bill uses his Mac strictly as a personal computer. Out of curiosity, Bill has tried programming in AppleScript and HyperTalk, but found them rather verbose and not very powerful. Bill would like to learn a language that can help him to learn more about programming.

Don has spent the last twenty years working as a landcape architect, using computers only rarely. He is considering starting a new career and sees MacPerl as a way to learn something about computers and programming before he invests time and money on attending courses at the local university.

Doug uses his Mac to design specialized electronic circuitry and supporting software. He programs MacPerl on a regular basis, using MPW (Macintosh Programmer's Workshop). Doug would love to have a MacPerl reference, particularly if it covers esoteric areas like Apple Event programming.

Ed has used personal computers for more than a decade, but now uses a Macintosh for all of his work. Ed has done some programming in BASIC and Pascal, but has never been motivated to learn C. MacPerl appeals to him, however, because of its powerful language features and high degree of Macintosh integration.

Erik has been doing network programming for years. Finding himself tied to a proprietary mail system, he created an Internet mail gateway using Perl.

---

[3] To make things easier for the authors, each of our profiles is taken from real life. The names have not been changed. We apologize if our sketches do not meet the current norms of "political correctness" but real people are rarely perfect, so there you are.

Erik reads manual pages for relaxation, so he doesn't need any tutorial material, but he thinks that a MacPerl reference would be nice to have around. (He also likes the idea of having a Mac OS-readable CD-ROM that contains copies of MacPerl, the CPAN, and other useful material!)

Joyce is a technical writer and editor who needs to maintain documents in various formats. She wants to ensure that each document matches the latest formatting standards, even after those standards change. Perl can be used for file checking: "Does this file match a specified format?" Perl is also adept at reading quasi-text formats, such as tab-separated exchange files.

Marilyn, a graphic designer, occasionally finds herself creating, designing, and/or specifying Web pages. She finds that Perl is used everywhere in the Web, not only for CGI scripts, but also (in Apache) for server administration and extensions. So, she needs to learn about programming in general and CGI (Common Gateway Interface) scripting in particular.

Rick has been programming the Macintosh for years, primarily in Assembly language, C, and Pascal. He also works with Unix systems, however, and finds that he misses the Unix scripting capabilities when he works on the Mac. Rick is interested in learning MacPerl as a fast prototyping tool.

Shira, the comptroller of a small high-tech company, uses computers in her work, but has never had any interest in learning how to program them. She has found, however, that the spreadsheets and other tools she uses are not able to perform the diverse kinds of analysis she requires. In addition, she needs a way to move data in and out of these tools, even when the formats are incompatible.

Tom, a retired professor, uses his Macintosh mostly to play games and send email. He's interested in learning more about his computer, however. Specifically, he'd like to understand a little more about programming and what makes "programs" different from other types of files.

Valerie has been using a Mac for several years, but has never learned how to program it. She is about to enter secondary school, however, and will be needing to do calculations for homework assignments, etc. She thinks that MacPerl will allow her to learn about programming while staying within her well-loved Macintosh environment.

Roadmap

Most programming books assume that the reader knows how to program in some other language. This eases the task for the authors, but it doesn't help non-programmers to get started. We want all sorts of users to get involved with MacPerl, so we have taken the effort to start with the basics.

If you are totally new to programming, we recommend that you begin with Chapter 1, *A Peek Into Programming*. It gives an overview of computer programming concepts and terminology, without resorting to language-specific constructs or syntax. Chapter 2, *A Dip Into Data*, then explains key concepts and terminology regarding data representation, structure, etc.

If you are an experienced programmer, but want an informal introduction to Perl syntax and concepts, we recommend that you begin with Chapter 3, *A Step Into Syntax*. Perl syntax is very eclectic and a bit unusual in spots. This chapter lets you take "a step into the water" before you jump into the pool.

All readers should work their way through Chapter 4, *Installation And Overview*. Not only do the following chapters assume that you have a running copy of MacPerl on hand, they will assume that you are familar with some of the user interface features (dialogs, menus, windows, etc.) covered in this chapter. Feel free to skim, but do read this chapter!

If you are comfortable with computer programming, but are unfamiliar with Perl, we suggest that you proceed to Part II, *Learning The Language*. Using a series of paced examples, this part introduces Perl concepts and syntax. In particular, it highlights some of the things that make MacPerl different from, say, Unix Perl.

Part III, *Advanced Topics*, will tell you how to do all sorts of useful and interesting things with MacPerl. Finally, Part IV, *Reference*, will serve as a place to look up some of the Perl constructs you will encounter.

Experienced MacPerl programmers may wish to skip much of Parts I and II, moving on to Part III, *Advanced Topics*. You know who you are; read the table of contents and have fun. If you get lost, Parts I and II are quite willing to take you in, soothe your pains, and get you started again ...

You should also consider investing in some of O'Reilly and Associates' Perl (and related) books at this point. O'Reilly is the definitive leader in Perl publishing; take advantage of their fine efforts! Here are some favorites, along with a rough graphical indication of their level of difficulty:

MacPerl: Power and Ease • • • • • •
Learning Perl • • • • •
Programming Perl • • • • •
Web Client Programming with Perl • • • •
Perl Resource Kit • • • •
Mastering Regular Expressions • • • • •
Advanced Perl Programming • • • •

Advice

Perl is a very eclectic language, so you may find things that are familiar to you. The influence of the C programming language is obvious, but Perl also draws upon constructs from Unixish programming tools (`awk`, `sed`, `sh`, `tr`, etc.). Be cautious, however, in assuming that a character sequence that looks familiar will act precisely as you expect: Perl is an integrated language, not a grab-bag of syntax.

Because TMTOWTDI, Perl code from other authors may contain constructs, idioms, or even syntax that we do not cover. If you are using code from other authors (not an unlikely event!), you will need to learn a broader range of Perl than we present.

Fortunately, O'Reilly and Associates (`www.oreilly.com`) has published some excellent books on Perl and related topics. Start with *Learning Perl*, moving on to *Programming Perl* (the "camel book") and *Advanced Perl Programming*. These books, and many others, are listed in Part V, *Resources*. For detailed information on related topics, visit O'Reilly's Web site.

More generally, you should take a look at Part V of this book (*Resources*). We have brought together a large list of books, CD-ROMs, email lists, web sites, and other useful sources of information. Do yourself a favor by becoming familiar with what's available!

Why Chapter 0?

This is a book about (Mac-)Perl, which considers 0 to be a "first class citizen" (Perl arrays, for instance, start with position 0). In order to learn Perl, you may have to change some of your ways of thinking. So, consider this to be your initial introduction to "thinking in Perl".

Chapter 1:

- *Cooking Up A Program*
- *Program Structure*
- *Error Checking*
- *The Programming Process*
- *Testing: 1, 2, 3, ...*

A Peek Into Programming

Are you sitting comfortably? Then I'll begin.

– Preamble to children's story in *Listen With Mother*,
B.B.C. radio program from 1950

The Macintosh is a truly wonderful invention: an approachable and highly interactive information-handling appliance. Using a Mac, even a beginning user can draw pictures, create and format documents, compose music, and more. With practice and study, users can learn how to achieve marvelous results in a wide range of disciplines.

Most **Mac OS** users are not, however, encouraged to program the computer itself. If a Mac OS application lacks a needed function, the typical user is forced to work around the problem. This may involve repetitive manual effort, the use of a "helper" tool, or switching to a different application.

More generally, although the **Finder** is a powerful and comfortable environment for interactive work, it fails to meet repetitive challenges gracefully. Renaming a single file is trivial: a matter of seconds. Renaming hundreds or thousands of files, however, requires minutes or even hours of labor. Worse, the process does not become significantly easier with practice.

By learning how to program your Macintosh, you can take control of the machine's powerful "batch" capabilities. This won't solve every problem you may encounter, but it will give you ways to avoid tedious, repetitive efforts. And, down the road, you may find yourself generating some helper tools of your own.

This chapter and the next two demystify computer programming, introducing a number of fundamental concepts at a theoretical and philosophical level. In Chapter 1, we discuss programming principles and philosophy,

Chapter 2 adds the concept of data, without which most programs are nearly worthless. Chapter 3 provides a first look at syntax – the structure of programming languages – with examples in Perl.

We won't get very far into practical programming techniques in Part I, however. If you are an experienced programmer, feel free to skip on to chapter 3, where we will begin to discuss Perl syntax in particular, or to Part II, where we begin learning the Perl language in depth, with real programming examples. Or, if you like, stick around; you might learn something …

Cooking Up A Program

Rachel is a bright young girl who needs to learn some cooking skills. After determining that Rachel likes to eat hard-boiled eggs, you set out to tell her how to prepare them. Here is a plausible **program** (recipe) that should allow a beginning cook to produce hard-boiled eggs:

> Place several eggs in a sauce pan.
> Add sufficient cold water to surround all of the eggs.
> Heat the pan until the water boils.
> Cover the pan and turn off the heat.
> Wait 25 minutes.
> Drain the pan, then refill with cold water.

In **debugging** (testing and correcting) this program, you might note that one bath of cooling water may not be sufficient to cool the eggs properly. Also, the program neglects to say anything about examining the raw eggs or storing cooked eggs. Finally, if you plan on giving Rachel more than one cooking note, a descriptive title would be useful. So, let's edit the program:

> **Hard-boiled eggs**
>
> Inspect eggs, discarding cracked eggs.
> Place several eggs in a sauce pan.
> Add cold water to the pan, covering all of the eggs.
> Heat the pan until the water boils.
> Cover the pan and turn off the heat.
> Wait 25 minutes for the eggs to cook.
> Drain and refill the pan with cold water until the water stays cool.
> Wait 5 minutes for the eggs to cool.
> If any of the cooked eggs are cracked, use them first.

Refrigerate any eggs that are not immediately consumed.

This program makes certain assumptions about the party (Rachel, in this case) that will be **interpreting** it. For instance, it doesn't bother to define eggs, sauce pans, or water. Thus, it might cause a sufficiently naive cook (or a computer) to make errors or even halt in confusion. When you are writing programs (or books!), be sure that the intended audience has the necessary background information to understand what you are saying.

Finally, always remember that your programs need to be both **executable** (runnable by the computer) and understandable by some future programmer. If you think of your programs as "executable essays", describing a problem and its solution, you won't go far wrong.

Program Structure

Some computer systems could follow our egg-cooking program, but most need more details and a slightly more explicit **structure**. Here is the program, translated into explicit, commented, and structured **pseudo-code** (i.e., any halfway step between English and a "real" programming language):

Hard-boiled eggs

Select some eggs and prepare them for cooking.

Until you have enough eggs:
    Select an egg from the carton.
    If the egg is cracked:
        Discard the cracked egg.
    Otherwise:
        Place the egg in the pan.
Return remaining eggs to the refrigerator.
Until all of the eggs are covered in water:
    Add cold water to the pan.

Cook the eggs.

Until the water boils:
    Heat the pan on a stove burner set to high.
Cover the pan.
Turn off the heat.
Wait 25 minutes.

Cool and store the cooked eggs.

Until the rinse water stays cool:
    Drain and refill the pan with cold rinse water.
    Wait 5 minutes.
If any of the cooked eggs are cracked:
    Use the cracked eggs first.
If any eggs are not immediately consumed:
    Refrigerate the remaining eggs.

Although this program is far more explicit than Rachel would need, it only begins to approach the level of detail required by a computer. For instance, it fails to specify a test for "cracked eggs" or to say what implement should be used to cover the pan. Also, the usage notes are not totally explicit.

Nonetheless, creating this sort of pseudo-code moves us several long steps towards creating a real program. We have commented[1] the intent of each section, just above the required actions. We have also been very explicit about which things will be done, under what conditions, and in what order.

If you think of each line in the recipe being "in control" for a brief instant of time, you can understand why programmers speak of the **flow of control** in a program. Many early programers allowed this flow to "jump around", using and abusing the infamous (and totally unstructured) "goto" statement.

In the early 1970s, however, the **structured programming** revolution hit programming. Its proponents[2] observed that three **control flow** constructs, taken together, were sufficient to express any desired flow of control, no matter how complicated:

- **Sequences** of actions, shown above as sequences of individual lines.

- **Selection**, indicated above by the "if" and "otherwise" constructs.

- **Repetition**, indicated above by the "until" construct.

---

[1] A bit of Perl syntax here; the "sharp" (hash, number, pound, etc.) sign is used to begin a comment that continues through the end of the current line of text.

[2] *Structured Programming* (O.-J. Dahl, et al, Academic Press, 1972, 0-12-200556-2)

By using only these constructs, programmers can create code whose "structure" is evident upon inspection. This eases the burden of initial development, but it really finds favor with programmers who need to delve into the code at some later date: structured code, quite simply, is easier to maintain!

Assuming that Rachel is successful in following your program, you could go on to describe the preparation of deviled eggs and egg-salad sandwiches. These programs could specify "hard-boiled eggs" as an ingredient, making the assumption that Rachel could remember (or look up) the needed recipe.

Because the program for egg-salad sandwiches can ignore the details of preparing hard-boiled eggs, it can be shorter, simpler, and easier to debug. And, if Rachel finds a better way of making hard-boiled eggs, she can use it without having to modify her method of making sandwiches.

Most comprehensive cookbooks are mixtures of low-level and high-level recipes. The low-level recipes (e.g., hard-boiled eggs, white sauce) can be used on their own, but they can also be referenced by higher-level recipes (e.g., poached salmon in egg sauce).

Similarly, by creating and using **code libraries**, programmers take advantage of generic **functions**, keeping their programs as short as possible. The Perl community is very rich in this sort of pre-defined code. Before you start to write a complex program, be sure to check for existing code resources!

Error Checking

Rachel would not continue trying to get eggs from an empty carton, but most computer systems have no such common sense. If our program were intended for use by a computer, it could be greatly improved by adding a bit of **error-checking**, as:

```
Until you have enough eggs:              # Select and prepare eggs.
    Quit loop if the carton is empty.    # Error-check
    Select an egg from the carton.
    If the egg is cracked:
        Discard the cracked egg.
    Otherwise:
        Place the egg in the pan.
    Quit program if the pan is empty.    # Error-check
```

The first added command (Quit loop …) tells the interpreter to leave the loop if the carton goes empty before we get the desired quantity. This may result in our getting less eggs than we wanted, but it prevents us from endlessly examining an empty carton. This is an example of **fail-soft** design; the program may not be able to do precisely what is desired, but it can still fail gently and gracefully.

The second added command (Quit program …) tells the interpreter to stop running the program if the pan never received any eggs. (Why boil a pan with no eggs in it?)

Error-checking can be very useful, but it is also possible to go overboard on it. In general, you should test for errors as early as possible, then relax a bit. If another program hands you bad data, it's not really your program's fault. More to the point, the other program should be fixed, not yours!

Don't fill your programs so full of error tests that you can't figure out what is going on; that's self-defeating. Finally, although this advice may seem a bit silly, don't check for errors unless you know what to do about them.

The Programming Process

Computer programming is, quite simply, telling the computer what you want it to do. Practically anyone can learn to write a program. It doesn't require a degree in computer science and you don't have to be a professional programmer. It does take some understanding of the problem you wish to solve, however, and some new ways of thinking about solutions.

Problem analysis may sound quite simple, but it is all too easy to fool yourself. Be quite certain you understand the problem before you start your design and programming efforts; a mistake at this stage can cause you to spend a great deal of effort in vain.

Specifically, be sure to go over the problem description with the program's "customers" (users). It doesn't matter how nifty or elegant your program is if it doesn't meet the customers' needs!

Once you understand what you want to do, you must **design** a solution. (Don't feel compelled to write a program or even to use a computer in solving your problem; the objective is to solve the problem in the easiest way you can!)

It is frequently useful, at this stage, to sketch out your solution in some sort of outline or pictorial form. Don't feel you have to use any particular notation; if a diagramming technique helps you clarify your thinking, use it!

We recommend that you start your design effort by thinking about the **data flow**. What are the format and content of the input data (information you now have) and of the output data (information you need)? What kinds of intermediate data storage will be needed? Should error-checking be performed on the input data?

In our program for hard-boiled eggs, these aspects would correspond to the packaging of the raw and cooked eggs, the type and size of the sauce pan, and the necessity to check the raw eggs for cracks. Understand, however, that computers do not share the kind of "common sense" that would allow Rachel to handle most of these details by herself.

Now that you have a handle on the **I/O** (**input/output**) requirements, you should decide what kinds of internal **data structures** are needed. (In cooking, this might correspond to the selection and arrangement of work surfaces and utensils.) In programming, the containers become lists, queues, arrays, trees, etc. If you choose your data structures carefully, the **logic** (specific instructions and flow) of the program will often be self-explanatory.

Occasionally, however, you will need to employ an arcane data structure or **algorithm** (piece of program logic). Don't be proud; a few minutes with a good reference work can save you hours of head-scratching and debugging!

Alternatively, if you think someone else may have solved a similar problem, take a look at how they did it. And, if they were nice enough to package up their work in a **library** (collection of pre-defined software), use it!

Selecting an **implementation language** normally comes next, but we're going to fudge a little on this issue. Perl is an extremely powerful and flexible language, capable of handling a wide range of problems. Unless you know that your problem requires very unusual language features, try writing it in Perl. Even if you discover that you need to switch languages, you will have clarified your thinking and created a useful prototype.

On the other hand, don't be afraid to switch languages if the need arises. If Perl seems to be running out of steam, look for a language which has the features you need. Perl is a wonderful "Swiss Army knife", but it may not be the best tool to change a tire!

Now you can try **coding** (writing down the exact text of) the program. If the programming effort seems a bit imposing, consider breaking it up into a few stages. Begin with a subset of the problem; add more features if and when the existing parts have been shown to work. In any case, you should **test** and **debug** the program, attempting to ensure that it performs correctly.

Testing: 1, 2, 3, ...

Just as cooking for oneself does not necessarily qualify one to cook in a four-star restaurant, there are many levels of "polish" that a program can have. If a program has only been used by its author, it is all too likely to have a few sharp edges and burrs.

There is nothing inherently wrong with this; most programs are only suitable for use by their original authors. Although they may be perfectly functional when used as designed, they aren't ready for use by anyone who isn't familiar with their limitations.

These programs should not be confused, however, with commercial-grade software or even widely distributed freeware and shareware. In general, a great deal of effort goes into documentation, testing, and polishing of most published software.

So, before you offer your "magnum opus" to the Internet, try to look at it as if you were a stranger: Is the program well-documented? Easy to install? Hard to break? Give it to some picky friends of varying skill levels and ask them to try it out. Accept their feedback and use it to improve the program.

Finally, when you do release your software to the world, be sure to include clear and complete release information. Be specific about any legal restrictions you may be imposing. Is the code Public Domain, GPL (GNU[3] General Public License), or what? Put a version number on the code, along with relatively permanent contact information for yourself. This will make the code substantially more useful than an "anonymous" contribution might be.

---

[3] The GNU (GNU's Not Unix) Project is engaged in duplicating (with enhancements!) the entire Unix operating system in freeware (freely redistributable software).

Chapter 2:

- *Bits And Bytes*
- *Quantifying Data Storage*
- *Values, Variables, And Calculation*
- *Data Structures*

A Dip Into Data

Representation is *the essence of programming.*

– Fred Brooks, *The Mythical Man-Month*

The Macintosh user interface tends to blur the distinctions between data files and programs. Compounding the problem, Apple uses terminology that is at variance with that used by most other operating system vendors. Consequently, it is not surprising that many Macintosh users get bewildered when they step outside of this somewhat sheltered environment.

Double-click on a Mac OS **document** (data file) and the Finder will locate and start up the appropriate **application** (program). Double-click on an application and it will start up, often asking for a document. Double-click on a **folder** (directory) and the Finder will show you a representation of the enclosed items.

This is all very convenient, but it muddies the conventional distinctions between nouns (data files) and verbs (programs). So, let's discuss some data-related terminology and concepts. Don't worry about remembering every detail; you can always refer back here if you get lost …

Data[1] is an encoded form of information.[2] The symbols you are reading right now (commonly known as the alphabet) are thus **data elements**, used to encode the information we are trying to convey. In any encoding system, the **context** determines whether and how the code should be interpreted.

The character sequences "plume" and "rouge", for instance, have different (though related) meanings in the English and French languages. Even in

---

[1] We use "data" for both singular and plural, eschewing "datum" (almost) entirely.

[2] That is, it has been turned into symbols for storage and/or transmission. The exact smell of a rose, in contrast, is information that is seldom, if ever, encoded into data.

English, many character sequences (e.g., "lead" and "read") depend upon context for both meaning and pronunciation.

Bits And Bytes

In computerese, data generally consists of sequences of **bits**: **binary (base-2)** numbers.[3] Thus, people speak of computers as understanding only ones and zeros. But, given our previous discussion, what does it mean for a computer to "understand" something? Predictably, the answer is: "It depends."

For engineering reasons, most computers store and manipulate bits in groups of 8, 16, 32, etc. **Bytes** (groups of eight bits) are, in general, the smallest useful aggregation. Because a byte can hold any of 256 unique values, bytes are commonly used to represent text characters.[4]

Let's say that, in looking through a computer's memory, we encounter a pair of 8-bit bytes: 01101001 01100110. Well, that's a little hard to read, but we can make things easier by changing the base. Here are the same numbers, in a variety of bases:

2 (binary)	8 (octal)	10 (decimal)	16 (hexadecimal)
01101001	151	105	69
01100110	146	102	66

Not that much easier to read, eh? OK, let's see what they look like if we interpret them as a sequence of text characters. In the **ASCII** (American Standard Code for Information Interchange) code, they translate to "`if`". This is still not enough, however, to tell us what the sequence "means":

• It might be an artificial character sequence, such as a control code.

• It could be part of a longer string: **ni**fty **a**rt**if**acts beaut**if**y Cal**if**ornia.

• Even if the sequence is a "word", is it English, Perl, or ???

---

[3] In conventional place-value notation, each digit has a value which gets multiplied by a power of ten (the **base**). Thus, **decimal** 101 is equal to 100*1 + 10*0 + 1*1. Binary notation works the same way, save that the multipliers are powers of 2, rather than 10. Thus, binary 101 is equal to 4*1 + 2*0 + 1*1.

[4] A character may, however, occupy more that one byte of storage. The UNICODE system, for instance, uses two bytes per character, to support oriental languages, etc.

In fact, the bit sequence could just as easily be an instruction to the computer, part of a numeric value, or part of a bit-encoded image. Clearly, context is critical to understanding any encoding of information.

To "understand" a bit sequence, computers apply a specified interpretation. In most cases, the computer has no way to detect an incorrect specification or faulty data. Hence, the expression: Garbage In, Garbage Out!

In Mac OS, a consistent set of user interface guidelines tell applications and the Finder how to interpret user actions. Similarly, there are standards for file encodings, programming interfaces, and other internal details. As you develop programs, you may find it necessary to research one or more of these standards, lest you generate the wrong encoding for a given context. For now, however, just be aware that context is important!

In particular, recognize that a document can be edited as text, interpreted and run as a program (using an interpreter such as MacPerl), and then (if need be) edited again. The distinction between a "document" and a "program" thus becomes a matter of (dare we say :-) interpretation; if a file is being edited or read, it's data; if it's being run, it's a program ...

Quantifying Data Storage

Collections of data (applications, documents, data structures, etc.) and physical storage devices (Disk, RAM, etc.) are measured in terms of the number of bytes they contain. Some of these collections can get very large, so they tend to be measured in terms of **kilobytes** (thousands of bytes), **megabytes** (millions of bytes), or **gigabytes** (billions[5] of bytes).

Here are some precise technical definitions:

2^{10} bytes (1024)	kilobyte[6]	KB	
2^{20} bytes (1024^2; 1048576)	megabyte	MB	(1024 KB)
2^{30} bytes (1024^3; 1073741824)	gigabyte	GB	(1024 MB)

---

[5] That is, American billions; in the rest of the world, it would be "thousand-millions".

[6] Prefixes such as "kilo" are used differently in the computer industry than in common usage. For reasons of engineering convenience, they are taken to mean powers of 1024 which (by a happy accident) are fairly close to a thousand, a million, etc.

To get an idea of the scales involved, consider a single-spaced (American; 8.5″ x 11″) page of text. Assuming 60 lines of 80 characters, such a page can hold 4800 characters, or about 5 KB of data. So, a 1 MB file can hold about 200 pages; a 600 MB CD-ROM can hold about 130,000 pages of text.

Mac OS documents commonly contain information other than text, however, including images, formatting codes, etc. Consequently, a word processor will typically use quite a bit more than a megabyte of disk space when storing a 200-page document. CD-ROMs, which often contain executable programs, graphic images, and audio and video data, will generally contain far less actual text than they otherwise might.

Values, Variables, And Calculation

Simple digits and characters (letters) cannot hold very much information. So, we use them in sequences (e.g., numbers and words). For similar reasons, computers combine bytes into larger-scale structures. The simplest of these are **scalar values**, known in Perl as **scalars**.

A **number** (numeric scalar) should be able to handle any reasonable value without overflowing.[7] In Perl, the standard number format supports integer (e.g., 123) values of up to seventeen digits, with no loss of **precision**. Decimal (e.g., 1.23) values have the same precision, but their **magnitude** can range from very small to very large values (roughly, 10^{-300} to 10^{+300}).[8]

A **string** (string scalar) is a sequence of bytes, generally interpreted as a sequence of characters. Most data enters and leaves a Perl program in string format, even if it is used within the program in a numeric context. As demonstrated below, Perl is more than willing to **coerce** (convert) strings into numbers (and vice versa), upon request.

It is very useful to be able to save and retrieve values by name, especially if the value may vary during the operation of the program. For this reason, most programming languages support the use of **variables**. Like their alge-

---

[7] If you put a four-digit number into a three-digit location, it won't fit. The result may vary, but you probably won't like it! In short, an overflow is usually bad news …

[8] Perl stores all numbers in **double-precision floating-point** format (even if they are being used as integers). This is a computer-oriented variant of **scientific notation**, using binary fractions and exponents. Perl also provides an **arbitrary-precision** "package" (`Math::BigFloat`) to support very demanding numeric calculations.

braic counterparts (e.g., "let x = y + 1"), programming variables "stand in" for values in calculations. Here are some examples of variable usage in Perl:

```
$a = "123";          # Set $a to "123"
$b = $a;             # Set $b to "123"
$c = $b + 1;         # Set $c to 124
```

Unlike its algebraic counterpart, the "equals sign" (=) in these **expressions** does not stand for equality. Rather, it is used for a command. The variable on the left-hand side (known in Perl as an **lvalue**) is set to the value of the expression on the right-hand side (**rvalue**). Thus, it is quite legal to modify (e.g., increment) a variable, using its current value as a starting point:

```
$c = $c + 1;         # Set $c to 125
```

In our egg-cooking example, scalar values are used in several places, as:

Wait 25 minutes.

A variable in this location might allow Rachel to cook either soft- or hard-boiled eggs, using the same basic recipe (oops, program :-). Assuming that the cooking time (in minutes) has been stored in $cook_time, we could use the Perl sleep (go away for a specified number of seconds) **function**. A Perl version of this line might thus look like:

```
sleep($cook_time * 60); # Wait for eggs to cook
```

Data Structures

Scalar variables are very useful, but they aren't good at expressing notions about collections of things. In our example above, cartons and sauce pans are both used to contain eggs. What kinds of collective **data structures** could let us **model** this aspect of cartons and pans? (Sauce pans can also contain water and sit on stoves, but these capabilities may not be critical to our model.)

We could model either of these containers as an ordered set of values, or **list**. Lists contain items and have ways to insert and remove items. The exact order of items in a list may not be critical in a given application. For instance, eggs have no particular ordering in a carton or pan.

If, on the other hand, we were modelling a package-handling system, the ordering of items in our lists might be very important, indeed. For this kind of application, we probably would use some number of "First-In, First-Out" (**FIFO**) lists, otherwise known as **queues**.

In other applications, we might want to use "Last-In, First-Out" (**LIFO**) lists (**stacks**), or numerically **indexed** lists (**arrays**). In each case, we would pick a data structure that provided a good **map** (representation) of the real-world col-lection we are modelling.

Perl programmers often use a **hash** (**associative array**), which"associates" array positions with particular text strings. This can be useful, for instance, in managing personnel data: "Raise Fred Smith's salary by $2 per hour."

Finally, by combining basic forms, it is possible to create structures that are even more complex. For instance, it is quite possible to consider using trees of arrays, stacks of queues, hashes of arrays, and more.

The ability to create and manage complex data structures is critical to good program design and implementation. If the data structures do not meet the needs of the problem, the program logic will be needlessly convoluted. Perl, fortunately for all of us, has a very rich set of data structuring operators.

Chapter 3:

- *Syntax, Meaning, And Truth*
- *Expressions, Statements, And Blocks*
- *Data Structures*
- *Control Flow*
- *Functions And Methods*
- *Parenthetical Remarks*
- *Combinatorial Complexity*

A Step Into Syntax

Take care of the sense,
and the sounds will take care of themselves.

— Lewis Carroll, *Alice's Adventures in Wonderland*

In Chapter 1, we developed a program to allow a new cook to prepare hard-boiled eggs. We started with an English description, later moving to a pseudo-code version. In this chapter, we will convert some of the pseudo-code into actual Perl code. In addition, we will make parts of the program a bit more general and quite a bit more detailed.

Here, for reference, is the pseudo-code version of our program:

Hard-boiled eggs

Select some eggs and prepare them for cooking.

Until you have enough eggs:
    Quit loop if the carton is empty.
    Select an egg from the carton.
    If the egg is cracked:
        Discard the cracked egg.
    Otherwise:
        Place the egg in the pan.
Quit program if the pan is empty.
Return remaining eggs to the refrigerator.
Until all of the eggs are covered in water:
    Add cold water to the pan.

Cook the eggs.

Until the water boils:
    Heat the pan on a stove burner set to high.
Cover the pan.
Turn off the heat.
Wait 25 minutes.

Cool and store the cooked eggs.

Until the rinse water stays cool:
    Drain and refill the pan with cold rinse water.
    Wait 5 minutes.
If any of the cooked eggs are cracked:
    Use the cracked eggs first.
If any eggs are not immediately consumed:
    Refrigerate the remaining eggs.

The most obvious problem with this program, from the perspective of the Perl **interpreter**, is that the statements don't look much like Perl. The interpreter, unlike a person, needs to have its instructions written down in a very exacting form. People can make assumptions and draw conclusions based on available information. However, an incorrect, misplaced, or missing character can cause the Perl interpreter to halt in confusion or, worse, perform an unintended action.

Syntax, Meaning, And Truth

In human languages such as English, the **syntax** defines the way that **tokens** (words and punctuation)[1] can be assembled. Although it can be very difficult to determine whether a statement is meaningful (let alone "true"), testing a sentence for correct syntax is usually pretty trivial.

Here are four English sentences. The first one is syntactically flawed, the second is meaningless, and the third is false. Only the fourth sentence is syntactically correct, meaningful, and true:

    This sentence no verb.
    This sentence is not green.

---

[1] more generally, lexically joined character sequences (e.g., "Fred" or "PowerPC")

This sentence has two verbs.

This sentence is syntactically correct, meaningful, and true.

Programming languages also have syntax. In fact, the syntax of programming languages tends to be defined much more rigidly than that of human languages (don't ya know!).

Because Perl syntax is fundamentally **algebraic**, many Perl statements look similar to algebraic statements. Perl is not algebra, however; don't assume that syntactic similarity implies similar (let alone identical) meaning. For instance, the Perl statement:

```
$a = $a + 1;              # Increment $a
```

tells the interpreter to retrieve the value of the **variable** (named storage location) $a, add one to it, then place the resulting value back into $a. That is, this is an executable statement, not an algebraic identity. Other Perl statements may not look much like algebra, but they *do* follow fixed and well-documented syntactic rules.

When the interpreter first encounters some (putative) Perl **code** (statements in Perl syntax), it must **parse** the code according to the Perl syntax rules. If the code is not syntactically correct, the interpreter will issue a diagnostic message and give up.

The interpreter will not, however, attempt to determine whether the code is meaningful. Here is a meaningless bit of Perl code, which the interpreter will parse and execute without any complaint whatsoever:

```
$a;                       # Evaluate, then discard, $a
```

You may be wondering, by the way, about the dollar sign ($) that begins the variable references above. Perl uses a raft of special characters (essentially every character on the keyboard!)[2] to help it keep track of all the different kinds of entities it manages. This can be rather confusing at first, but it turns out to add greatly to Perl's capabilities in the long run.

> **Hint:** The dollar sign looks a lot like an "S". Think of it as a short-hand way of saying "scalar".

---

[2] Foreign readers may encounter some difficulty in attempting to find all of the keyboard characters that Perl uses. We suggest that you use the Mac OS "Key Caps" program and play with the keyboard settings until you see what you want on the screen. You may then wish to paste helpful stickers on some of your keys!

The question of **program correctness** is even more arcane. One way to define program correctness might be: Does the program perform the desired set of operations, under all expected circumstances? This is not an easy question to answer, given that any significant program can have many different execution paths. Automated proving of program correctness is, in fact, a hot topic in Computer Science research, and is likely to remain so for some time.

Nonetheless, it's the job of the programmer to ensure that the code is meaningful and correct. This is best accomplished by adhering to careful design and coding practices. Rigorous testing can then be used to confirm that the program performs as expected in a typical range of conditions.

On the other hand, no amount of care and/or testing can guarantee a perfect program. Consequently, programmers are forced to accept the possibility of a few bugs in their released code. At present, the best practice is to balance the implementation and testing costs against the cost of program failure.

So much for cautionary philosophy; now let's examine a few pieces of Perl code. Please remember that There's More Than One Way To Do It. Hence, these versions aren't "official syntax", just plausible ways to express the desired actions.

Expressions, Statements, And Blocks

An **expression**, in Perl, is a syntactically valid and meaningful sequence of characters. In general, an expression has a value. Here are some sample expressions:

```
123
123 + $i
$j * (123 + $i)
```

The following lines, in contrast, are not valid expressions:

```
123 $i
123 ++ $i
$j * 123 + $i)
```

In use, expressions are collected into **statements**, as:

```
$k = 123;
$l = 123 + $i;
$m = $j * (123 + $i);
```

But, because statements are also expressions, you may encounter some rather peculiar **compound statements** on occasion:

```
$m = $k = 123;
$n = ($j = 123 + $i) * 2;
```

Syntactically, the difference between a statement and an expression is that a statement ends in a semi-colon, **;** . Semantically, the difference is that a statement usually does something, while an expression only does things as **side-effects** (e.g., by calling a function).

A **block**, in Perl, is a sequence of statements, enclosed in a matched pair of braces (curly brackets), as:

```
{
    $k = 123;
    $l = 123 + $i;
    $m = $j * (123 + $i);
}
```

Blocks are used to group lines of code for repetition or selection, function definitions, or controlling the **scope** (visibility) of variables. Indenting, as in the code above, is a good way to clarify the **block structure** of a program.

Data Structures

Perl provides two powerful data structures (ways of aggregating data): **arrays** and **hashes**. Either of these can contain any number of other items, including numbers, strings, (references to) other data structures, and more. In short, by building up combinations of hashes and arrays, you can create just about any type of data structure you might need.

Although arrays and hashes can act similarly, they are implemented very differently. An array is an **ordered** sequence of items, accessed via indexing or specialized operators. A hash is an **unordered** sequence of **key / value pairs**, accessed via (a "hashed lookup" on) the keys (index text strings).

The **array** is Perl's most versatile data structure. Each scalar in an array is accessed by its position. You can add an element to either end of an array, remove an element from either end, or index numerically to a specific array position. You can even modify (groups of) elements in the middle of an array,[3] possibly changing the positions of any following elements.

In general, arrays are:

- **indexed** numerically, like suites in an office complex.

  ```
  $suite[150] = "Prime Time Freeware";
  ```

  This code stores a text string ("Prime Time Freeware") in location 150 of the `suite` array.[4]

- used as **stacks**, also known as "Last-In, First-Out" (LIFO) lists.

  ```
  $egg = pop(@carton);      # Get an egg from the carton
  push(@pan, $egg);         # Add it to the pan
  . . .
  $egg = pop(@pan);         # Get an egg from the pan.
  ```

  This code **pops** a scalar off of the `carton` stack, saves it in `$egg`, then **pushes** it onto the pan stack. Later, it pops a scalar off of the pan stack. Although it doesn't matter in this instance, the scalar that is popped from the pan stack is the one that was most recently pushed onto it.

- used as **queues**, also known as "First-In, First-Out" (FIFO) lists.

  ```
  push(@belt, $item);       # Put an item on the belt.
  . . .
  $item = shift(@belt);     # Get an item from the belt.
  ```

  This code pushes an item onto the start of a queue that is modelling a (conveyor) `belt`. Later, it **shifts** an item off the end of the `belt`. Note that the ordering of the items is maintained.

  Note: The use of an at-sign (@) before a variable name (e.g., `@belt`) tells Perl that we are referring to an entire array, rather than a single element. You might think of @ as looking a bit like the "a" in "array". (Don't worry; we'll cover this syntax in detail in following chapters.)

---

[3] using the **splice** function

[4] Pedants might argue that this is actually the 151st location, because (like C) Perl uses 0 as the first array subscript. This will not be an issue in most cases, but you may want to stuff the information into the back of your mind, in case it comes up at some point...

Hashes are also known as **associative arrays**. Each scalar value in a hash is "associated" with a string **key** (rather than a numeric array index). A hash can store or retrieve items according to these keys.

Here is an example of a hash being used to store telephone numbers. Note the use of braces (curly brackets) to surround the index (key), instead of the square brackets that are used for arrays:

```
$phone{"Vicki"} = "555-1234";
$phone{"Chris"} = "555-4321";
```

We'll cover hashes and arrays in more detail later in this book.

Control Flow

Control flow modifiers affect the order in which the program is executed. They can cause the interpreter to skip statements, repeat actions, etc. Our program contains several instances of control flow, including the repetition:

> Until the rinse water stays cool:
>> Drain and refill the pan with cold rinse water.
>> Wait 5 minutes.

In Perl syntax, this might be expressed as:

```
until(cool($rinse_water)) {
   drain(@pan);
   refill(@pan);
   sleep(300);
}
```

Perl's `until` construct performs the **test** given in the parentheses "`(...)`". If the test **fails**, the interpreter executes the statements in the associated block, then repeats the test. If the test **succeeds**, the interpreter moves on to the code following the block.

There are many forms of tests: numeric and string comparisons, file tests, etc. And, because a test can contain any Perl expression, tests can have an unlimited amount of flexibility. Tests are also used in selection:

> If the egg is cracked:
>> Discard the cracked egg.
> Otherwise:
>> Place the egg in the pan.

This might be expressed in Perl as:

```
if (cracked($egg)) {
  push(@trash, $egg);
} else {
  push(@pan,    $egg);
}
```

Perl's if-else construct uses two blocks. The first block is executed if the test succeeds; the second is executed if the test fails. In many languages, blocks that contain only one statement do not require braces. This saves on typing, but it can lead to confusion when control structures are **nested** (layered). Perl syntax requires braces for all blocks, eliminating this risk.

Functions And Methods

Functions are used to remove complicated or frequently-used calculations from the main flow of the program. This is similar to the way in which most cookbooks are organized. A generic recipe for "boiling eggs" might be given, then referenced by recipes that require boiled eggs as ingredients.

Some of the code snippets above have quietly used functions, as:

```
until(cool($rinse_water)) {
  drain(@pan);
  refill(@pan);
  sleep(300);
}
```

This snippet depends on the `cool` function to test $rinse_water, returning a **true** (non-zero) value when the condition is met. The `drain` and `refill` functions may or may not return values. This code, in any case, ignores their **return values**.

A Perl function may perform some desired action, **return** a value, or both.[5] If a return value makes sense, by all means return one. Don't return a value for no good reason, though; it just confuses your readers ...

As noted in the previous chapter, Perl has a `sleep` function, which "puts the program to sleep" for a specified number of seconds. Our program has two very similar lines, both of which could use this function:

---

[5] A function which does not return a value is sometimes called a **subroutine**; Perl makes no such distinction.

    Wait 25 minutes.   # Allow the eggs to cook.
    Wait 5 minutes.   # Allow the eggs to cool.

A brute-force translation of the top line would yield:

```
sleep(1500);                  # Allow the eggs to cook.
```

This is pretty ugly, however. For one thing, the requirements of the `sleep` function (i.e., times must be expressed in seconds) have caused us to lose a bit of readability. Also, hard-coding numbers into programs tends to be a Bad Idea, from a maintenance perspective. So, let's clean things up:

```
sleep($cook_time * 60);       # Allow the eggs to cook.
```

Now, if we need to adjust the cooking time, we can do so by changing the value of `$cook_time`. In addition, by using a shorter value, we can produce a wide range of soft-boiled eggs (three minutes is a good starting point).

The number of seconds in a minute isn't likely to change, and the number 60 is pretty well understood by most readers, so getting rid of it doesn't pay off much. Still, we can consider using a function to get rid of it, as an exercise:

```
sleep(min2sec($cook_time));   # Allow the eggs to cook.
sleep(min2sec($cool_time));   # Allow the eggs to cool.
```

The function `min2sec` accepts a single argument, which it multiplies by 60 and returns for use by the calling program. (Don't worry about the syntax of Perl functions right now, we'll cover it in detail in following chapters.)

Perl also supports **methods**, as part of its **object-oriented** programming capabilities. Loosely speaking, an **object** is a set of data and associated ways of interacting with the data. For instance, although we have been treating $pan as a simple array, it is quite possible that we might need to maintain more information on the pan (e.g., is it full?) than that would allow.

But, rather than make the cooking programs deal with the implementation details of @pan and @trash, we could package up our data structures and access methods into objects, as:

```
if ($egg->cracked()) {
  $trash->put($egg);
} else {
  $pan->put($egg);
}
```

Although this looks very similar to the non-object version, it is actually quite different. We are now free to change the implementation details of the base objects ($egg, $pan, $trash, ...) without worrying about the possibility that we might need to modify the programs that use them.

As a beginning programmer, you are very unlikely to get into object design for a while. On the other hand, you are quite likely to use pre-packaged objects and methods. Although the syntax can get a bit peculiar at times, the benefits will be large. (Objects are your friends!)

Parenthetical Remarks

Alert readers may have noted our use of parentheses with several of Perl's "named operators" (pop, push, shift, ...). For instance, instead of:

```
push @pan, $egg;
```

We have written:

```
push(@pan, $egg);
```

The parentheses clarify the fact that @pan and $egg are parameters that "belong to" push. Although this relationship is relatively self-evident in the simple statements above, it can become significantly less obvious in more complex statements.

This is particularly important in a language such as Perl where there are so many (two dozen!) levels of **operator precedence**, coupled with left-, right-, and non-associative operators.

An example may help to clarify the reasons behind our concern. Multiplication takes precedence over addition and both take precedence over named operators (read, functions). Hence, these four statements are equivalent:

```
$hypot = sqrt((($s1 * $s1) + ($s2 * $s2)));

$hypot = sqrt( ($s1 * $s1) + ($s2 * $s2) );

$hypot = sqrt(  $s1 * $s1  +  $s2 * $s2);

$hypot = sqrt  $s1 * $s1  +  $s2 * $s2;
```

We are not convinced, however, that they are equally easy to read. (For what it's worth, the first version seems quite pedantic to us, while the last seems very chaotic.) Adding parentheses to clarify meaning is very much a matter of taste, however, as long as the code actually works.

But, as there is seldom any reason to leave parentheses off of function calls, we tend to leave them on. We also add parentheses whenever things start to get too complicated for easy and error-free reading.

This is, of course, acceptable practice in Perl (There's More Than One Way To Do It, after all!), so we will continue to code our examples in this manner. Be aware, however, that Perl code generated by Other People may not use as many parentheses as our code does. (TMTOWTDI works both ways...)

Combinatorial Complexity

For similar reasons, we suggest that you restrict yourself to a subset of Perl's operators and syntactic structures, at least until you get your feet wet. Adding a new operator or construct to a program (or a language) contributes in a very non-linear manner to the complexity, because the reader must understand all possible interactions between the new item and the existing ones.

And, although we understand (and to some degree, sympathize with) Larry Wall's motivation in providing myriad Ways To Do It, we think that some of the increases in Perl's complexity have not been matched by equivalent increases in expressive power. And, since TMTOWTDI, we (and you) can pick and choose among Perl's linguistic features, selecting those that seem worth the trouble of understanding and remembering.

Chapter 4:

Installation And Overview

> *One doesn't discover new lands*
> *without consenting to lose sight of the shore*
> *for a very long time.*
>
> – André Gide, *The Counterfeiters*

This chapter describes the installation of MacPerl and provides a brief "get acquainted" overview. If you already have a working copy of MacPerl on your disk, you may want to skip this chapter. Or, you may wish to read the sections on menus and preferences, in case you might see something new.

MacPerl Flavors

There are two flavors of MacPerl – the standalone application (**app**), which works similarly to most other Macintosh programs, and the **MPW tool**. The MPW tool is only useful if you also have a copy of MPW, Apple's **Macintosh Programmer's Workshop**, installed. MPW is a complete Macintosh programming environment, consisting of a **shell** (command line interpreter) and various **tools**. The MPW `perl` tool may be more familiar to users of Unix or DOS, as it is accessed from the command line.

Although MPW is somewhat more readily available than it once was, it is not in widespread use except among Macintosh software developers. Thus, we do not expect that many readers of this book will be MPW users. If you do not plan to use MPW, you may wish to skip ahead to the next section, *System Requirements*.

If you plan to use Perl with MPW, *be sure to follow the instructions below to install the standalone app.* The installation script for the MacPerl MPW tool requires that the MacPerl application package be installed first!

The examples in this book were written (and tested) using the standalone app. In most cases, this will make little difference. Occasionally, MPW users may have to make slight adjustments to our examples in order to make them work under MPW.

Complete instructions for installing the MacPerl MPW tool, as well as special features pertaining to the tool, are described in Chapter 22 in Part IV of this book. This book does not, however, provide detailed information about using the MPW environment. If you are not already familiar with MPW, we suggest that you familiarize yourself with MPW *before* you attempt to install or use the MacPerl MPW tool.

If you are familiar with MPW, but have never used Perl, we suggest that you install only the standalone app at first, then work your way through the tutorial material in Part II. After you have become comfortable with Perl, you can install the MacPerl tool under MPW.

System Requirements

MacPerl requires that your Macintosh be running Mac OS System 7 or later. Be sure you have at least 4 MB of memory available, more if you wish to run complex scripts or work with large amounts of data.

MacPerl can be installed in any of several ways. The Easy Install option installs an application most suited to your system: either PowerPC systems (Power Macintosh, later Powerbooks, and Performa systems with 4-digit model numbers (7500, 2300, 6400, ...)) or Motorola 68K-based Macintoshes (the Mac II, early Powerbooks, the Centris or Quadra series, etc.). Alternatively, you may wish to install a "fat" version of MacPerl, which will run on any Macintosh model. To do this, you will need to perform a "Custom" installation.

M68K processor-based Macintoshes

If you are installing MacPerl on a 68K-based Macintosh, however, the default installation may not be sufficient for your needs. The standard, or "small" 68K MacPerl has only a "minimal" set of modules linked in statically; these modules provide functionality which has always been present in previous releases of MacPerl. These modules are: `DB_File`, `DynaLoad er`, `Fcntl`, `IO`, `MacPerl`, `NDBM_File`, `Opcode`, `POSIX`, and `Socket`.

Two alternative versions of the MacPerl application are also available for 68K Macintoshes. "Big MacPerl" (bigappl) has additionally linked in the GD module and all Mac Toolbox modules. Dynamic 68K, or CFM68K (appl_cfm68K), includes the same modules as the small version, but is also able to load arbitrary modules dynamically.

> **Note**: Some functionality in the Perl core modules, such as File::Copy, is implemented via the Toolbox Modules. If you use a 68K Mac, make sure that either CFM-68K MacPerl or BigMacPerl is installed.

If you plan to install the CFM68K MacPerl application, you must make sure that your system supports it. You will need to have the following Mac OS System Software installed:

- AppleScript Lib version 1.2.2 or later

- ObjectSupportLib version 1.2 or later

- CFM-68K Runtime Enabler version 4.0 or later

This software should already be present on 68030- or 68040-based Macintosh models running MacOS 7.6.1 or later. Under Mac OS 8.0 and later, **do not** install CFM-68K Runtime Enabler or ObjectSupportLib; they are built-in to the System file.

Installing The Standalone Application

If you have downloaded a recent copy of the MacPerl application from one of the archive sites on the Internet, the file will most likely be compressed and encoded, usually with **StuffIt** (from Aladdin Systems) and **BinHex**.

In this case, you will need to decode and uncompress the archive before continuing. StuffIt Expander, an expansion utility from Aladdin, is included on the enclosed CD-ROM and is also freely available from many Macintosh archive sites or from Aladdin Systems at `www.aladdinsys.com`.

If you are installing MacPerl from the included CD-ROM, you won't need to uncompress or decode an archive. (We have supplied the MacPerl Installer as a ready-to-run application.)

Once you have unpacked the MacPerl Installer, life gets pretty easy. All you need to do is launch the Installer application, review the instructions for any important last-minute notes, select the installation location, and click Install. The Installer will install everything you need to use MacPerl, including examples, all libraries, documentation, and the "standard" MacPerl application.

If you wish to install one of the alternative (Big or CFM68K) standalone versions of MacPerl, or you wish to install the MacPerl MPW tool, be sure to complete the standard installation first. The alternative distributions contain only the alternative application (or tool) and a small number of additional files.

You should install the distributions as suggested in the figure below, from bottom to top. That is, if you wish to use the big MPW tool, you should first install the standard application (appl), then the standard MPW tool distribution, then the bigtool distribution.

		bigtool
bigappl	**appl_cfm68K**	**tool**
appl		

All distributions are available on the CD-ROM included with this book, or can be downloaded from the MacPerl archive sites.

Steps to Install the MacPerl standalone app

1. Double-click the Installer application to start the installation. Be sure to review the instructions in the initial screen for any important last-minute notes. Print or save these notes, then click Continue.

2. If you wish to install a fat binary, be sure to select Custom Install from the popup menu; otherwise, select Easy Install as shown. Choose the volume and folder where you wish to install MacPerl, then click Install.[1]

3. The Installer will install everything you need to use MacPerl.

---

[1] We have removed some blank space from this and other dialog images; don't worry if the dialogs on your screen have substantially more white space than we show.

4. When the Installer completes successfully, choose Quit. You do not need to restart your Macintosh.

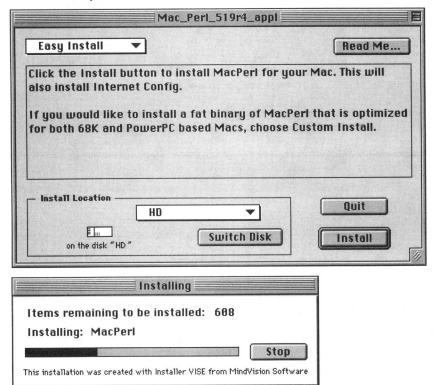

If you have a 68K based Macintosh and desire to do so, you may install the Big MacPerl application (…bigappl) or the CFM68K MacPerl application (…appl_cfm68K) at this time. Simply double-click the appropriate Installer and follow the directions, making sure to install onto the same disk where you installed the standard (small) MacPerl application.

Examine The Results

The Installer installs two new folders in the location you chose. The first of these, MacPerl ƒ, contains the MacPerl distribution, including the application, libraries, and documentation.

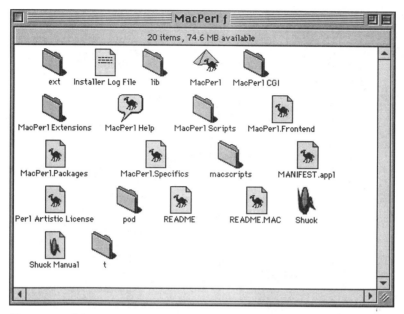

You can safely ignore most of the files and folders for now. There are, however, several items that you should recognize and understand, as they will be useful to you shortly. Examine the contents of the MacPerl *f* folder.

- The **MacPerl** application has an icon of a camel and a pyramid.[2] This is the actual double-clickable application which you will be running when you use MacPerl.

- The files **README.MAC** and **README** contain general information about MacPerl and Perl, respectively. These files contain release notes, information on known problems, special comments about the current release, etc. Be *sure* to take a look at these README files.

- The **Perl Artistic License** file contains information related to the circumstances under which you are permitted to use Perl, give it away, or sell software that is based on it. Be sure to read this file as well.

- The Perl online documentation is stored in the **pod** folder (POD stands for Plain Old Documentation). The POD files comprise your best user

---

[2] Due to trademark issues, this icon may change on future versions of MacPerl.

manual. POD files are text and can be read with many applications, including MacPerl itself. However, they will look better if you use a program designed to read POD files, such as **Shuck**. The Shuck application is included with the MacPerl distribution; its icon resembles a partially-shucked ear of corn.

• The **lib** folder contains MacPerl libraries, additional functions, and modules which you may include in your programs to give you additional capabilities. We'll cover libraries and modules in a later chapter.

• There are also a few files which contain information specific to Mac-Perl itself (as opposed to Perl documentation in general). You should read **MacPerl.Frontend**, **MacPerl.Packages**, and **MacPerl.Specifics**.

• Many of the remaining folders contain examples of Perl code. Feel free to peruse these at your leisure. We recommend, however, that you do not move, remove, or rename any of these folders or their contents, unless you are sure you know what you are doing, as this could cause problems with running MacPerl.

The Installer has also installed the **Internet Config** application in a separate folder, named for the current version of Internet Config (e.g., Internet Config1.4).

Internet Config can be used for many things, including setting up standard preferences for many Internet programs, such as USENET news or email readers. It can also be used to assign **helper applications** for reading various types of files such as text, html, and pod. We'll use Internet Config later in this chapter to assign Shuck as the helper for reading pod files.

A Walk Through The Menus

Now that you've familiarized yourself, at least a little, with the contents of the MacPerl folder, it's time to try out MacPerl. Double click the MacPerl application icon to launch MacPerl. The Menu bar should contain the standard File, Edit, and Help menus (Balloon Help prior to Mac OS 8.0), as well as a new menu called Script. If you have previously installed the Internet Config extension, you may see an additional menu as well.

```
┌─────────────────┐
│ ☐File           │
├─────────────────┤
│  New       ⌘N   │
│  Open...    ⌘0  │
├─────────────────┤
│  Close     ⌘W   │
│  Save      ⌘S   │
│  Save As... ⇧⌘S │
│  Revert         │
├─────────────────┤
│  Page Setup...  │
│  Print...   ⌘P  │
├─────────────────┤
│  Stop Script ⌘. │
├─────────────────┤
│  Quit      ⌘Q   │
└─────────────────┘
```

```
┌────────────────────┐
│ ☐Edit              │
├────────────────────┤
│  Undo        ⌘Z    │
├────────────────────┤
│  Cut         ⌘H    │
│  Copy        ⌘C    │
│  Paste       ⌘U    │
│  Clear             │
│  Select All  ⌘A    │
├────────────────────┤
│  Find...     ⌘F    │
│  Find Same   ⌘G    │
│  Jump to...  ⌘J    │
├────────────────────┤
│  Format...   ⌘Y    │
├────────────────────┤
│  Preferences...    │
└────────────────────┘
```

The **File** menu should look familiar to you. Most of the menu items will be **greyed-out** (inactive) until you create a new MacPerl document. The items in the File menu are fairly standard, performing much the same actions as their counterparts in other Macintosh applications.

You may not recognize the **Revert** item. This causes MacPerl to revert to the last saved version of a MacPerl document (or not, if you choose Cancel).

The **Edit** menu should also look very familiar, although you probably won't recognize the **Jump to...** or **Format...** items. We'll come back to these later. Again, many of the menu items will be greyed-out. Most of these will become active when you begin to work on a new document.

If you have already installed Internet Config, you may see a menu between the Edit and Script menus, named for the text editor (e.g., SimpleText or BBEdit) which has been selected as the Internet Config **editor helper**.

```
┌──────────────────────────┐
│ ☐Script                  │
├──────────────────────────┤
│  Run Script...      ⌘R   │
│  Run Front Window  ⇧⌘R   │
│  Syntax Check...    ⌘K   │
│  Check Front Window ⇧⌘K  │
├──────────────────────────┤
│  Compiler Warnings       │
│  Perl Debugger           │
│  Taint Checks            │
├──────────────────────────┤
│  One Liner          ⌘1   │
└──────────────────────────┘
```

The next menu is the **Script** menu, which drives MacPerl, letting you run the scripts (programs) you write or get from other people. Let's look at each item in the Script menu:

- **Run Script...** brings up a dialog allowing you to choose, and run, a script you may have stored on disk.

- **Run Front Window** runs the script in the frontmost MacPerl window. The menu item name will change to reflect the actual name of the script window. If there is no active script window, this item is inactive.

- **Syntax Check...** brings up a dialog allowing you to choose, and perform a syntax check on, a script you may have stored on disk. The script will not be run, but is simply checked for syntactic errors. It is often useful to syntax-check a new script before attempting to run it.

- **Check Front Window** performs a syntax check on the script in the frontmost window. Again, the menu item changes to reflect the actual name of the window; this item is only active when there is a window available. The script is not run.

- The next three items, **Compiler Warnings**, **Perl Debugger**, and **Taint Checks** are options you can set before running scripts. The Compiler Warnings option provides additional warnings of potential problems and incorrect code.[3] Taint Checks monitor the use of outside (i.e., tainted) data in controlling program activities. This is *very* useful when you are writing **CGI scripts**. The Perl Debugger provides a complete debugging environment for searching out the cause of errors in scripts. For now, we recommend you select and check Compiler Warnings and Taint Checks but not Perl Debugger.

- The last item, **One Liner**, allows you to specify and run one line of MacPerl code. This isn't as powerful as writing a script, but it can come in handy on occasion. Note that One Liner requires Unix-style Perl "one

---

[3] If this setting is not checked, only fatal errors are noted. Note that setting this option is the same as using the -w switch inside each Perl program.

liner" syntax.[4] The One Liner dialog is written in MacPerl; you can find the script in the MacPerl Scripts folder inside the MacPerl *f* folder.

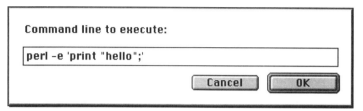

On-line Help - Installing Internet Config

The last menu is the **Help** menu.[5] The Help menu provides links to Mac-Perl's extensive online help files.

Most of the help files are in pod format and are best read with the Shuck application. MacPerl uses the Internet Config extension, included in the MacPerl distribution, to tell it which **helper application** to use in browsing the help files.

If you select one of the Help topics (e.g., MacPerl Overview) and you have not installed Internet Config (or have not set up Shuck as your helper application), you will get the following dialog:

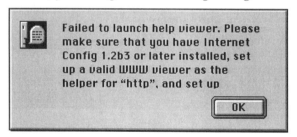

If Internet Config has not been installed:

If you have never installed Internet Config, you should install it. Open the InternetConfig folder that was installed along with MacPerl and double-

[4] One Liner also relies on the presence of AppleScript; early versions of System 7, specifically those prior to 7.5, may not have AppleScript installed by default.

[5] Prior to Mac OS 8.0, the Help menu is found under the Balloon Help icon at the right-hand end of the menu bar.

click the Internet Config application. You should see a dialog asking if you would like to install Internet Config.

Click Install to install Internet Config. You should soon see another dialog informing you of a successful installation. You do not need to restart your computer.

Once Internet Config has been installed:

In the Internet Preferences window, click Helpers.

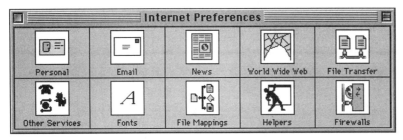

You should see the Helpers dialog box appear. Click the Add button, type pod in the Helper For: box, then click Choose Helper....

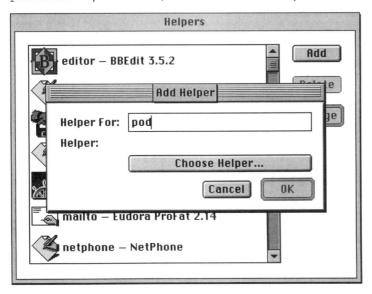

Navigate the file selection dialog until you find the MacPerl folder you previously installed. Select Shuck and click Open.

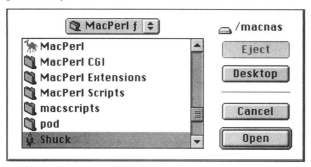

The Add Helper dialog should now show Shuck as the helper for pod files. Click OK. Save your changes and quit Internet Config.

Viewing the online help (pod) files

Once the pod helper is set up, you can view the online help. Once more, select MacPerl Overview from the MacPerl Help menu. (If you still see the Failed to Launch alert, quit and relaunch MacPerl.)

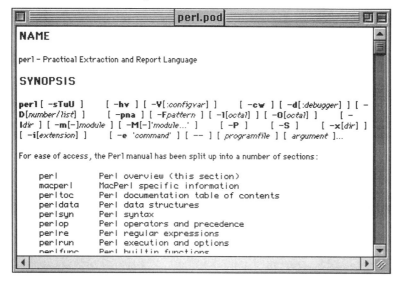

We encourage you to peruse the online help information. The pod files contain a wealth of useful information about the Perl language. In particular, you should be sure to refer to the Macintosh-specific help topics.

A New Menu

When Internet Config has been installed, you should see an additional menu between the Edit and Script menus. This menu represents the editor helper chosen in Internet Config, and allows you to edit MacPerl scripts using an alternative to the default MacPerl editor. You may want to launch Internet Config again and set the editor helper to your preferred text editor, such as Alpha or BBEdit.

Running A Script

Next, let's create a very simple script, save it, and run it. (It's not strictly necessary to save a script before running it, but this is a good habit to get into.) We'll do this both to get a feel for how MacPerl works and to observe the resulting changes in the menus.

Create a new document (using the File menu). You'll see a new Untitled window and many of the formerly greyed-out items in the File, Edit, and Script menus will now become available.

Note that the Script menu items now refer specifically to Untitled, rather than to the generic Front Window.

You'll also see a new menu appear – the **Window** menu. The Window menu keeps track of all MacPerl windows. A check mark is placed by the name of the frontmost window, in this case, Untitled. The MacPerl window is the window which shows output from your scripts; it is in *italic* font because we have no output at the moment.

Creating a script

At the cursor in your Untitled window, type

```
print 'hello';
```

If you don't like the default font or size, use the **Format...** item in the Edit menu to choose something you prefer. We strongly suggest, however, that you use a **monospace** (fixed-width) font such as `Courier` or `Monaco`.

Next, save the file as myscript (or any name you prefer). Note that the Script and Window menu items change again to reflect the new name. Select Run "myscript" from the Script menu. A new window, entitled MacPerl, will appear, containing the text

```
hello
```

Note that the MacPerl item in the Window menu is no longer in italics.

Close the MacPerl window and edit the script in the myscript window, deleting one of the quote marks, ', to produce:

```
print 'hello;
```

Run myscript again. This time, the MacPerl window will contain an error message:

```
# Can't find string terminator "'" anywhere before EOF.
File 'HD:MacPerl ƒ:myscript'; Line 1
```

The message tells you that MacPerl expected to find a closing quote mark, ', but that the interpreter reached **EOF** or **End Of File**, without encountering the quote. If you had selected Syntax Check "Untitled", you would have received the same error message. Try it!

Select the line[6] that says:

```
File 'HD:MacPerl ƒ:myscript'; Line 1
```

---

[6] Depending on the location of your script, the pathname you see for the file will vary.

then pull down the Edit menu. The **Jump To...** item is now enabled and has changed to refer directly to the specific file name and line number in the error message.

Select Jump to "myscript". MacPerl will jump to, and highlight, the line in your script window where the error was found.

Because you saved myscript before deleting the quote mark, you should be able to revert to the previously saved version, using the Revert item under the Edit menu. Try it.

Check The Preferences

Before we leave the Installation chapter, you might want to take a look at the MacPerl preferences. The default preferences should be fine for now, but it's nice to know what they do.

The **Libraries** preference tells MacPerl where to look for libraries of additional code. Each **path** is a sequence of folders, starting with the disk volume, that leads to the location of the library files.

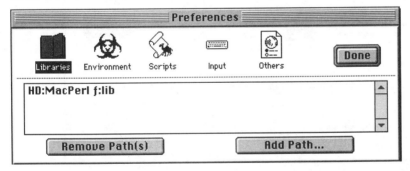

Libraries already contains one path – the path to the libs folder in the Mac-Perl *f* folder you just installed. You'll add a few more paths to the libraries if you start installing and using Modules (discussed in detail later in this book). For now, just familiarize yourself with this preference dialog so that you can find it when you need it.

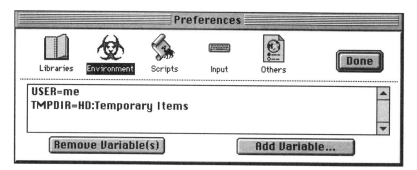

The **Environment** preference sets various **environment variables**, variables which are available to all parts of your Perl scripts and which tell Perl certain things about the environment under which it is running. The USER variable is taken from the owner name in the File Sharing control panel.[7] The TMPDIR variable references a typical MacOS location for temporary files.

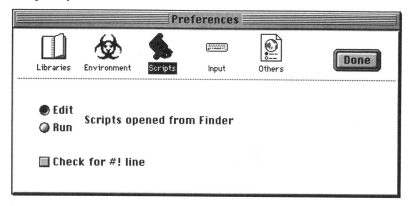

The **Scripts** preference tells MacPerl how you want to treat scripts. The radio buttons customize how scripts are treated when you double-click them under the Finder. Specifically, a double-click can cause the script either to be opened by the MacPerl editor or to be run by the Perl interpreter.

The check box determines whether MacPerl will check for the presence of # ! as the first two characters of the first line in each script. The # ! line

---

[7] The Sharing Setup control panel, prior to Mac OS 8.0

(also known as the **shebang**[8] line) provides special instructions to the Perl interpreter when the script is run. An example of a #! line might be:

```
#!perl -w
```

The word `perl` is required.[9] The **option**, `-w`, tells Perl to turn on extra **warnings**. These warnings will tell you about non-fatal errors which could cause execution problems. Many other options (or **switches**) are available, but not all of them are meaningful (or even supported) by MacPerl. To get a list of all possible Perl switches, execute a script beginning with

```
#!perl -h
```

We recommend that you click the box to check for the #! line. Note that the #! line is necessary if you plan to use the MPW `perl` tool and make any of your scripts directly executable.

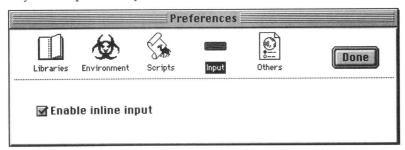

The **Input** preference tells Perl whether or not you want to enable inline input. This Preference is only meaningful under Japanese systems; it allows characters to be composed directly in the MacPerl TextEdit window instead of in a separate floating window.

The Input preference has been confirmed to work well on a Macintosh running the Japanese Language Kit, using the Kotoeri Input-System and the Osaka font. It should also work with other settings.

---

[8] Perl jargon is rife with puns, many of which have Unixish origins. Shebang, aside from its colloquial meaning (as in "the whole shebang"), comes from the Unix "shell", coupled with a "bang" (exclamation point). *The New Hacker's Dictionary* is a wonderful compendium of such jargon, along with amusing and edifying hacker folklore.

[9] If you intend to run your script on a Unix system as well, you may specify the full pathname to the `perl` application on the Unix system. MacPerl doesn't care if you use a full pathname; it only looks for the string "perl".

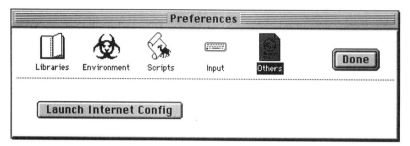

The **Others** preference handles miscellaneous things. As of version 5.1.9r4 of MacPerl, this preference only allows you to launch the Internet Config application, where you can set helper applications for viewing files such as the pod documentation.

Part II

Learning the Language

We dissect nature along lines laid down by our native language...
Language is not simply a reporting device for experience
but a defining framework for it.

– Benjamin Whorf, *Thinking in Primitive Communities*, 1964

The use of traveling is to regulate imagination by reality,
and instead of thinking how things may be,
to see them as they really are.

– Samuel Johnson, quoted in Hester Lynch Piozzi's
Anecdotes of Samuel Johnson, 1786

Chapter 5:

Building Blocks

*It has long been an axiom of mine
that little things are infinitely the most important.*

– Sir Arthur Conan Doyle, *The Adventures of Sherlock Holmes*

Part I of this book provided a gentle introduction to programming theory and philosophy. Part II expands on those concepts by introducing the Perl language, one step at a time.

There are many ways to introduce a new programming language. We could simply provide a reference guide to the various commands, along with the online manual pages, and let you puzzle things out on your own. If you're a person who prefers this method of learning, our language guide is in Part IV, *Reference*, and the online documentation is extensive. Have fun!

Alternatively, we could start to write a simple program, expanding on it and adding more features as we learn more about the language. This is one of the most popular ways of teaching a language. Unfortunately, the resulting program can become complex rather quickly, and often seems artificial.

A third method employs many small examples of various aspects of the language; each example is self-contained and easily understandable. As new features are discussed, they become part of future examples, but no example contains language features that have not yet been discussed.

The resulting bits of code may work together as part of a larger program, but no attempt is made for that program to do anything useful.[1]

This last method is the one we are using in Part II. Each of our examples demonstrates a feature of MacPerl. Each is self-contained and should run if you want to try it out. Some of our examples may not produce output, but they should not produce errors, either.[2]

In summary, rather than trying to build one complete program by the end of Part II, we provide you with the tools and understanding to leverage our examples into any number of programs of your own.

The goal of Part II is to provide you with the basic skills for writing Perl scripts, and to give you an understanding of Perl which will enable you to move forward and learn more. We won't try to teach you everything there is to learn about programming Perl (Perl is big!) but we hope that you'll leave Part II with a good understanding of what Perl can offer.

Many of the examples in this chapter build on concepts covered in Part I of this book. If you find yourself getting lost, or don't think that we're providing sufficient explanation for a new idea, please go back to the early chapters and look through them again.

> *A journey of a thousand miles must begin with a single step.*
>
> Chinese proverb

Perl is a language, much like other languages you may be familiar with. As a programming language, it has much in common with other programming languages such as AppleScript, awk, or C. It was invented by humans, so it also has a lot in common with other human languages, such as English or mathematical (e.g., algebraic) notation.

Languages tend share certain syntactic elements. These elements combine, like building blocks, to form larger structures. Most languages have nouns, verbs, expressions, statements, and punctuation – although these may go by different names in different languages. Perl's building blocks may not be

---

[1] Many years ago, young girls who were learning embroidery skills would create pieces composed of the stitches they had learned. The resulting "**samplers**" served to demonstrate examples of particular stitches. In a similar fashion, the programs we will present in this chapter serve as a sampler of Perl code.

[2] Unless, of course, we're teaching you about errors!

immediately familiar to you, but they are analogous to similar elements in other languages.

Literals – Numbers And Strings

We will begin very simply.

```
3
3.14159
three
```

We can describe the **values** shown above in several ways.[3] 3 is a **number**, specifically, an **integer**. 3.14159 is also a number, in this case a **floating point** number. three is a **character string**, or, more simply, a **string**.

Each of these is also a **literal**, (specifically, a numeric literal or string literal) because its value is literally what is shown. Literals are distinguished from **variables**, whose value may vary.[4] Literals are some of the nouns, or objects, in the Perl language.

When used in Perl, strings are usually **quoted** (e.g., delimited by either single or double quotes[5]). Strings which contain **whitespace** (e.g., blanks or tabs), or characters with special meaning to Perl, *must be* quoted. Numbers, in contrast, are never quoted – if quoted, they are converted to strings.

Variables

Literals are very useful, but they are not very flexible. As we saw in the boiled egg example in Chapter 2, we can use variables in a program to represent values that could change, such as cooking time, temperature, number of eggs, and so on. Variable names are composed of **alphanumeric characters** (letters and digits) or **underscores**, _. They must begin with a letter or an underscore.[6]

---

[3] One way is to call them **values**.

[4] We don't expect the value of 3 to change anytime soon.

[5] The type of quote mark has an effect on how the contents of the string will be evaluated or **interpolated**. More on this shortly.

[6] Some *special* variable names are defined and may include a character that is not alphanumeric (e.g., $#) or may be comprised only of digits (e.g., $1). These variables are not user-defined (although you may modify their values). In general, the rule is: begin your variable names with a letter or _ and stick to alphanumeric characters!

Variables are also used as they are in algebra, to hold the value of an expression. We'll cover expressions later in this chapter.

A **scalar** variable contains a *single* value; the value can be either a number or a string.[7] Scalar variable names are always preceded by a dollar sign, **$**.

```
$cook_minutes = 3;
$some1 = 'Vicki';
$pi = 355/113;
```

A string can be **coerced** (converted) into a number and vice-versa. This may sound a bit silly, but it turns out to be very handy on occasion. The rules for coercion are basically what you would expect:

```
$s = '123';
$n = $s * 2;        # e.g., 246
$s = "$s $n";       # e.g., '123 246'
```

Exercise caution however, when working with anything other than simple integers. What you expect may not be what you get![8]

An **array** variable can contain *multiple* (zero or more) values. Array variable names are always preceded by an at sign, **@**.

```
@colors = ('red', 'green', 'blue');
```

Because the initial character (**$** or **@**) identifies the type of variable, it is perfectly legal for a scalar variable to have the same name as an array variable! This can actually be quite useful, once you get over the shock.

Case – A Sensitive Issue

Unlike some operating systems, such as Unix and VMS, the Mac OS is not **case sensitive**.[9] Upper- and lower-case letters are usually considered to be identical; the letter **a** is treated the same way as the letter **A**. If you create a file on your Macintosh named MyStuff and later try to create a file named

---

[7] A scalar can also hold a **reference**.

[8] See *Unreal Numbers*, by Tom Phoenix, in *The Perl Journal*, issue #8 (vol. 2, no. 4), Winter, 1997.

[9] URLs (Uniform Resource Locators) are a bit schizophrenic on this issue. Everything up to the first slash is case-insensitive; everything thereafter is (generally) sensitive to case differences (unless, of course, the server is a Macintosh!).

mystuff, you will usually receive an Alert dialog (or possibly overwrite the MyStuff file!)

Perl, on the other had, *is* case sensitive. This means that in Perl (and thus in MacPerl!), the letter **a** is *not* the same as the letter **A**. So, $cook_time and $Cook_Time are *two separate and distinct variables.*

If you are only familiar with the Mac OS, case sensitivity may be a strange concept. Be sure to keep it in mind as you work in MacPerl, however, and be sure to specify your variable names consistently!

> **Note**: The usual Perl convention is to use lower case for most ordinary user-defined variable names. For complex names, some people prefer mixed case (e.g., $loopCounter), but with the first character of the name in lower case. Alternatively, the underscore may be used (e.g., $loop_counter) to separate portions of a variable name.
>
> Special variables, such as **environment variables** (e.g., $USER), Perl **built-in variables** ($MATCH), and special constructs such as **filehandles** (STDIN) and **labels** (LOOP1), are generally named entirely in upper case to alert readers to their special nature.[10]

Quoting

As we said previously, strings are usually quoted. Perl has several different ways to perform quoting. The simplest way is to use either single, **'**, or double, **"**, quote marks.[11] Under many circumstances, the result will be the same whichever you choose. However, there are special circumstances where the choice of quote is important.

Perl supports variable **interpolation**; interpretation of a variable within (in general) a text string. Double quotes permit variable interpolation to occur. Single quotes suppress variable interpolation. For instance:

```
$fruit = 'apple';          # set to string apple
$price = '$1.00';          # set to string $1.00
$cost = "$1.00";           # evaluate the variable $1!
```

---

[10] Note that the MacOS toolbox calls follow their own case conventions, and MacPerl's Mac:: toolbox modules follow suit....

[11] A number of fancy quoting mechanisms (e.g., q/*string*/) were introduced in Perl version 5. See Part IV, *Reference*, for more details.

```
$cake = 'pine$fruit';    # set to string pine$fruit
$cake = "pine$fruit";    # set to string pineapple
$pie = "$fruitpie";      # evaluates $fruitpie!
$pie = "${fruit}pie";    # set to string applepie
```

The last two examples show what can happen when a scalar variable is embedded in a "word". If Perl disagrees with you about where the variable stops and the rest of the word begins, you will get strange results. By enclosing the variable name in braces (a form of quotation), you can specify where the variable stops and the rest of the word begins.[12]

Double quotes also permit backslash (i.e., escape sequence) interpretation. Again, single quotes suppress this interpretation. We'll come back to escape sequences when we discuss the `print` command, later in this chapter.

Take care to consider which type of quote to use. For string literals, we recommend using single quotes unless you have a reason for doing otherwise. In certain cases, such as print statements, you may find that you have a good reason more often than not. The best rule is: Think Before You Quote!

Operators

Operators operate on data elements (e.g., variables and literals), combining and modifying those elements in various ways. Perl has several hundred operators, many of which can be used in more than one way![13]

By way of introduction, this section will cover the most common arithmetic and string operators. As we work our way through the examples in Part II, we will introduce additional operators as needed. For a more comprehensive treatment of Perl operators, be sure to check the *Reference* portion of this book (Part IV), the online help, or *Programming Perl*.

Arithmetic Operators

Let's start with the most common arithmetic operators; these should be largely familiar to you already.

---

[12] You only need the braces if the characters following the variable name are alphanumeric (letters or numbers) or underscore. However, you are always free to enclose the variable name in braces, if this makes your meaning more clear.

[13] Perl takes a rather casual approach to the use of such terms as **operator**, **function**, and **subroutine**. You will find that these terms are frequently used interchangeably, or have subtle differences in meaning based on how they are being used.

+	**addition**
–	**subtraction**
*	**multiplication**
/	**division**
=	**assignment**

Note that Perl, like most programming languages, uses ***** for multiplication. Here are two additional operators whose symbols may be less familiar.

**	**exponentiation**
%	**modulus (remainder)**

The first one, ******, is the power or **exponentiation** operator (e.g., `10**3` is the Perl way of writing 10^3). Don't be confused by **%** – it's not percentage as you might think! Rather, it is the **modulus** (integer remainder) operator. The value of the arithmetic expression

```
11 % 5
```

would be 1 (11 divided by 5 leaves an integer remainder of 1). Modulus is the only arithmetic operator that performs calculations in integer mode; floating point is the default for all others.[14]

Shortcut Assignment

Suppose we wanted to write a Perl expression to increment a counter by 10. We could say

```
$counter = $counter + 10;
```

This is a common operation, however, and Perl has shortcuts for many common operations. A simpler way to write this expression would be

```
$counter += 10;
```

By mixing the various numeric calculation operators with the assignment operator, we can derive a collection of "shortcut" assignment operators.

+=	**"increment by"**
–=	**"decrement by"**
*=	**"multiply by"**

---

[14] It is possible to reset the default for all operations to integer calculation by including the **pragma**, `use integer`, in your program. Generally, however, it is best to use the `int()` function to extract the integer portion of an expression.

```
/=       "divide by"
%=       "modulo by"
**=      "raise to the power"
etc.
```

Each of these shortcut operators works in a similar fashion. For example:

```
$x -= 5;     # $x = $x - 5;15
$y *= 100;   # $y = $y * 100;
```

There are more than a dozen of these shortcut assignment operators; we'll cover more of them as we go along …

Because in Perl, There's More Than One Way To Do It, there are even shorter shortcuts for increment and decrement, a pair of very common operations. These are the **autoincrement**, **++**, and **autodecrement**, **− −**, operators, created for the specific case when the value of a variable is incremented (or decremented) by exactly 1. The following commands are thus equivalent:

```
$x = $x + 1;
$x += 1;
$x++;
```

Numeric Comparison

The comparison operators should also be familiar to you, although some of these may look a little bit different from when you saw them in math class. (**!** is Perl's "not" operator).

```
<        less than
>        greater than
<=       less than or equal to
>=       greater than or equal to
!=       not equal to
==       equal to (equality)
```

Be sure to note the difference between the **=** (assignment) operator and the **==** (equality) operator. The former, =, is used to assign a value to a varia-

---

[15] Using comments to "explain" idioms is generally not a good idea. If you don't expect a reader of your code to understand the idiom, perhaps you should use clearer code! In general, comments should be used to explain high-level intent, abstract algorithms, data formats, and the like; they should complement the code rather than reiterate it. In other words, avoid putting comments such as this one into *real* code.

ble (or list of variables). The latter, ==, is used to compare two expressions. For instance, using the assignment operator, we might say:

```
$dozen = 12;
```

This assigns the value, 12, to the scalar variable named $dozen. It does not make any comparisons. Let's say that we wanted to keep adding eggs until we had 12 eggs in the pan. Using the equality operator, we could ask the question, does the number of eggs equal 12?

```
if ($eggs == 12) ...
```

This fragment of code compares the value of the variable $eggs to the number 12 and tests for equality. One of the most common Perl programming mistakes, however, is to use the assignment operator, **=**, where you meant to use the equality comparison operator, **==**, or vice versa, as:

```
if ($eggs = 12) ...
```

Rather than testing whether the current value of $eggs is 12, this code *sets* the value of $eggs to 12, then tests the "truth" of the resulting expression (12). In Perl, non-zero numbers are always considered to be "true", so the if will always succeed, regardless of how many eggs there really are!

> **Note:** You might think of **==** as "really equals", or remember that the equality comparison operator, **==**, is the opposite of inequality, **!=**. Or, you may think of some other way to recall the difference between **==** and **=**. But *find a way to remember*!

String Operators

Although arithmetic operations are more common, Perl also has operators which work specifically on strings. Several of these are analogous to the numeric operations.

x	**repeat by**
.	**concatenate with**

The **x** operator is the string **repetition** operator.[16] The statement

```
$ohs = 'o' x 5;
```

is equivalent to

---

[16] This is somewhat analogous to "multiplication" for a character string.

```
$ohs = 'ooooo';
```

The **.** operator (dot) is used for string **concatenation**. The statement

```
$bf = 'butter' . 'flies';
```

sets the variable `$bf` to the string `'butterflies'`.

The string comparison operators act very similarly to their arithmetic counterparts; they are distinguished, however, by alphabetic (string) names (i.e., the numeric < operator corresponds to the string `lt` operator).

lt	**less than**
gt	**greater than**
le	**less than or equal to**
ge	**greater than or equal to**
ne	**not equal to**
eq	**equal to**

Note that each operator is abbreviated from its full English name.

String comparison is based on (ASCII[17]) character ordering. The following are some examples of string comparison expressions.

```
'abc' eq 'abc'     # the strings are identical
'ABC' ne 'abc'     # remember about case sensitivity
'four' lt 'three'  # f precedes t in the alphabet
```

When you are performing a comparison, be sure to use the correct (string or numeric) operators, depending on the type of data you are comparing. If you forget and choose the wrong operators, Perl will not complain, but the program's results may not be what you expected!

Precedence

Precedence rules determine the order in which operations will take place. You may recall from elementary school arithmetic that multiplication takes precedence over addition. That is, the following equation

```
17 + 2 * 5
```

is arithmetically equivalent to

---

[17] American Standard Code for Information Interchange. There are alternative ways of ordering characters, which are less dependent upon a particular alphabet. However, these are not currently used by Perl.

```
17 + 10              # not 19 * 5
```

because the multiplication is performed before the addition. Parentheses can be used to make precedence rules clearer

```
17 + (2 * 5)         # still 17 + 10
```

or to **override** them

```
(17 + 2) * 5         # now 19 * 5
```

Perl has a very large and complex list of precedence rules.[18] Even if you have an excellent memory (and an interest in learning the entire list!), we recommend that you use parentheses to avoid difficulty. *You* may be able to remember all of the precedence rules, but the parentheses could help someone else, if they need to read and/or maintain your code.

Expressions

We have referred to **expressions** several times now. In English, an expression is a "particular word, phrase, or form of words". In programming languages, expressions have a similar meaning.

Expressions are composed of Perl syntactic elements, such as literals, variables, operators, etc. An expression can be used wherever a value can be; that is, an expression can be **evaluated** to produce a value.

In the simplest case, an expression contains only one element, as in the case of the (literal) number 3. Sometimes the expression contains several elements and must be evaluated further. The numeric expression below

```
355/113
```

consists of two integer numeric literals (355 and 113) and the **division operator**, **/**. This expression, discovered by Chinese mathematicians, evaluates to a rather close approximation (3.1415929...) of π.

Expressions must be legal within the syntax of a specific language. The text

> If dog rabbit.

is not a valid English sentence, even though it is composed of valid English syntactic elements (words and punctuation). Similarly, the following lines

---

[18] The complete precedence table is provided in Part IV, *Reference*.

are not valid Perl expressions, even though they are composed of valid Perl syntactic elements.

```
123 $i
123 ++ $i
$j * 123 + $i)
```

Statements

Before a Perl expression can be used, it must be incorporated into a **statement**.[19] A statement is a command to the Perl interpreter, (generally) telling it to do something. To ensure that Perl knows where one statement stops and another begins, statements make use of punctuation, much as human languages do.

Perl statements end with a semicolon, **;**[20]. Statement **blocks** are enclosed in braces, **{ }**. **Comments** begin with a hash mark, **#**, also known as a pound sign or sharp sign, and finish at the end of the line.[21] Programmers include comments solely for the benefit of human readers; Perl itself ignores them.

Statements are composed of expressions, blocks, and other statements, with comments scattered among them. Taken together, this collection of statements comprises your program.

Commands: Operators, Functions, And More

Once you have some objects (variables, literals, and operators) gathered together into expressions and statements, you need to tell Perl what to do with them. You do this by using **commands**, the verbs of the Perl language.

Perl, like many programming languages, is rather **terse**. If you were talking to a friend, you might say "Write the word 'hello', please." In Perl, you issue a command:

```
print "hello\n";
```

---

[19] To be precise, Perl also makes use of **declarations**, which look a lot like statements, but act a bit differently. A declaration tells Perl about something, but doesn't specify what to do with it; a statement tells Perl what to *do*.

[20] As with most rules, there are exceptions. For instance, no semicolon is required at the end of a block or a program. However, we advise that you put one in anyway…

[21] Comments don't require a semicolon either. (Picky; picky…)

The `print` command writes a string of characters, in this case `"hello"`, to the screen (the MacPerl output window). The odd looking pair of characters at the end of the string, `\n`, is an **escape sequence**[22] representing a **newline**. It tells Perl to move to a new line after printing (the equivalent of pressing return when you are typing text on a keyboard). This is often useful to keep what is printed from bumping into whatever comes next.[23]

Note that we enclosed the string `"hello\n"` in double quotes. As we discussed earlier, single quotes would have prevented the `\n` from being interpreted as a newline. Try

```
print 'hello\n';
```

to see what happens.

There are many commands in Perl and they fall into various categories depending on certain attributes. One such category is **operators**, as introduced earlier. Much of the Perl language is made up of operators. Some of these are made up of symbols, as we have seen; others look like words.

Perl has more than four dozen **named unary operators** (e.g., `defined`, `exit`, `log`, `sleep`, and `sqrt`). A unary operator takes a single argument. Named unary operators have (relatively) memorable names, rather than symbolic representations.

Perl also has named **list operators**, which can take a list (i.e., multiple values), as an argument. In the preceding example, `print` is a **list operator** (although there is only one item in its argument list). Try

```
print 'hello', "\n";
```

Then there are **functions**. A function is a self-contained piece of a program that performs a specific task. Functions can take arguments and usually return a result. A function is **called** by the main program (or another function). Its arguments are **passed** to it, normally enclosed in parentheses.

---

[22] `\n` is one of a class of multi-character codes called escape sequences. (The backslash character, `\`, is also called the escape character). Escape sequences provide a shorthand way to describe special characters (e.g., tabs or newlines) or groups of characters (e.g., all digits or any **white space** character).

[23] The Macintosh actually uses a Carriage Return (^M or octal `\015`) rather than a Line Feed (^J or octal `\012`) as the "end of line" character. To help ensure the portability of Perl programs, MacPerl uses the `\n` construct, but actually reads and writes Carriage Returns rather than the Line Feeds that Unix Perl would use.

Some languages make distinctions between different types of functions, such as **procedures** or **subroutines**.[24] Perl, however, employs a very liberal definition of the term function. A function acts upon its input, returning some sort of result. Perl commands can all, essentially, be thought of as functions. *If it looks like a function, it is a function.*

What makes something "look like a function"? Traditionally, a function is called by enclosing its arguments within parentheses. So, a *function* is a list or named unary operator, with parentheses around its arguments.

Unfortunately, things aren't quite that simple. Recall the discussion of precedence earlier in this chapter. By enclosing a function's arguments in parentheses, you raise their precedence. So, results may vary if you use the parentheses or leave them out; that is, "functions" and "operators" may not always act in quite the same way. When in doubt, use parentheses.[25]

To summarize

Most functions take one or more arguments. If more than one argument is expected, the order is usually important. Arguments are generally separated by commas.[26]

```
rename("myfile", "yourfile"); # rename a file
```

Many functions **return** a value which may be saved in a variable or used in any other expression.

```
$sq = sqrt($x)     # sqrt returns the square root
```

Functions may be used with or without the enclosing parentheses. If parentheses are omitted, the function acts like a **list operator** or a **unary operator**. These operators follow precedence rules which determine how they will act. As we discussed previously, precedence rules are complex. To be absolutely certain how a function will act, you should use parentheses.

---

[24] Whereas the built-in functions are also known as operators, user-defined functions are frequently referred to as **subroutines**.

[25] In part II of this book, our examples use Perl functions with parentheses. However, you should expect to see our coding style become somewhat less rigid in part III, as we attempt to show you more "real world" examples. In particular, print statements are frequently written without the enclosing parentheses.

[26] If one of the arguments is a **filehandle**, it should not be followed by a comma. Filehandles will be discussed in the next chapter.

Control Flow

As we discussed in Part I, the structure of a program can be described by three simple **control flow** constructs:

- sequence - a sequence of individual statements, taken in order

- selection - a decision or selection, made between one or more choices

- repetition - the same action, performed a specified number of times

Each of these constructs, spearately or in combination, can be used to control the flow of the program.

Sequence

Sequences are the simplest form of control flow. Any series of statements, taken in order, comprises a sequence.

```
$x = 25;
sleep($x);
print "$x";
$x -= 5;
```

Selection

Selection tells the program to choose from among alternatives.[27] Depending upon the choice that is made, a different block of code will be executed. In previous sections, we introduced a control flow construct that is used for selection: the **if** statement. This statement is used to make a decision – the program checks for a certain **condition** and performs some **action** if the condition is true.[28] This type of control flow construct is also often referred to as a **conditional** statement.

```
if ($x == 25) {
   sleep($x);
   print($x);
}
```

Often, decisions are more complex. For example, you may want to perform one action if the condition is true and a different action if the condition is false. Our egg cooking example contained this set of instructions:

---

[27] Often including the alternative of doing nothing at all!

[28] Note that Perl, unlike some languages, requires the action to be in a **block**.

If an egg is cracked, discard it.

Otherwise (if it is not cracked), put the egg into the pan.

Here is an example that might come up in "real" code. Suppose you have a program which counts how many mice are connected to your Macintosh and prints the result.[29] Being a careful programmer, you want to be sure the message is grammatically correct.

```
if ($count == 1) {
  print("My Mac has 1 mouse.\n")
}
if ($count != 1) {
  print("My Mac has $count mice.\n")
}
```

Just as English has the word "otherwise" which is equivalent to "if the previous condition is not true", Perl has the **else** statement. The above code fragment could thus be made simpler (and more efficient), as follows:

```
if ($count == 1) {
  print("My Mac has 1 mouse.\n")
} else {
  print("My Mac has $count mice.\n")
}
```

Alternatively, you could instead use **unless**.

```
unless ($count == 1) {
  print("My Mac has $count mice.\n")
} else {
  print("My Mac has 1 mouse.\n")
}
```

The decision to use an `if` or an `unless` statement is based on how you think about the problem you are solving. By expressing the control flow as simply and naturally as possible, you will make things easier for the next person (perhaps yourself!) who looks at the code.[30]

---

[29] Admittedly, you probably won't write many programs to count mice. But programs which count things and generate reports are relatively common.

[30] Just to prove that TMTOWTDI, you might also consider the `? :` **conditional** operator (a handy shortcut!). See Chapter 9, *Odd Corners*, for an example.

So far, we have selected between two choices (a **Boolean** choice). The condition either is met or is not met. But we could also have several choices.

```
if ($count == 1) {
  print("My Mac has 1 mouse.\n")
}
elsif ($count > 1) {
  print("My Mac has $count mice.\n")
}
elsif ($count == 0) {
  print("How do you run a Mac with no mice?\n")
}
else {
  print("Eeek! Negative mice found?!\n")
}
```

You can include as many `elsif` statements as you need. Use care if the conditions are not exclusive; only the first condition which is true will be executed. The `else` block will be executed only if no prior conditions are met. A final `else` condition is commonly included to catch errors.[31] There is no multiple choice equivalent for `unless`.

Repetition

The third control flow construct is repetition. Using repetition, a section of a program repeats an action or sequence of actions **while** some condition is true (or **until** a condition becomes true). These sections of repeating code are called **loops**, because the control loops through them some number of times.

The code fragment below implements a simple egg timer. It sleeps for 60 seconds, then increments (**bumps**) a counter. The counter is set (**initialized**) to 1 before we begin the timing loop.

```
$n = 1;             # start with counter set to 1
while ($n < 4) {    # Loop while $n is less than 4
  print("tick\n");
  sleep(60);        # sleep 1 minute
  $n++;             # increment the counter
}
print("RRIINNGG\n");
```

---

[31] For example, conditions you didn't think of or conditions that should not happen.

After each pass through the sequence of statements, the program returns to the **top** of the loop and checks the condition again: is the value of $n still less than 4? The block of code (called a **while loop**) repeats 3 times, once each for values of 1, 2, and 3. When $n becomes 4, the condition ($n < 4) is no longer true, so the loop **terminates** (stops repeating).

Again, you have a choice in how to state the condition, depending upon how you think about the problem. The following is an equivalent timing loop.

```
$n = 1;              # start with counter set to 1
until ($n == 4) {    # Loop until $n equals 4
  print("tick\n");
  sleep(60);         # sleep 1 minute
  $n++;              # increment the counter
}
print("RRIINNGG\n");
```

This time, the loop continues **until** the condition is true.

Putting the pieces together

Once you have sequence, selection, and repetition, you can combine these constructs into more interesting and (arbitrarily) complex programs. Here's a fairly simple example using all three control flow constructs.

```
$t = 10;
while ($t > 0) {
  if ($t == 1) {
    print("Ready for blastoff in $t second.\n");
  } else {
    print("Ready for blastoff in $t seconds.\n");
  }
  sleep(1);         # sleep 1 second
  $t--;             # decrement the counter
}
print("Blastoff!\n");
```

Chapter 6:

Stacking The Blocks

> *Since we cannot be universal*
> *and know all that is to be known of everything,*
> *we ought to know a little about everything.*
>
> – Pascal, *Pensées* (1670), 37, tr. W. F. Trotter

The previous chapter covered the basic building blocks of most programming languages: literals and variables, expressions and statements, operators, commands, and control flow. By putting these basic constructs together in various ways, you can build programs of arbitrary size and complexity.

Input And Output (I/O)

Most programs act upon **data** (information). They take data from somewhere (**input**), process it in some manner, and produce a report or perhaps new data that has been transformed in some way (**output**).

Input can be provided in several ways. It can be **hard-coded** – stored inside the program itself. It can be provided by interaction with the user (e.g., typing on a keyboard) or from a file which the program opens and reads.

Output can also be provided in several ways. The most common of these are to write (e.g., `print`) to the screen or to open and write to a file.

So far, our examples have been very simple. They don't do very much and they depend entirely on data that is hard-coded within the program (or acquired mysteriously prior to the example). This isn't very flexible, however. Most programs operate on data acquired from the outside world.

We'll cover reading and writing files in the next chapter. For now, our programs will get their input directly from the keyboard and write their output to the screen (specifically, to the MacPerl window).[1]

We introduced the `print` command in the previous chapter. We will continue to use `print` in these examples, both to prompt for input and to write the results of our programs to the screen.

Input

If a program expects input to be typed on the keyboard, it should **prompt** for input in some way; we will accomplish this by printing a request.

```
print('Please type something: ');
```

Note that we omitted the newline sequence, **\n**, from the `print` statement. This is a common way to put the prompt and the text the user types on the same line.[2]

Next, we need to tell Perl to expect some input from the keyboard, and to store that input somewhere. Input that comes from the keyboard is said to come from **standard input**. Note that standard input can be **redirected** to come from a file instead, but for now, we'll use the keyboard.

```
print('Please type something: ');
$input = <STDIN>;
```

Perl uses <STDIN> to read from the keyboard. This construct is known as the **line input operator**, or, simply, the **angle operator** (for the angle brackets which enclose it). The word within the angle brackets (e.g., STDIN) provides a **handle** to the location of the data.[3] The variable $input is set to the input line.[4]

---

[1] There are many other ways to handle input and output, such as mice, joysticks, bells and lights, sound and video devices, etc. The most common input and output methods for Perl scripts, however, involve typed user interaction and files.

[2] If your script uses the -1 switch, or sets the special variable, $\, a newline would be printed even if not specified.

[3] We will cover **filehandles** in the next chapter. For now, just remember that <STDIN> retrieves a line of text entered .

[4] Of course, we could call this variable anything we want to. If we don't specifically set a variable to the input line, Perl will set the special (magic) variable $_. $_ is the default pattern-searching and input space, and tends to crop up a lot. For now, we'll be explicit about naming our variables, but remember that $_ is implicitly there.

Finally, we should do something with the data we have stored.

```
print('Please type something: ');
$input = <STDIN>;
print("You typed: $input\n");
```

If you have been using MacPerl to try this out, you may have noticed that the program printed an extra blank line to the MacPerl output window.

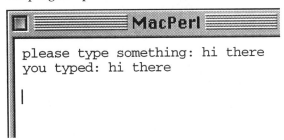

This is because MacPerl reads everything you typed, including the return, and stores the result in $input. When Perl executes the next statement

```
print("you typed: $input\n");
```

the result is that two newlines are printed – one that is specified in the code and one that is included in the $input variable.

Unless you really want the extra newline, it could become annoying. The chomp function removes the newline from its argument, leaving the rest of the string intact.[5]

```
print('please type something: ');
$input = <STDIN>;
chomp($input);
print("you typed: $input\n");
```

More Commands?

While it can be useful to get some data from the keyboard and print it back, this wouldn't be very interesting for long. Most programs do something with the data they take in, such as performing calculations, comparing the data

---

[5] Actually, chomp removes the current **line ending** character, if present. It returns (evaluates to) a truth value indicating whether it found (and removed) anything.

with other data, and so forth. As we discussed in the previous chapter, you tell Perl what to do with your data by issuing commands.

Perl has nearly 200 **built-in** commands (functions and named operators that act like functions). These are available as an integral part of Perl; you don't need to install them or do anything special to make them available. All you need to do is tell Perl to run a command, specifing any necessary arguments (data values for the command to act upon) in the proper order.

`length()`

For example, once you have your keyboard input, you could determine how many characters were typed. The following examples assume that we are adding code to the program we began writing above.

The `length` function determines the length of a character string and **returns** it as a scalar value. We can capture that value in a variable, and store it for future use or print it.

```
$len = length($input);
print("Your input is $len characters long.\n");
```

`index()`

Alternatively, you could determine whether there is a **space** (octal `\040`, also known as a **blank**) in the input string, using the `index` function. The `index` function returns the position of the first occurrence of a given **substring** (a portion of a larger string) in a given string.

```
# $position = index($str1, $str2, $offset);6
```

The `index` function requires two arguments. The first (`$str1`) is the string to search; the second (`$str2`) is the desired substring. An optional third argument (`$offset`) tells Perl where in the string to begin the search. If omitted, this starting **offset** is taken to be 0.[7]

If the specified substring is not found when the string is searched, `index` returns a value of `-1`. We'll add some **error checking** code to alert us if this is the case.

-----

[6] This line is commented to indicate that it is a syntax definition, not real code!

[7] Because Perl begins counting from 0, the index of the first character in a string (i.e., the index origin) is 0, rather than 1. As with so many things in Perl, the index origin can be changed to something other than 0. *Don't.*

```
$position = index($input, ' ');
if ($position < 0) {
  print("There are no blanks in your input.\n");
} else {
  print("There is a blank at position $position.\n");
}
```

Note: If you are typing this example in, take care; there's a single blank space between the single quotes in the statement

```
$position = index($input, ' ');
```

substr()

Now that we've found the first blank, we might want to print only the first word of the input, that is, everything before the first blank in the string. We know the position of the blank, and we can use the substr function to extract a substring from a string.

```
# $substr = substr($str1, $offset, $length);
```

Like index, substr requires two arguments, but has an optional third argument. The first two arguments specify the string to examine ($str1) and the offset ($offset) from which to begin. The third ($length) specifies the length of the substring to extract. If this is omitted, a substring will be extracted from the position spefified by offset to the end of the string (i.e., the maximum possible length).

```
if ($position < 0) {
  $substr = $input;
} else {
  $substr = substr($input, 0, $position);
}
print("The first word you typed was $substr.\n");
```

If there are no blanks in the input ($position < 0), we print the entire input string. Otherwise, we extract a substring from position 0 (the beginning of the string) to the first blank. The length is easy to calculate in this case, as it is equivalent to the value stored in $position.[8]

---

[8] If you don't see why, take some paper and a pencil and try a few examples. Remember to count characters in the string beginning with 0 until you reach the first blank, then go back and determine the length of the part before the blank. Hint: the *length* does not start with 0 unless there are no characters to count!

Note that it is acceptable to name a variable ($substr) with the same name as a function! The $ prevents any confusion (on the part of Perl :-).

Putting it all together

If you have been following along with our example, your script should now look something like this.

```
print('please type something: ');
$input = <STDIN>;
chomp($input);
print("you typed: $input\n");

$len = length($input);
print("Your input is $len characters long.\n");

$position = index($input, ' ');
if ($position < 0) {
  print("There are no blanks in your input.\n");
} else {
  print("There is a blank at position $position.\n");
}

if ($position < 0) {
  $substr = $input;
} else {
  $substr = substr($input, 0, $position);
}
print("The first word you typed was $substr.\n");
```

Pattern Matching

Perl excels at **pattern matching**, that is, comparing a string of data to a particular pattern of characters to see if it matches. A pattern, in this context, describes any regular set or sequence of characters which might be present.

The pattern to be matched is described by an expression which can be used anywhere a Perl expression can be used. When these expressions exploit regularities (patterns) in the data, they are referred to as **regular expressions**.[9] A pattern is specified by enclosing a pattern description between a pair of **delimiter** characters, usually /slashes/.

---

[9] There has been some discussion of whether Perl patterns are (truly) regular expressions. Those who are interested in this discussion are referred to Tom Christiansen's *Perl Wizard's Quiz* in *The Perl Journal*, (vol. 2, no. 4), Winter 1997.

There are three variations on the basic pattern matching expression. Each uses a different named operator, which is placed before the initial delimiter character, and each has a slightly different format.[10]

m//	**match**	m/*pattern*/
s///	**substitute**	s/*pattern*/*replacement*/
tr///	**translate**	tr/*pattern*/*replacement*/

In most cases, the goal is simply to search for (match) a particular pattern. Occasionally, however, you may want to modify the data, based on the success of the particular match. At these times, you'll want to use a **substitution** or **translation** operator.

Although the slash,/, is perhaps most common, any non-alphanumeric, non-whitespace character can be used for the delimiters.[11] And, because matching is a very common operation, the **m** operator is optional as long as the delimiters used are slashes. If you decide to use some other character (e.g., **#**), you must use m to tell Perl that this is a pattern matching expression , as m#pattern#. However, to explicitly indicate that a pattern is to be **matched**, the **m** may be specified. If the operation is a substitution or translation, the operator (s or tr) is always required.[12]

Perl also has two **binding operators** for use with pattern operations:

| =~ | **successful (matches)** |
| !~ | **unsuccessful (does not match)** |

Binding operators act somewhat differently from other operators we have seen so far. Sometimes they act like comparison operators; at other times they may seem more like asignment operators.

A binding operator **binds** a scalar expression to a pattern operation (match, substitution, or translation). The argument to the left of the binding operator consists of a scalar expression or string which will be searched (and pos-

---

[10] The **translation operator, tr///**, does not use regular expressions in its matches; translation patterns are matched character for character. However, the **tr** operator looks and feels a lot like the **m//** and **s///** operators, so it makes sense to discuss it along with the others.

[11] A ? is a special case, however. If you match a pattern using ? as the delimiter, ?abc?, the pattern will be matched only once, finding only the first occurrence of the pattern. No other delimiter choices have special meaning.

[12] You may see expressions of the form y/.../.../. The **y** is synonymous with tr.

sibly modifed). The argument to the right of the operator consists of the pattern expression that performs the match, substitution, or translation.

Let's begin with a matching expression, as these are the most popular. Here is another way to tell if there is a blank in your input string (if not what its position is). We could add this code to the program we've been writing.

```
if ($input =~ / /) {
  print("There is a blank in your input.\n");
} else {
  print("There are no blanks in your input.\n");
}
```

The `if` statement compares the input string, stored in `$input`, to the pattern described as `/ /` (one blank space). The binding operator (=~) returns success if the pattern matches the string (i.e., occurs anywhere in the string). Note that we could also have written the `if` statement as:

```
if ($input =~ m/ /) {
```

This pattern is quite simple: a single blank space, occurring anywhere in the input line. Don't be fooled; patterns (and the corresponding expressions) can be *very* complex and exceedingly powerful! So, hang on ...

Perl provides a number of tools for composing patterns, to make descriptions easier to write.[13] First, patterns generally contain literal characters, which match themselves in the target string:

```
/ /
/hello/
```

Next, Perl provides a set of **escape sequences** which may be used as a form of shorthand in describing certain common types of characters or patterns. Many of the escape sequences which can be used in `print` statements are available for use in regular expressions as well (e.g., \t, tab, \n, newline, \f, formfeed, and \a, "alarm" or "bell"). Some, however, have different meanings (\b is a backspace in a print statement but matches a word boundary in a regular expression).

Here is an abbreviated list, to get you started. See Chapter 19, *Operators*, for a complete list.

---

[13] Some people would disagree that any of this gets easier. Perhaps we should say, more flexible.

\t	match a tab character
\0n	match an octal number n[14]
\d	match any digit [0-9]
\D	match any nondigit
\w	match any "word" character (letter, digit, or underscore)
\s	match any whitespace character (e.g., tab, space, newline)
\b	match at a word boundary

Finally, Perl provides **metacharacters** which do not match themselves, but which modify the nature of a pattern. For example, metacharacters may be used to group parts of a pattern, to **anchor** a pattern to the beginning or end of a string, or to specify a certain number of repetitions.[15] The **backslash** character used in the escape sequences above is itself a metacharacter.

\	"escape" character
[]	describe a character class[16]
()	parenthesize for grouping
*	repeat the previous match 0 or more times
+	repeat the previous match 1 or more times
?	repeat the previous match 0 or 1 times
^	anchor a pattern to the beginning of the line
$	anchor a pattern to the end of the line
.	match any (single) character
|	alternation (choice of alternative matches)

Several of these metacharacters can also be combined to produce variations in meaning (e.g., a character class, repeated one or more times).

Matching

We'll define a few patterns that you might use in the program we've been constructing, to let you see how pattern matching works in context. Feel free

---

[14] A backslashed two- or three-digit octal number matches the character with that octal (ASCII) value. For example, \015 matches the **carriage return** character, **^M**.

[15] If you ever wish to match one of these metacharacters literally, you must **escape** it by preceding it with a backslash. This removes the special meaning from the character.

[16] A **character class** is a set of characters, where the pattern may match any member of the set. For example, the regular expression class [0123456789] describes the set of digits from 0 through 9, inclusive. For series classes, a dash, -, may be used to represent missing but assumed members (e.g., [0-9] also represents the same set of digits).

to experiment by substituting one of these for the / / expression we used in the previous example, or by writing new `if` statements (be sure to modify the associated `print` statements appropriately!).

```
/[A-Z]/       # any capital letter
/^[A-Z]/      # string starts with a capital letter
/[aeiou]/     # any vowel
/\d\d\d/      # a sequence of three digits
/ ....../     # a space, followed by any 6 characters
/\./          # a literal period
/\.$/         # a period at the end of a string
/[1-3]+/      # one or more instances of 1, 2, or 3
/Tue|Thu/     # either Tue or Thu
```

Try entering the following strings as input to your program. Which patterns will match which strings?

```
hello!
I cooked 12 eggs.
This is a sentence.
454 Maple Street
Thursday, Dec. 25 1997
Tom Thumb
```

What expressions could you write that would match the different patterns found in the following string, extracted from a typical email message?

```
Date: Sun, 28 Dec 1997 20:37:03 -0500 (EST)
```

Which of the expressions you've written would be the hardest to fool (that is, which is the least likely to match a string that is not a typical date string?).[17] Which expression would be the easiest to fool? What sort of data could you create that would incorrectly match your patterns?

Substitution

The patterns we have used so far have only made use of Perl's matching facility. However, text can also be replaced (**substituted**) if a match is successful. A substitution expression looks very similar to a matching expression, except that it begins with an initial (required) **s**. The substitution

---

[17] Hint: The "Tom Thumb" example above will "fool" a pattern designed to match days of the week using /Tue|Thu/.

expression also describes the **replacement** text which will be substituted for the target text if a pattern match is successful.

The example below will substitute the string December for the string Dec. if found. Try adding this code to the script we have been creating, then enter one of the sample date strings shown previously under Matching.

```
$input =~ s/Dec\./December/;
print("The substituted string is: $input\n");
```

Used as shown, the substitution changes the value of a variable. If you wanted to preserve that value, you could first set a new variable to have the same value as the first, then change the new variable.

```
$newstring = $input;
$newstring =~ s/Dec\./December/;
print("The substituted string is: $newstring\n");
print("The original string is: $input\n");
```

Perl provides a convenient idiom (shortcut) for this type of operation.

```
($newstring = $input) =~ s/Dec\./December/;
print("The substituted string is: $newstring\n");
```

First, the lefthand side of the expression, ($newstring = $input) is evaluated, setting $newstring to the value of $input; next, $newstring becomes the lefthand side of a new operation and the substitution takes place. The final value of $newstring is the substituted value.

The next example translates text files into Macintosh line-ending format. Typically, Unix text files use a linefeed (octal \012) at the ends of lines, Macintosh text files use a carriage return (octal \015), and DOS (and Windows) text files use both. This pattern matches lines which end with (no more than one) carriage return, followed by a linefeed, replacing matching strings with a single carriage return.[18]

```
($line = $input) =~ s/\015?\012/\015/;
```

Translation

Translation expressions are usually discussed along with pattern matching and substitution, even though translation does not use regular expressions.

---

[18] You may have some difficulty entering any sample text for this substitution to work on! Try this example again after we begin to work with files, in the next chapter.

Instead, translation searches a string, one character at a time, **translating** (replacing) all occurrences of one set of characters into the corresponding characters in another set.

The code below will translate all uppercase letters in the input string into their lowercase counterparts.[19]

```
($lower = $input) =~ tr/A-Z/a-z/;
print("The translated string is: $lower\n");
```

Breaking Data Apart

Earlier in this chapter we learned how to find the first word in an input string by searching for the first blank space. But what if we wanted to find the second word, or the last? And what if the words are separated by more than one space or by another character such as a tab?

There is an easy way to break an input string into words or **fields**. split breaks a character string into one or more substrings, based on a given separating pattern (e.g., a tab, space, or other character). The split function can be especially useful when working with data that has been exported from a spreadsheet, a data base, or a calendar application, as these programs frequently have an option to export data as **tab-separated text**.

Unlike the functions we have used so far, split returns, not a scalar value, but an array. Each element of the array contains one substring of the original string.

We discussed arrays briefly in previous chapters. An array variable can hold multiple values, in this example, split-up pieces of a string:

```
@pieces = split(/\t/, $input);
print("The first word is: $pieces[0]\n");
print("The last word is: $pieces[$#pieces]\n");
```

The split function breaks the input string ($input), into pieces, or substrings, based on a given pattern (e.g., a tab character, /\t/). It returns an array (@pieces) containing those substrings.

Recall that Perl begins counting at 0, so the first element of the array is at position (or offset, or **index**) 0 and is expressed as $pieces[0]. Note that a

---

[19] Try adding this code to the script we have been creating, then enter some of the sample input suggested previously under Matching.

single element of an array is itself a scalar value (single items are scalars); use the **$** prefix when referring to an array element.

Perl returns the index value of the last element of an array in the variable $#*arrayname*, in this case, $#pieces. Because array indexes begin at 0, the index of the last element will always be numerically one less than the actual number of elements in an array.[20]

```
$count = $#pieces + 1;
print("There are $count fields in your string.\n");
```

An Array Of Possibilities

Ordinary arrays are indexed by number; the first position is at 0 and the last is at $#*arrayname*. You could use a loop to walk through the array.[21]

```
for ($i = $#pieces; $i >= 0; $i--) {
    print("\$pieces[$i] contains: $pieces[$i]\n");
}
```

The loop above walks through the array in reverse order, from the last element to the first. Of course, you could access an array in any order: first element to last, last to first, or by some other method of your choosing. Here is another style of loop that will print every item in an array, in order.

```
foreach $item (@pieces) {
    print("$item\n");
}
```

You can fill an array in any of several ways. As we have seen, an array can be returned by a function, such as split. Or, you can fill the array yourself, specifying the positions of each element (e.g., using a loop). Array elements can be set to any values: numbers, strings, or the results of expressions. Note that you do not have to fill every position in an array; the "empty" positions contain **null** (the empty string, ' ', which coerces to 0) values.

---

[20] As an interesting side effect, if you use the array in a scalar context (i.e., treat the variable as if it were a scalar value) it will return the length of the array (i.e., the actual number of items in the array). Try:
```
$count = @pieces; print("There are $count fields."\n);
```

[21] TMTOWTDI: Alternatively, use the range operator, **..**, to create the loop:
```
foreach $i (0 .. $#pieces) {
    print...
```

```
for ($i = 0; $i <= 15; $i += 5) {
  $my_array[$i] = 1;
}
foreach $item (@my_array) {
  print("$item");
}
print("\n");
```

Note: Perl does not require you to specify the size of an array before you use it. An array will simply keep getting larger as you add more items (until you run out of memory!). For efficiency's sake, however, you may wish to "pre-allocate" large arrays by setting the value of the highest position you expect to use: `$my_array[1000000] = '';`

You can provide a **list** of values and Perl will fill your array for you, beginning with position 0 and continuing until there are no more values remaining. This is a very common way to **initialize** an array.

```
@colors = ('red', 'green', 'yellow', 'blue');
for ($i = 0; $i <= $#colors; $i++) {
  print("position $i contains: $colors[$i]\n");
}
```

Perl provides several functions for working with arrays. `push()` and `pop()` add and remove items from the "end" of an array (treating it as a **stack**). `shift()` and `unshift()` also add and remove items, but at the "front" (index 0). By using these operators in concert, you can treat the array as a **queue** or even a **deque (double-ended queue)**. `splice()`, the most general of these functions, can add or remove items at arbitrary positions in an array.

Several interesting and useful arrays are predefined in MacPerl, including:

@ARGV   the array containing the command line arguments for a Perl script (or list of files dropped onto a MacPerl droplet).

@INC   the array containing the list of places to look for Perl libraries; this is set by the Libraries preference.

Hashes

What if you wanted a more memorable way to index an array than by numbers? Alternatively, what if your array is **sparse** (containing many unused positions)? For times when ordinary arrays are not what you need, Perl provides **hashes** (also known as **associative arrays**).

A hash also holds multiple values, but each value is indexed by a (possibly) non-numeric **key**.[22] You provide the keys as you fill the hash. The items in a hash are **unordered**; that is, they are accessed by their keys but there is no way of knowing what the internal structure of the hash is.[23] You might think that this lack of order would make hashes slow or difficult to use. Actually, they are fast, easy to use, and quite powerful.

To distinguish a hash from an ordinary array, hash names begin with **%**. When you refer to a single element of a hash, however, that element is a scalar value and is prefixed with a **$**; individual hash elements are distinguished from array elements by the use of braces, **{}**, instead of brackets, **[]**, surrounding the key (index).

Let's get on to some examples.

Because the elements of a hash are unordered, Perl cannot provide the keys for you as it could with the indexes of an ordinary array. You must provide the keys as you fill the hash. A hash is initialized by providing a list of key / value pairs. Every other item in the list (beginning with the first) is a key; the alternating items are values.

```
%colors = ('ball', 'red', 'sky', 'blue');
print("The ball is $colors{'ball'}.\n");
```

It's not very easy to see the key / value pairs here, so we'll take advantage of Perl's insensitivity to whitespace (Perl usually doesn't care where you put extra blanks, tabs, and carriage returns) to reformat this statement as:

```
%colors = ('ball',    'red',
           'sky',     'blue');
```

To make things even more readable, Perl provides the **=>** operator. It's just a synonym for the comma, but it's easier to distinguish and more memorable (if used correctly).[24]

```
%colors = ('ball'  => 'red',
           'sky'   => 'blue');
```

---

[22] If the key is numeric, it will be coerced to a string before it is used.

[23] In contrast, the elements of an ordinary array are **ordered**. The element at position 1 is always between the elements at positions 0 and 2.

[24] As a side effect, the => operator forces the argument to its left to be interpreted as a string. So you don't actually *need* to put in the quotes ... but we will anyway.

You might want to pronounce **=>** as "gets the value".

Hash items can be printed in the same way that ordinary array items are printed (just remember to use braces, **{ }**, around the key!).[25]

```
print("The ball is $colors{'ball'}.\n");
print("The sky is $colors{'sky'}.\n");
```

This method of printing could get tedious, however. You may be wondering if there is an equivalent to the loop commands we used with arrays, to print each member of a hash. Because a hash is unordered, you cannot use a loop with an incremented (or decremented) counter. However, you can use a `for` or `foreach` loop if you combine it with a function called `keys`.[26]

The `keys` function returns a list of all the keys in a specified hash. The keys cannot be assumed to be returned in any particular order; that is, they will most likely *not* be returned in the order in which they were stored!

```
foreach $key (keys(%colors)) {
  print("key: $key, color: $colors{$key}\n");
}
```

If a particular ordering is important, you can sort the retrieved `keys`.

```
foreach $key (sort(keys(%colors))) {
  print("key: $key, color: $colors{$key}\n");
}
```

Perl has several functions for working with hashes: `each` and `values` also return the elements of the hash (in different ways); `exists` determines if a particular key exists; `delete` removes a specified key (and its value).

Many interesting and useful hashes are predefined in MacPerl, including

`%ENV`   contains information about your current environment; this is set by the **Environment** preference. In particular, `$ENV{TMPDIR}` is the name of a folder where temporary files can be stored.

---

[25] The key need not be explicitly quoted, as the braces themselves provide quoting for any single identifier (element) in a subscript. That is, `$colors{ball}` is usually acceptable. Under certain circumstances, however, leaving out the quotes may generate a warning if you use the `-w` switch, so be warned!

[26] The `foreach` keyword is actually just a synonym for `for` so you can use whichever you feel most comfortable using. In practice, the keywords are used as we show them; that is, `foreach` is most often used when iterating over an array or hash.

See Part IV, *Reference*, for more information on hash-related functions, pre-defined hashes, etc.

Multiple Dimensions

It may sound like a term from a science fiction story, but Perl arrays can have multiple dimensions. A multiply-dimensioned array is simply an array of arrays – each element in the array is, itself, an array.[27] Multiply-dimensioned arrays can become very complex, and we'll only be giving you a brief taste here. For a more complete and in-depth discussion, we refer you to *Programming Perl* and (perhaps) *Advanced Perl Programming*.

The following code creates a simple array of arrays which can be mapped as a two-dimensional matrix. The first dimension is "vertical" (the rows); the second is "horizontal" (the columns). What will the third `print` statement print?

```
@matrix = (
    ['yellow', 'purple', 'red',    'blue' ],
    ['pear',   'grape',  'apple', 'berry'],
    ['small',  'medium', 'large', 'huge' ],
);
print ("$matrix[0][0]\n");    # prints yellow
print ("$matrix[1][1]\n");    # prints grape
print ("$matrix[2][2] $matrix[0][1] $matrix[1][3]\n");
```

Context

Perl has two types of variables: ones which contain a *single* value (scalars) and ones which contain *multiple* values (arrays and hashes). Some functions (e.g., `length`, `index`) return scalar values; others (e.g., `split`, `keys`) return lists of values which can be assigned to an array.

Every operation in Perl is evaluated in a specific **context**. Assignment to an array or a hash is said to be evaluated in a **list context**.[28] List context is also provided by assignment to a list of scalars. For example:

```
($a, $b, $c) = split (/ /, $line);
```

---

[27] Or, more pedantically, a **reference** to an array (or perhaps a hash …).

[28] A third context, interpolative context, refers specifically to what occurs inside quotes or "quote-like things" such as a pattern match, `m//`. Interpolative context is neither scalar nor list context, but then, you'll seldom need to worry about it …

If, however, a value is assigned to a scalar variable, the operation is said to be evaluated in a **scalar context**. Simply assigning a list value to a scalar variable can switch from list context to scalar context:

```
$nfields = @fields;
```

If this **implicit context switch** is not to your taste, the `scalar` function provides an explict way to make the same conversion.

```
$nfields = scalar(@fields);
```

Two special cases of scalar context deserve their own names. In a **Boolean context**, an expression is evaluated as either true or false; the actual scalar value does not matter.[29] A scalar value is **true** unless it is the null string, the number 0, or the string `"0"`, in which case, it is **false**.

In **void context**, it really doesn't matter what value is returned, or even whether it's true or false. Void context doesn't require any return value.

Context becomes more interesting when you realize that many operators and functions *know which context they were invoked in*. That is, the context is determined by the caller and the operator (or function) returns a different type of value based on that context. For example, the `split()` function can return either a list of substrings (fields) in list context, or a count of the fields found in scalar context.

```
$string = "This is a string.";
@fields = split(/ /, $string);
foreach $field (@fields) {
  print("$field\n");              # prints each field
}
$n_fields = split(/ /, $string);
print("$n_fields\n");             # prints 4
```

---

[29] The term Boolean is named for a mathematician, George Boole, who developed an "algebra of logic" as a way of expressing logical constructs mathematically.

Chapter 7:

- *Filehandles*
- *Reading Input*
- *Error Handling*
- *Pathnames*
- *Writing Output*
- *Redirecting Standard I/O*
- *Working With Folders (Directories)*
- *Working With Aliases*

Filing The Edges

You cannot create experience.
You must undergo it.

– Albert Camus, *Notebooks 1935-1942*, I. tr. Philip Tody

You can only go so far by interactively typing all of your data into a program. Sooner or later, you'll have one or more files full of data you want to work on. These files could come from many places: exported tabular data from a spreadsheet program or a database application, calendar or contact data from an organizer application, email archives, or even another Perl program. In order to process this data, your Perl program will need to be able to open, read from, and possibly write to, files on your disk.

Perl works with files by means of a data type called a **filehandle**. Filehandles are also used when working with **devices** (things like printers or windows on the screen) and **sockets**.[1] Sockets are discussed later in the book, in relation to networking applications. The analogous data type for working with directories (folders), by the way, is the **directory handle**.[2]

Filehandles

A filehandle is, simply, a symbolic name (a handle) that you attach to a file so that you can refer to it and access it throughout your program. By

---

[1] and **pipes**, on systems that support them

[2] Filehandles have a separate namespace from directory handles.

associating a filehandle with the actual file on disk, Perl hides much of the internal complexity of working with files from you, the programmer.

You choose the names for your filehandles, using the same naming rules as for variables. That is, a filehandle name can consist of letters, numbers, or underscores, and must begin with a letter or underscore.

To make things easier, Perl provides three predefined, standard filehandles for working with input and output.[3] These predefined filehandles are initially associated with devices, not with files. We've already seen an example of a filehandle in the previous chapter. **STDIN** is a predefined filehandle that refers to **standard input** (usually typed at the keyboard).

There are two predefined filehandles for working with output. **STDOUT** is the filehandle associated with **standard output** (normally the MacPerl window). **STDERR** is associated with **standard error output**; this is normally set to the MacPerl window, but it can be separated so that error messages from your program don't get mixed up with the regular output.[4]

By now, you should have noticed some patterns in the names of these filehandles. For one thing, each name is written entirely in uppercase letters (remember that Perl is case sensitive).[5] For another, each name begins with STD, to indicate that it is a standard filehandle.

By convention, filehandles are named in all uppercase letters, to distinguish them from function names and other keywords. (Case is not necessary to distinguish filehandles from variable names, as variable names always begin with $, @, or %.) You aren't required to use this naming convention (TMTOWTDI, after all), but we recommend it strongly. Conventions such as this one help make your programs easier to read and maintain.

---

[3] The three pre-defined standard filehandles are pre-opened as well. Each can be **re-opened** as needed to associate it with something else, such as a different window or a file on your disk. We advise you not to **close** the standard filehandles unless you really understand what you are doing!

[4] The separation is done by re-opening either STDERR or STDOUT (or both) in association with a file or a different device (e.g., a different window). We'll cover this in more detail under *Redirecting Standard I/O*, later in this chapter.

[5] You may be interested to know that the filehandles stdout, stderr, and stdin are also predefined and pre-opened as synonyms for the ones discussed here. We recommend, however, that you stick with the uppercase versions.

We also recommend that you choose names that are **mnemonic** (easy to remember) and related in some way either to the file you are opening (e.g., LOG) or to how you are using that file (e.g., IN). As with variable names, a filehandle name can be arbitrary (within the set of alphanumeric characters and _); however, as with variable names, your choice should be well-considered. You may enjoy calling all of your filehandles FRED and BART, but the next person to read your program probably won't thank you for it!

You attach a filehandle to a file by using the open function, which takes two arguments: the name of the filehandle you are creating and the name of the file you wish to open. The file will be opened and the filehandle will be associated with the file until you close it (or exit the program).

If you open a file using a filehandle that is already associated with another file, the first file will be silently closed and the filehandle will be reassociated with the new file! Be careful to keep track of your filehandles, and use memorable names to avoid accidentally closing files you thought were open (and thereby confusing your data).

Files may be opened for **reading** (the default), **writing**, or **appending**. You can also open for reading and writing simultaneously.[6] You tell Perl which you want to do by inserting extra characters (e.g., **>**) before the filename.[7]

```
open(IN,      'mydata');  # open mydata for reading
open(IN,     '<mydata');  # explicit open for reading
open(IO,    '+<mydata');  # open for read and write
open(IO,    '+>mydata');  # open for read and write
open(OUT,    '>newfile'); # create or truncate newfile
open(ADD,   '>>oldfile'); # create or append to oldfile
```

If you open a file for writing, and the file already exists, the existing data will be deleted upon opening. If you want to write to an existing file without destroying its current contents, be sure to use the append mode. When you

---

[6] Exercise caution if you do this; you could easily make a mistake! Use of temporary files is generally safer.

[7] These characters, <, >, and >>, will be familiar to readers who have used a DOS- or Unix-based operating system. If they are unfamiliar to you, think of them as arrows; < "comes from" and > "goes to" the named file (>> adds to the end of the file).

are finished using a file, you can close the filehandle (disassociating it from the file) by using the `close` function.[8]

```
close(IN);
```

Reading Input

Once you have opened a file and attached a filehandle to it, you can read data from (or write data to) the file. You can use the filehandle anywhere in your program that you need to work with the associated file.

This may seem a little strange at first (you may be asking "why can't I just work with the file directly?"), but there are good reasons for using file-handles. File I/O can get complicated and messy; filehandles hide most of the details and make working with files much easier.

The following piece of code opens a file called `README` and attaches it to the filehandle, `IN`. It then loops over each line in the file, reading and printing each line in turn. We use the **line input** or **angle** operator to read the data from the filehandle; evaluating a filehandle within angle brackets, `<>`, yields each line of the associated file, in turn.[9] (Recall from the previous chapter that we read lines from the keyboard using `<STDIN>`.)

```
open(IN, 'README');
while ($line = <IN>) {
  print($line);
}
close(IN);
```

If you enter this code into a new MacPerl script and run the script without saving first, the script will attempt to open the file `README` in the MacPerl ƒ folder. However, if you save the script and then run it, it will try to open a file called `README` in the same folder where you saved the script.

> **Note:** Unix and MPW have a concept called the **current directory** which refers to the directory where things will happen by default. For most Macintosh applications, the current directory is less well defined. It may be the folder where the application resides or the folder where

---

[8] It's good practice to close your filehandles, but don't worry if you forget. Perl closes all open filehandles when a program finishes and exits.

[9] TMTOWTDI: `print while <IN>;`

the currently open document (file) can be found. Alternatively, the "current" folder may be the most recent folder visited by the application, or it may be the Documents folder.

If you tried saving the script as we just mentioned, you may have noticed some peculiar results (depending on where you saved the script). If there is no file called README in the same folder as the saved script, *nothing is printed*. Perl doesn't complain that it can't find the file README.

If you try to open a file that doesn't exist (or which cannot be opened for some other reason), the open function will return an error. However, unless you capture the error and act upon it, Perl will go happily on processing your script (and the results will probably not be what you planned!).

Error Handling

To avoid confusion, most Perl programmers check the **status** of the open, printing an appropriate error message if something went wrong.[10] Perl provides several functions to make **error handling** easier. If the problem is serious (e.g., the input file cannot be opened) there is probably very little point to continuing. In this case, you should use **die**, which causes your program to stop immediately.

```
open(IN, 'README') or die;
```

This statement can be read as "open README or die". If the file (README) cannot be opened, the program will stop, printing Died to the screen.

This is an improvement over what we had before; at least the program doesn't keep trying to go on without input. But Died is not a particularly informative error, especially if there was more than one location in your program where something could have gone wrong.

```
open(IN, 'README') or die('Could not open README');
```

If you supply die with a message string, it will print that string to STDERR before exiting.[11] We recommend including the name of the file that couldn't

---

[10] Many Perl functions return status (1 for success; 0 for failure). In general, it's a very good idea to check the status of these function calls and handle any errors. If you don't, and the function fails, the results may be very mysterious indeed.

[11] In fact, die takes a **list** as its argument and will print the concatenated value of that list. In many cases, however, this means that it will print the string you told it to print.

be opened, as well as any other pertinent information, in the message. If the message string does not end with a newline, Perl will append the name of the current script and the current line number to the message.

```
# Could not open file.
File 'HD:scripts:foo.pl'; Line 1
```

This may or may not be useful (line numbers can be very helpful for debugging purposes, but they may only confuse a future user of your program).

If the situation is not so serious that you want the execution of your program to cease, use warn instead. Like die, warn prints a message on STDERR, but it won't cause the program to stop.

```
warn("Warning: Debugging is on!\n") if ($DEBUG != 0);
```

Again, if you leave out the newline, \n, warn will include the name of the script and the current line number in its message.

Pathnames

So far, we've covered opening a file which can be found in the "current directory" (probably the same folder where you've saved your Perl script). This isn't very flexible, however. It shouldn't be necessary to store all of your data files in the same folder as your programs! How do you open a file that is located somewhere else on your disk (or even on another volume)?

There are several ways to open an arbitrary file. You can:

- specify the file within your Perl script, using its **pathname**

- put up a **dialog**, allowing users to navigate to and choose a file

- create a MacPerl **droplet**, then drag and drop the file onto it

We'll get back to the latter two methods (dialog boxes and droplets) in the next chapter. For now, let's continue our discussion of pathnames.

A filename (e.g., README) is the name of a file found within a particular directory. The name need not be unique; another directory may contain a file with the same name. Thus, to allow unambiguous references to a specific file, we must specify the **path** to that file through the filesystem.

A **full pathname** begins with the name of the volume, followed by the names of all folders which need to be opened until you reach the folder containing the file of interest. Each part of the pathname is separated from the other parts by a colon, **:**.[12] The output message from die in the example in the previous section contained a full pathname to the script that died.

```
File 'HD:scripts:foo.pl'; Line 1
```

In this case, HD is the name of a volume (a disk); scripts is a folder at the top level of that volume; foo.pl is a file in the scripts folder.

A **relative pathname** is similar to a full pathname, but contains the path from the current directory to the desired file or folder; that is, the folders are named "relative" to the current directory. For example, the following open statement uses a relative pathname.

```
open(IN, ":stuff:README");
```

In this example, the folder stuff is presumed to be in the current directory. The file, README, is expected to be in the stuff folder.

On the Macintosh, full pathnames always begin with the name of a disk **volume**.[13] Elements are separated by colons, **:**. If the pathname contains only a volume name, it must still contain (end with) a colon. If any elements contain spaces or tabs (let alone at signs or dollar signs!), be sure to quote the entire pathname. (Hint: play it safe and use quotes for all pathnames...)

```
MyHardDisk:                                  # volume
'MyHardDisk:Desktop Folder:LaserJet 4'       # file
'MyHardDisk:System Folder:Extensions:'       # folder
Perl:MacPerl:Mac_Perl_519r4_appl             # file
HD:chapter6.pl                               # file
```

Files that appear on the desktop actually reside in an invisible folder named Desktop Folder on the particular disk volume. Note that, although all desktop files appear to be on the same "virtual" desktop, each disk volume actually maintains its own Desktop Folder.[14]

---

[12] Different operating systems use different separators. For example, Unix uses slashes, **/**. MS-DOS uses backslashes, ****.

[13] For example, a hard disk, CD-ROM, removable media, etc.

[14] And its own Trash as well.

Note: You may have noticed what appear to be pathnames in Get Info windows. Get Info will show where a file resides, but its information may be incomplete.

Keep in mind that Get Info does not show the full pathname of the file itself, only of the folder or volume that contains it. Also, Get Info shows the location of files on the desktop as if they were located in the **root** of the volume, rather than in the Desktop Folder.

Relative pathnames begin with a colon, **:** (that is, they look a lot like full pathnames, except they do not begin with a volume name). The double colon construct, **::**, means "up one level" in the folder hierarchy.[15,16]

```
:stuff:README                          # file
::                                     # folder
::CPAN:authors:                        # folder
```

The following code example illustrates full and relative pathnames, using a function, `chdir`, which changes the current directory to a named directory, and a command, `` `pwd` ``, which prints the full pathname to the current working directory. If you try this example in MacPerl, be sure that the MacPerl disc is loaded.

```
chdir('Perl:MacPerl') or warn;
print(`pwd`);
chdir('::') or warn;
print(`pwd`);
chdir(':CPAN:authors:Chris_Nandor') or warn;
print(`pwd`);
```

Note: Generally, expressions in backquotes, `` ` ``, do not work in MacPerl (unless you are running MPW Perl and have ToolServer installed). The backquote is used to evaluate a command "outside" of the Perl program (e.g., a Unix shell command), which Mac OS does not allow. However, several expressions, such as `` `pwd` ``, are so popular that they have been specially implemented (emulated, really) in MacPerl.

---

[15] Readers familiar with Unix will recognize this as analogous to the **..** construct in Unix pathnames. Note, however, that **:::** is analogous to **../..** (up two levels), etc.

[16] Do not confuse the **::** in pathnames with the **::** construct used by Perl modules! They only look the same; the context is entirely different.

Note that the returned value includes a newline, so you do not need to use \n in the `print` statement.[17] Also, note that the last `print` statement may not display what you expected. This statement prints

```
Perl:CPAN:authors:id:CNANDOR
```

because the folder named by the (relative) path

```
:CPAN:authors:Chris_Nandor
```

is actually an **alias** to the folder

```
Perl:CPAN:authors:id:CNANDOR
```

When you access (e.g., `open` or `chdir` to) an alias from within a MacPerl script, the result is the same as if you had accessed the file (or folder) that the alias references.

We've included a small MacPerl droplet, path2clip, on the MacPerl disc, to help you in using pathnames.[18] When you drag and drop any file or folder onto path2clip, its full pathname is determined and copied to the Clipboard. You can then cut and paste the path string into any text document, such as a MacPerl script you may be writing.

Writing Output

We've been using `print` a lot, so you may feel fairly comfortable about writing output. However, at this point we've only sent output to the MacPerl window (also known as standard output or `STDOUT`). So, let's consider doing something more interesting, such as:

- separating error messages from other output[19]

- printing status messages to a log file

---

[17] Do not enclose expressions such as `` `pwd` `` in double quotes; you will only get the literal string `` `pwd` `` (backquoted expressions do not evaluate within double quotes).

[18] You can examine the code for path2clip by opening it from MacPerl (droplets cannot be edited using a text editor such as BBEdit). We've used the Dartmouth XCMDs package, discussed in more detail in Chapter 12, *The MacPerl Package*.

[19] Using Unix or MPW, you can **redirect** the standard error and standard output to (separate) files. The standalone MacPerl application has no provision for separating standard error from standard output, but you should know it can be done in case you port your script to another system (or MacPerl adds this feature in the future).

- sending different "streams" of output to different files based on characteristics of the data

- printing output with a specific format

The first three of these alternatives can be accomplished using filehandles. The fourth, printing output with a specific format, makes use of special formatting functions. We'll cover filehandles first and come back to formatted printing shortly.

Recall that earlier we introduced STDOUT, a filehandle associated with standard output (normally the MacPerl window). In fact, STDOUT is the default filehandle for output (just as STDIN is the default filehandle for input). We could have specified the filehandle in the print statements in any of our previous examples:

```
print STDOUT ($line);
print STDOUT (`pwd`);
```

You may have noticed something a little unusual about these statements. Isn't STDOUT an argument to print? Did we forget to include a comma? (There's a comma after the filehandle when you use open.) And why didn't we put the filehandle inside the parentheses, as we did with open? What's going on?

The comma is specifically omitted after the name of the filehandle because of the way the print statement works. The syntax of a print statement is

```
print FILEHANDLE list of things to print
```

So far, our lists of things to print have been confined to single strings. But print can just as easily include more than one thing (variables, strings, expressions, etc.) in its list. (The use of multiple arguments to print is especially useful if one of the arguments is an expression to be evaluated.)

```
$name = 'Vicki';
print('My name is ', $name, ".\n");
print('Pi is approximated by ', 355/113, ".\n");
```

If you forget and follow the filehandle with a comma, Perl won't know whether the first argument to print is a filehandle or something to print! This gets worse if you've stored a filehandle in a variable:

```
$loghndl = 'LOG';
open($loghndl, '>logfile') or die;
```

```
print($loghndl, "Finished.\n");          # wrong!
print $loghndl ("Finished.\n");          # right
```

In fact, the need to write statements like this, where a filehandle is stored in a scalar variable, is exactly the reason why the filehandle is not followed by a comma.

Now you may have guessed why, in the previous examples, we put the filehandle outside of the parentheses. The reason is to make it even more clear that the filehandle is separate from the argument list (and to remind ourselves not to include the comma).

```
print $loghndl ("Finished.\n");
```

Printing large blocks of text

If you need to print more than one or two lines of output in sequence, consider using a **here document**[20] rather than multiple print statements in a row. A here document provides a special way of quoting a large block of text.[21] It begins by specifying a **terminating string** (preceded by the characters, **<<**, to indicate that this is a here document).

```
print <<EOF;
```

The start of the here document, and the specification of the terminating string, are part of a statement, in this case a `print` statement. Be sure to end this statement with a semicolon, `;`, as usual. Lines of text to be printed follow, until the terminating string appears by itself on a line.

The terminating string must be the only thing on the line; that is, it must not be quoted or indented, and no other character may follow it *except for a newline*. Note that the terminating string *must* be followed by a newline (i.e., be sure to type RETURN after EOF).

```
print <<EOF;
Mary had a little lamb,
its fleece was white as snow.
```

---

[20] The term comes from Unix shell scripts, which can take input from a file (document) as well as from the command line. When that input is specially encapsulated as part of the script, the "document data" is said to be "right here", thus, the feature was referred to as a "here document". Perl continues to use the name for historical reasons.

[21] Here documents can be used for more than just printing output (e.g., to set a variable to a multi-line string). The syntax is similar.

```
And everywhere that Mary went
the lamb was sure to go.
EOF
```

If the specification of the terminating string is enclosed in quote marks, the following lines of text will be processed as if they were quoted in the same way. By default, lines of text are processed as if they were contained in double quotes (i.e., variables and escape characters are interpolated). To protect at signs, dollar signs, or quote marks within the text, use single quotes in the specification.

```
print <<'EOF';
Mary spent $2.95 for soap to wash her
lamb's fleece and keep it snowy white.
EOF
```

Formatted output

Now suppose you want to exercise more control over what you print. For example, if you tried out this example in MacPerl

```
print('Pi is approximated by ', 355/113, ".\n");
```

you would have seen this output

```
Pi is approximated by 3.14159292035398.
```

That's a little long. What if we would be satisfied to print only the first six decimal places (with rounding)? We can do this with the formatted print function, `printf`.[22]

The syntax of `printf` is much the same as that of `print` except that a **format specification** precedes the list of items to be printed. A format specification consists of a string of (optional) text and **field specifiers**. The remaining elements of the argument list are each substituted into the format string, one per field specifier.[23]

---

[22] The `format` and `write` functions provide yet another way to create formatted output and reports. See *Programming Perl* for information on these functions.

[23] Unlike C, if the number of field specifiers exceeds the number of elements in the argument list, Perl uses nulls to "fill in"; like C, it silently ignores any extra list elements.

There are more than a dozen field specifiers, each of the form %*x* , where *x* is a single character representing the type of field. The following are some of the most common field specifier types.

%s	**a string**
%c	**a single character**
%d	**an integer (decimal number)**
%f	**a floating point number**
%e	**an exponential format floating point number**

Many of these field specifiers can be modified by including the minimum and/or maximum size of the field. The field specifier is then of the form %*m.nx* where *m* is the minimum size and *n* is the maximum.[24] Padding (if necessary) is done with spaces (and occasionally zeroes, for numbers).

Some examples should make things clearer; try these out!

```
$name = 'Vicki'; $pi = 355/113;
printf("My name is %s.\n", $name);
printf("My name is %16s.\n", $name);
printf("Decimal %d represents %c.\n", 42, 42);
printf("Decimal %d rings the bell %c.\n", 7, 7);
printf("Pi is approximated by %2.6f.\n", $pi);
printf("Pi is approximated by %d.\n", $pi);
printf("A millenium is %d years.\n",    1000);
printf("A millenium is %8d years.\n",    1000);
printf("A millenium is %08d years.\n",    1000);
printf("A millenium is %1.2e years.\n", 1000);
```

Redirecting Standard I/O

Unless you do something to separate them, standard output and standard error will both be sent to the same place (by default, the MacPerl window). However, if they both show up in the same place, what is the good of having different filehandles for printing the messages?

Environments such as MPW (or Unix) allow you to **redirect** standard I/O from the **command line**, when you run a command. For example, you can redirect STDIN to come from a file, rather than from keyboard input. Or, you might specify that the standard output and standard error be separat-

---

[24] For exponential formats, *n* represents the desired precision. A negative value for minimum length will cause the field to be left-justified.

ed, sending standard output to a file, but sending error messages to the screen. However, the Finder does not have a command line; can you redirect input and output from the standalone MacPerl application?

You can, because you can also redirect standard I/O from *within* a Perl script. This is the method you must use when working with the standalone MacPerl application. This form of redirection is accomplished by reopening the appropriate filehandle and associating it with a new device (or with a file on your disk).

For example, the following code forces STDIN to be read directly from a file rather than the keyboard.

```
open(STDIN, '<Datafile');
```

Recall that we said filehandles are also used for working with devices (such as windows or printers). The following line of code will cause standard error to be printed to a separate window within MacPerl.

```
open(STDERR, '>Dev:Console:Messages');
```

The special pathname, Dev:Console:, doesn't actually refer to a location on your disk, but rather to a window in the MacPerl application. The last part of the pathname, Messages, provides the title for this particular window. Feel free to name the window with a name of your own choosing.

You can also print directly to a printer. This code reassociates STDOUT with your default (chosen) laser printer.[25]

```
open(STDOUT, '>Dev:Printer');
```

As before, the filehandle is being associated with a device (in this case, a printer), rather than with a file on your disk.[26] For example, you might use this technique to send PostScript code directly to the printer. The following code prints an isosceles triangle.[27]

---

[25] Dev:Printer opens a PAP connection to your default laser printer. It is not guaranteed to work with any other type of printer (e.g., inkjet style printers).

[26] A third device, the **null** device, is named by the pathname Dev:Null. Sending output to the null device makes it disappear. This can be useful for temporarily suspending the printing of error messages or even output, in some cases. Reading from the null device guarantees an immediate **end of file** (EOF).

[27] Example from *PostScript by Example*, McGilton and Campione.

```
open(STDOUT, '>Dev:Printer');
print STDOUT <<'EOF';
%!PS
 72 144 moveto
306 648 lineto
540 144 lineto
closepath stroke showpage
EOF
```

Working With Folders (Directories)

Now let's suppose that you want to open, and work with, many files. If those files are all in the same folder (directory), this is easy. All you have to do is open the folder, get the list of files found inside, and then work through the files one by one.

Working with directories in Perl is very similar to working with files. First, you open the directory with the opendir function, associating a **dirhandle** with the directory. Then, you read data (in this case, a list of filenames) from the directory by means of the dirhandle. Finally, you close the directory using the closedir function, retaining the list of filenames to process. The following code illustrates these steps.

```
opendir(DIR, ':') or die 'cannot open :';
@files = readdir(DIR);
closedir(DIR);
foreach $file (@files) {
  print("$file\n");
}
```

The second argument to the opendir function is the pathname of the directory to open. In this case we are opening the current directory. (Just as : : was a shorthand representation for the pathname of "the folder above this one", a single colon, **:**, is a shorthand representation for "the current directory".)

The readdir function reads the contents of the directory asociated with a dirhandle and returns an array containing the names of all files, folders, etc., that were found in that directory. Note that the names of *all* files and folders are returned, including any that are invisible under the Finder![28]

---

[28] You might be surprised at the number of invisible files stored on your disks!

Once you have this array, you can close the dirhandle (you won't need it again). Then you can process the files that were found, in whatever manner you choose. For example, you might open each one in turn and examine its contents, check or set file attributes such as Type and Creator, or perform whatever other processing suits your needs.

Alternatively, you can use file globbing (wild card expansion), as described in Chapter 8, *Curious Constructions*.

`mkdir()`

Unlike `open()`, the `opendir()` function does not create a directory if it does not already exist. If you need to create a directory (i.e., make a new folder), use the `mkdir()` function.

```
mkdir('HD:new folder', 0755);
```

The second argument to `mkdir()` is the **mode**. Under Unix, the mode provides the directory permissions, that is, who can see files or make changes. Directory permissions are unsupported in MacPerl. If you don't plan to port your script to Unix, just pick a reasonable value (e.g., `0755`).[29]

If you aren't sure whether the directory already exists, you can use the `-d` file test operator.[30]

```
if (! -d 'HD:new folder') {
  mkdir('HD:new folder', 0755);
}
```

Working With Aliases

The Unix analog to the Mac **alias** is the **symbolic link**.[31] Perl has several built-in functions for working with symbolic links; to create an alias, use the `symlink()` function. The first argument to `symlink()` should be the name of an existing file or folder. The second argument should be the name of the alias to create.

```
symlink('HD:Trash', 'HD:Trash alias');
```

To test whether a file is an alias, use the `-l` file test operator.

---

[29] Then, if you ever *do* port your script, the permissions will probably be all right.

[30] There are many file test operators; see Chapter 19, *Operators*, for details.

[31] Use caution. As with any analogy, this one is not quite perfect. But it's close.

Chapter 8:

- *Subroutines*
- *The Standard Perl Library*
- *Adding Libraries - The CPAN*
- *Mac-specific Functions*
- *Droplets, Runtime Versions, And CGI Scripts*
- *Program Arguments:* `@ARGV`
- *References*
- *Filename Globbing*
- *Passing Filehandles*

Curious Constructions

"Curiouser and curiouser!" cried Alice
(she was so much surprised, that for the moment
she quite forgot how to speak good English)...

– Lewis Carroll, *Alice's Adventures in Wonderland*

In Part I of this book, we introduced a number of programming concepts to provide you with a firm grounding and a basis for learning about Perl. The first three chapters of Part II provided an introduction to the Perl language: its basic structure and syntax, data types, expressions and statements, control flow, functions, input and output. By now, you know enough to construct small Perl programs that work.

The remainder of Part II explores more exotic territory, expanding your horizons (and your programming toolbox). By the time you finish Part II, you should be able to write (and understand) more complex scripts. You will then be ready to venture into Part III, where we will cover more advanced topics and specific applications of MacPerl.

Subroutines

In the examples we've seen so far, we've made extensive use of Perl functions. A subroutine is a user-defined function.[1] Specifically, a subroutine is a

---

[1] Some languages make a technical distinction between functions and subroutines, but Perl rarely wastes time on technicalities. However, you will more often see the term subroutine used for a user-defined function, rather than to a built-in function.

named piece of code which can be called (by name) from another piece of code.[2] The name, subroutine, is self-descriptive.

A **routine** is a set of instructions or operations; the prefix "sub-" implies assistance, or a "part of" something. Thus, a subroutine refers to a set of code which assists the main part of the program.

A subroutine is a self-contained portion of a program. Each subroutine performs a specific task. Like the programs they are part of, subroutines can take input (arguments), process information, and produce output (return values). A subroutine can be thought of as a "mini program" (a sub-routine!).

By breaking specific functionality into smaller portions, programming languages allow for **modularity** and **reuse**. In other words, instead of always writing large, special-purpose programs, we can make use of smaller, generalized units of code which can be moved around and used in many programs.

It wouldn't be much fun writing programs if you could only use functions that someone else had created. So, many languages, including Perl, provide for **user-defined subroutines**.

You may recall this sample code from chapter 3:

```
sleep(min2sec($cook_time)); # Allow the eggs to cook.
```

At the time, we said that the function min2sec accepts a single argument, which it multiplies by 60 and returns for use by the calling program. Now, let's write the function min2sec.

```
sub min2sec {
  $minutes = shift(@_);
  return($minutes * 60);
}
```

A subroutine **definition** begins with the keyword **sub**, followed by the subroutine name and a block of code to be executed, enclosed in braces, {}. The **return value** of a subroutine is (implicitly) the value of the last expression evaluated within the block. If you want to be explicit (we recommend it), use the return function.

---

[2] OK, we lied. Perl also has anonymous subroutines, which are accessed via references and are a bit too arcane for the current discussion.

The **argument list** is passed to the subroutine in the special Perl array, @_.[3] The shift command takes the first value off of an array and returns it, shortening the array by one element in the process. If we did not specify the array to use, Perl would still use the special @_array. So we could have said, simply

```
$minutes = shift();
```

The value that is shifted off is assigned to the variable, $minutes.

As long as we only want one variable, shift is a good way to get it. Be a bit careful, though; if you simply assign to the variable like this:

```
$minutes = @_;              # error: scalar context!
```

you would be evaluating the assignment in scalar context, setting $minutes to the *number* of arguments in the @_ array! If, however, there are several variables being passed to the subroutine, you can use a list to retrieve them.

```
($a, $b, $c) = @_;         # list context
```

Scope

Any variables created (or used) within a Perl program, which are not explicitly made private, are **global**; that is, they (and their current values) are available to your entire program, including subroutines.

In practice, variables that are used inside a subroutine are conventionally made **private** to that subroutine, using the my() command.

```
my($minutes) = shift();
```

These private variables exist only within the **scope** of the subroutine; they are not available to the calling routine or to any other subroutines, not even to those *called by* the current subroutine. When the subroutine returns and exits, these variables no longer exist (they "go out of scope").

This type of scoping is called **lexical scoping** or **static scoping**. Lexically scoped variables are declared in a "private dictionary" for each subroutine. They are visible only from the point at which they are declared until the

---

[3] Perl has two special "magical" variables, the array, @_, and the scalar, $_. The former is **local** to a subroutine; the latter is **global** to your program.

end of the **block** in which they were declared (or the end of the file, if the variable was declared outside a block).[4]

The following example illustrates how lexical scoping can be used.

```
my($a) = 1;
$b = 2;
print("main:     \$a: $a, \$b: $b\n");
print_ab();

sub print_ab {     # a called function
  my($a) = 3;
  print("sub_ab:  \$a: $a, \$b: $b\n");
  print_ab2();
}

sub print_ab2 {    # a second called function
  print("sub_ab2: \$a: $a, \$b: $b\n");
}
```

This displays

```
main:     $a: 1, $b: 2
sub_ab:   $a: 3, $b: 2
sub_ab2:  $a: 1, $b: 2
```

This script defines two scalar variables – $a is lexically scoped, $b is global. The value of $a is changed to 3 within print_ab, but that value exists only within the scope of the block. The call to print_ab2() is outside of the block, so the value of $a is restored to 1.

Note that the value of $a is available to the subroutine, print_ab2, because the subroutine is within the same block (in this case, the file) as the declaration of $a.

What would happen if you enclosed the first four lines of code within braces, causing them to be in a separate block from the subroutine definitions? How would the output be affected?

---

[4] It may be useful to think of blocks as levels on a "stack"; when the program exits a set of braces, the definitions made at that level are "popped off the stack".

```
{
  my($a) = 1;
  $b = 2;
  ...
}
sub print_ab {
  ...
}
...
```

Perl also supports **dynamic scoping,** by means of the `local()` command. A dynamically scoped variable is declared to have a temporary value which is separate from its external value (outside the block in which it was `localized`). Again, the scope lasts from the point of declaration until the end of the enclosing block (or file). However, "local" variables can be seen by other subroutines that are called by this subroutine because the variable is still global; only its *value* has changed.

> **Note:** It's important to keep in mind that `local()` isn't really local; it's still global. Dynamic scoping should be used only when you need to save, modify, and then restore the value of a global variable. Most of the time, what you really want to use is `my()`.

> In particular, you can get into trouble using `local()` declarations if you set the `use strict` pragma on your programs. The `strict` pragma requires you to fully qualify any global variables (including variable that have been declared `local()`) with their explicit package name.

A Little More About Context

Recall from the chapter 6 that every operation in Perl is evaluated in a specific **context**. We've just seen how context is important in evaluating the arguments to your subrutine. But what about the subroutine itself – will it also be evaluated in a particular context?

The answer is yes. The value your subroutine returns will be evaluated in the context of the subroutine invocation (the same as any other function). This means that your own functions can be context-sensitive, just like Perl's built-in functions and operators.

If you want to change a subroutine's behavior (e.g., actions, return value) based on the context in which it was called, use `wantarray()`. The `wantarray()` function returns true if the subroutine was called in list context, false if the call was made in scalar context.

```
sub hms {
  # return the time (hours, minutes, seconds)
  # separately if in list context, or as
  # colon separated time if in scalar context

  my($sec, $min, $hr) = localtime();
  if (wantarray()) {
    return($hr, $min, $sec);
  } else {
    return(sprintf("%02d:%02d:%02d",
      $hr, $min, $sec));
  }
}
```

The hms subroutine uses the built-in `localtime` function to determine the current time in hours, minutes, and seconds. If called in a list context, it returns the hours, minutes, and seconds as a list. If called in scalar context, however, the function joins these values into a "timestamp" of the form `12:36:07`, suitable for printing.

> **Note:** `localtime` is a very useful function which returns much more information than just the current hour, minute, and second. In fact, it returns a nine-element list of useful time and date values, corrected for the local timezone! We refer you to *Reserved Words* in Part IV, or to the section on Built-in functions (`perlfunc.pod`) in the online help, for more details.

We're using the `sprintf` function to join the values together; `sprintf` works very much like `printf`, except that `sprintf` creates a formatted string, rather than printing its output to a file or to the screen. We could have written instead:

```
return("$hr:$min:$sec");
```

but we want to be sure to print each part of the timestamp with a leading 0 for values less than 10. (Hint: what string will the simpler `return` statement, without `sprintf`, return at 7 minutes after 9?)

Now, let's try calling our function. We'll call it both ways and display the results. Decide for yourself whether the context sensitivity adds clarity.

```
$the_time = hms();      # scalar context
print("The time is $the_time.\n");

@the_time = hms();      # list context
print("The time is $the_time[1] minutes ");⁵
print("past $the_time[0].\n");
```

This displays:

```
The time is 12:38:35.
The time is 38 minutes past 12.
```

When Should You Define a Function?

You might be wondering when you should create a subroutine (function), rather than coding everything in the main routine. After all, if your Perl program isn't really huge; why should you write a subroutine?Why not just keep all your code together in one big program?

One reason to create a subroutine is if you need to do something more than once. After all, how many times do you want to write the same code? In our egg cooking example in Part I, there were multiple places in the program where we needed to convert minutes to seconds, in order to wait (`sleep`) for the correct length of time. Instead of specifying the multiplication every time, we used a function.

Another reason is to reduce the complexity of the main routine. If a piece of code is complex and has few ties to the surrounding code, break it out as a separate routine. You'll turn one complex routine into two simpler ones, and you can ignore the inner workings of the subroutine most of the time.

Once you have written a function, you can use it in other programs, simply by including it with their code. Eventually, you can build up a **library** of useful functions. Instead of deciding how to write something each time, you'll be able to reuse code you have written (and tested!) before. You may even decide that your library is useful enough to share!

The Standard Perl Library

Perl has nearly 200 **built-in** functions (and named operators that act like functions). Hundreds more are available as part of the **standard Perl libr-**

---

⁵ We broke this `print` statement in two, in order to fit the example on the page.

ary. In programming terminology, a library represents a set of functions that can be included in your programs. The files that are part of the standard Perl library can be found in the lib subfolder of the MacPerl ƒ folder.

Many of the functions in the standard library were written by other Perl programmers, who decided to make their function libraries available to the Perl community. These library functions are not built into Perl; that is, they are not immediately accessible to your program at any time. However, they are included with all Perl distributions and can be readily accessed with a minimal amount of effort. The Libraries preference tells MacPerl in which folders it should look for libraries to include.

If you add your own libraries, we recommend that you store them in a folder of your own creation. This folder need not be within the standard MacPerl distribution hierarchy. Just be sure to update the Libraries preference to add the path to the new folder, so that MacPerl can find your libraries.

Library functions are usually part of **modules**.[6] Module filenames always end in .pm. Modules that affect the compilation phase of a program as well as its execution are known as **pragmas** (e.g., integer). A pragma usually limits the scope of its effects to a portion of your program (e.g., the inner-most enclosing block). By convention, pragma names are all lowercase.

A module is defined as the unit of **reusability** in Perl. Strictly speaking, a module is a file that defines a **package**. A package is a way of managing a chunk of Perl code which is kept separate from other chunks of Perl code. We will come back to packages and modules in more specific detail in Chapter 11, *Extensibility And Re-use*.

For now, you'll need to understand that a package contains code which is **external** to your program. In order to access this code (e.g., variables, sub-routines, etc.) from your program, you must (usually) first tell Perl that you want to include it, by means of the use command.

```
use Package;
```

When you refer to a subroutine (or variable) that is part of a package, you must also specify the package name, using the "double-colon" syntax, as:

---

[6] Modules were introduced in version 5 of Perl. You may still encounter libraries which are not part of modules, usually contained in files which end with the suffix, .pl. These still work in version 5, but modules *only* work in Perl version 5 and up.

```
Package::subroutine()
```

If the package name is omitted, MacPerl will assume that the current package (your program, package main by default) is meant.[7]

The standard library contains many of the most popular and useful Perl modules. For example, the specific functions which allow MacPerl to take advantage of the Macintosh platform are part of the MacPerl package. Other packages and modules contain functions that are useful for file manipulation, data base manipulation, CGI scripting, working with the World Wide Web, and more. We'll discuss these in more detail in Part III.

Adding Libraries - The CPAN

> *Many shall run to and fro,*
> *and knowledge shall be increased.*
>
> *Bible*, Daniel 12:4

The MacPerl distribution contains several hundred libraries and modules, with more being added in each new release. These represent the most popular, powerful, and tested add-on functionality available for Perl. Even so, there may be things you want to do with Perl for which no module has been provided in the standard library.

Before you resign yourself to writing the code from scratch, take some time to look farther afield. The Comprehensive Perl Archive Network (CPAN), is a vast online repository of Perl code and documentation, contributed by Perl programmers worldwide. The CPAN is available on the world-wide web via www.perl.com/CPAN. We've also included a recent snapshot on the CD-ROM that accompanies this book.

This is how the CPAN describes itself in CPAN.html, the "front-end" document for the CPAN. CPAN.html describes the CPAN, provides pointers to available modules, and explains how you can contribute modules yourself.

> The CPAN contains the collected wisdom of the entire Perl community: hundreds of Perl utilities, several books' worth of documentation, and

---

[7] If you plan to make many calls to package functions, prefixing each name could get tedious. Fortunately, you can bring an entire package into the current **namespace** of your program by using the package declaration at the beginning of your script, as:

```
package MacPerl;
```

the entire Perl distribution. If it's written in Perl, and it's helpful and free, it's in the CPAN.

The CPAN currently lists 22 module categories of modules, including:

- Perl Core Modules
- Development Support
- Networking, Devices, and Interprocess Communication
- Data Type Utilities
- Database Interfaces
- User Interfaces
- String, Language, and Text Processing
- World Wide Web, HTML, HTTP, and CGI
- Images, Pixmap, and Bitmap Manipulation

… and much more.

Not every module will work with MacPerl. Some modules are operating-system specific. Others may call functions that MacPerl does not support, or may depend upon your having previously installed some other module. The ease with which a given module can be unpacked, installed, and used with MacPerl varies widely. When you're ready to go looking for new modules, be sure to review Chapter 11, *Extensibility and Re-use*, for hints and step by step instructions for importing and installing new modules.

Mac-specific Functions

Because MacPerl runs on Mac OS, it has some different requirements than do Perl versions for other platforms. Some of these requirements have to do with traversing the filesystem, dealing with files, inter-application com-munication (i.e., AppleEvents), etc. The MacPerl package was created to handle these special requirements, adding functionality that would not be needed on other platforms.

In fact, the functions in the MacPerl package are considered so much a part of MacPerl that they almost seem built-in. This is the only package which you do not need to specifically use in order to access its contents. MacPerl's special functions are accessible just like any Perl function except for one thing: you must still be sure to refer to these items by using the double-colon syntax (prefixing each name with `MacPerl::`).

Aside from the MacPerl package of generally useful Mac OS-related functions, there is also a set of more than a dozen modules, known collectively as the **toolbox modules**. The toolbox modules access the Mac OS Toolbox, a set of instructions for controlling various Mac OS functions. Mac OS has thousands of toolbox calls; these modules attempt to provide a useful subset of the calls in MacPerl.

The toolbox modules cover more in-depth Mac OS programming needs, from getting file information to process control, interapplication communication, graphics, speech recognition, and more. To access any of the toolbox modules, you must first specify its package with the appropriate `use` directive. Because of the way the toolbox modules are written, it is not necessary to specify `Mac::` before each function name.[8]

The MacPerl package and the toolbox modules are very important to MacPerl, providing fine control of many Mac OS features. For this reason, we have devoted two entire chapters to them! We'll put off a detailed discussion of the available Mac OS-specific functions to those chapters. Here, however, are two simple examples to whet your interest.

The following example uses the function `MacPerl::SetFileInfo` to set the Type and Creator IDs for an existing file, `myscript` (specified by its full pathname). `McPL` is the Creator ID for a MacPerl script (plain text).

```
MacPerl::SetFileInfo('McPL', 'TEXT', 'HD:myscript');
```

The next example uses the `FSPCreate` function, part of the `Mac::Files` module, to perform a similar function. This code creates a new (empty) file, `HD:newfile`, with the specified Creator and Type.

```
use Mac::Files;
FSpCreate('HD:newfile', 'McPL', 'TEXT');
```

Droplets, Runtime Versions, And CGI scripts

So far, we've created and run all of our scripts from within MacPerl. But there are alternative ways to save and run MacPerl scripts as "double-clickable applications": droplets, runtime versions, and CGI scripts.

---

[8] Symbols in a module (e.g., functions, constants) can be explicitly exported through a combination of defining them as part of the `@EXPORT` array and calling the `Exporter` module. These exported symbols become part of the **namespace** of the calling package.

Each of these can be opened and edited from within the MacPerl application, but they are no longer of type TEXT and cannot be edited with text editors such as BBEdit or Alpha.[9] If you use an alternate text editor to write and edit MacPerl scripts, we recommend that you keep your source code in plain text form, and use Save As... to save a copy of the script as an alternative type.

Droplets

Droplets function as "mini" applications. They can be double-clicked in the Finder, or you can drag and drop files and folders onto them. A droplet is a MacPerl script which contains a small amount of additional code (causing MacPerl to run the droplet script).[10] A droplet still requires you to have the complete MacPerl distribution installed on your disk, but it can make running MacPerl scripts much simpler.

Runtime Versions

A runtime version of a MacPerl script contains a complete copy of MacPerl, everything necessary to run the script. Consequently, a runtime version can be very large; even a small script will be over 1 MB in size! A runtime version isn't a very efficient way to save your own scripts, but it's a useful way to send scripts to friends and co-workers who do not have the MacPerl distribution installed (and may not want to).

CGI Scripts

MacPerl CGI scripts contains a small amount of code to allow them to interact with the Common Gateway Interface (www.w3.org/CGI/), without needing to understand the (very different) CGI AppleEvent protocol that is used by Mac OS HTTP daemons.[11] See Chapter 16, *CGI Scripting*, for more information.

---

[9] The type of these scripts is APPL and the creator ID is MrPl.The text of the script is stored in a TEXT resource in the resource fork of the file, rather than in its data fork.

[10] The additional code in a droplet translates the "Open Document" AppleEvent sent by the Finder into a "Do Script" AppleEvent for MacPerl. More abstractly, it receives the Finder notification of which files, folders, etc. were dropped on it and executes the script of the droplet with the path names of these dropped items in the @ARGV array.

[11] This code translates the CGI Apple Events sent by Mac OS HTTP daemons into "Do Script" Apple Events for MacPerl, by copying the appropriate Apple Event parameters into the @ARGV and %ENV variables and the standard input and output stream.

Program Arguments: @ARGV

When a Perl script is run, any arguments to the script are automatically placed in the @ARGV (argument vector) array.[12] MacPerl scripts that are run with the Run Script menu item cannot have arguments, but droplets and runtime versions can.

The following code fragment loops through the @ARGV array and prints out what it finds.[13]

```
for ($i = 0; $i <= $#ARGV; $i++) {
  printf("item %d is %s\n", $i, $ARGV[$i]);
}
```

The arguments to a MacPerl script will usually be files or folders to open.[14] What if you simply double-click a droplet or runtime version of a MacPerl script that expects arguments, that is, a script that expects to have something dropped on it?

The following code uses the MacPerl::DoAppleScript function to put up a dialog box, asking the user the choose a (text) file to open.[15]

```
if ($#ARGV < 0) {
  $file = MacPerl::DoAppleScript(<<SCRIPT);
    choose file with prompt "Pick a file" ¬
    of type "TEXT"
SCRIPT
  exit(1) if ($file eq '');
  $file =~ s/^alias "//;
  $file =~ s/"$//;
  push(@ARGV, $file);
}
print("you picked: $ARGV[0]\n");
```

---

[12] The name, ARGV, is taken from the argv array in the C programming language.

[13] This fragment is part of the drplt.tst.pd droplet example included on the CD-ROM.

[14] Actually, you can send just about any sort of information as an argument, provided you encode that information as the name of a file or folder. But most often, arguments are simply ordinary files that contain data or folders containing files (or more folders).

[15] If you want to "break" and continue a long line of AppleScript code across more than one line of Perl, end each unfininished partial line of AppleScript code with the AppleScript continuation character, ¬, (formed by the sequence option-L).

Note the nifty use of the here document to send the AppleScript code to `Mac Perl::DoAppleScript`. (The characters that follow `SCRIPT` on the initial line are not passed to `DoAppleScript`.)

The two substitution commands

```
$file =~ s/^alias "//;
$file =~ s/"$//;
```

are needed because AppleScript returns the name of the chosen file as

```
alias "HD:examples:chapter8.pl"
```

We use `push()` to add the name of the chosen file into `@ARGV`. The `push()` function pushes the values in a list (in this case, the single element, `$file`) onto the end of an array. The length of the array is increased by the length of the list.

The next example does essentially the same thing, this time using the `StandardGetFile` function from one of the toolbox modules, `Mac::Standardfile`, to put up the dialog box. `Mac::Standardfile` is described in detail in chapter 13, *The Toolbox Modules*.

```
if ($#ARGV < 0) {
  use Mac::StandardFile;
  $file = StandardGetFile('', 'TEXT');
  if ($file->sfGood()) {
    push(@ARGV, $file->sfFile());
  } else {
    exit(1);
  }
}
print("you picked: $ARGV[0]\n");
```

References

Just as HFS (the Mac OS Hierarchical File System) has "aliases" that can be used in place of files and folders, Perl has "references" that can be used in place of variables, functions, etc. Perl's references are a bit too complicated to explain fully here, but a brief introduction should be useful.

Perl supports two forms of references: **symbolic** and **hard**. A symbolic reference is implemented in a manner that is very analogous to HFS aliases (or Unix symbolic links). Specifically, a symbolic reference is a string variable that contains the name of another variable. In the following example, Perl "dereferences" $$ref (getting $var), then increments the result:

```
$var = 1;
$ref = "var";
$$ref++;
print("ref=<$ref>, var=<$var>\n");
```

Displays:

```
ref=<var>, var=<2>
```

A hard reference, in contrast, is implemented in a manner that is analogous to a Unix hard link.[16] That is, it refers to the entity (e.g., function, number, string) itself,[17] rather than to the *name* of the entity. This saves Perl the time needed to "look up" the entity; more critically, it allows the reference to act differently in some cases.

Because a hard reference is a scalar, it can be stored in a variable (including an array or hash location). It is neither a number nor a string, however, so it cannot be operated upon. Here is the same example, using a hard reference:

```
$var = 1;
$ref = \$var;
$$ref++;
print("ref=<$ref>, var=<$var>\n");
```

Displays:

```
ref=<SCALAR(0x87de08)>, var=<2>
```

As shown above, the hard reference $ref does not have a value that is likely to be meaningful to a human reader. Nonetheless, it works quite well! Perl's "reference" operator, used above, is a backslash, \.

Because references can be made to functions, you can actually "store" functions in a hash. If you were building a lookup table for an interpreter, for instance, you might pre-load (and then use) its table of functions in a manner something like this:

---

[16] Unfortunately, there is no Mac OS analog for hard links.

[17] *Programming Perl* refers to this entity as a "thingy" or, grudgingly, as a "referent". You may prefer to think of it as the *Ding an sich* (the thing itself).

```
$funcs{'foo'} = \&foo;
...
$out = &{ $funcs{$func_name} } ($in);
```

Note: Perl's built-in functions cannot be referenced and invoked in this manner. So, if need be, create a "wrapper" function:

```
sub my_sqrt { sqrt(@_[0]); }
```

Filename Globbing

If you have ever used a command line **shell** such as MPW or one of the Unix shells, you may be familiar with **wild card characters**, also known as shell **metacharacters**, which are used to match simple filename patterns. For example, in the MPW shell one might specify all of the filenames that end in the suffix `.pl` as `≈.pl`. Under Unix, the same set of filenames would be specified as `*.pl`.

When you generate filenames in this manner, using wildcards, you are **globbing** the filenames.[18] Perl also allows filename globbing, using the standard Unix (C shell) metacharacters in specifying globbing patterns:

`*`	match any number of characters (except leading dot, `.`)
`?`	match any single character (except leading dot, `.`)
`[...]`	match any of the characters in the class
`{...,...}`	match any of the comma-separated alternatives in the group

In MacPerl, only `*` and `?` are supported. Filename globbing under Perl is specified by describing a **glob pattern** within the filename globbing operator, `<>`, the `glob()` function, or (MacPerl only), the `glob` command.[19]

As an example, suppose you have several files with names ending in `.pl`. From a MacPerl script, you could specify only these files in several ways:

```
@files = <*.pl>;
foreach $name (@files) { print "$name\n"; }
```

---

[18] In Version 6 Unix, this task was performed by the `/etc/glob` program.

[19] Recall that the <> (angle) operator is used to read input from a filehandle. If the string within the angle brackets is anything *other than* a filehandle (or a scalar variable that can evaluate to a filehandle), then the <> operator becomes the globbing operator instead. TMTOWTDI.

```
@files = glob('*.pl');
foreach $name (@files) { print "$name\n"; }

@files = `glob *.pl`;
foreach $name (@files) { print "$name\n"; }
```

The first two globs, `<*.pl>`, and `glob('*.pl')` print the same results, e.g.

```
chapter6.pl
chapter7.pl
...
```

The backquoted glob command, e.g. `` `glob *.pl` `` includes its own embedded newline, resulting in slightly different values for each `$name`

```
chapter6.pl

chapter7.pl


...
```

Passing Filehandles

A **typeglob** is a way of accessing the internal data type that Perl uses to hold an entire **symbol table entry**.[20] A typeglob represents all data types that share a given name. That is, the typeglob `*foo` affects the entities `$foo`, `@foo`, `&foo`, etc.

Prior to version 5 of Perl, typeglobs were used to pass references to arrays and hashes to functions. Weird, but useful. With the advent of real references, however, this is no longer necessary.

Typeglobs can also be used to alias one set of names to another:

```
*abc = *def;
```

This ties `$abc` to `$def`, `@abc` to `@def`, `&abc` to `&def`, etc. It is not clear why one would wish to do this; perhaps it's just another Way To Do It ...

---

[20] A `typeglob` has only a passing relationship to a filename glob: both use the same root word, glob, and both use the same wildcard * character (which "globs" things together). A typeglob globs symbols of the same name from the symbol table. A filename glob globs filenames that match a specified pattern. (Yes, we know it's confusing!)

Typeglobs are still useful, however. You can pass a filehandle reference to a subroutine, store it in a data structure, etc. (Because filehandles themselves cannot be stored or passed, this is quite a useful characteristic.)

The precise method Perl uses to do this is, unfortunately, more mysterious than we have any interest in explaining (see *Programming Perl*). Nonetheless, we *can* tell you how to use typeglobs for this purpose, and we will.

Typeglobs are prefixed by an asterisk, *. References are, as always, prefixed by a backslash, \. To save a reference to a filehandle in a scalar variable, you actually save a reference to a typeglob of the filehandle:

```
$fh = \*FH;
```

You can treat a reference to a filehandle like any other reference, as:

```
$fh{'abc'} = \*FH;
$fh[12345] = \*FH;
```

Now, let's get some real use out of one! Here's a simple function that will print its argument string to a specified (pre-opened) file, preceded by the current time. This might be useful if you needed to maintain several log files. To get the time information, we'll use our hms() subroutine.

```
sub log_it {
  my($string, $fh) = @_;

  $the_time = hms();
  print $fh ("$the_time\t$string");[21]
}
```

You might call log_it() in any of several ways, changing the filehandle that describes where to print the output.

```
$log = "logfile";
open(LOG, ">HD:$log") or die "Cannot create $log\n";
...
log_it("Begin Processing\n", \*LOG);
...
log_it("Started\n", \*STDERR);
...
```

_____

[21] Note that only one dollar sign is used with the filehandle reference $fh; that is, no explicit dereferencing is done. Don't ask …

Chapter 9:

- *$_*
- *use English*
- *MacPerl Oddities – Portability Issues*
- *To Parenthesize Or Not To Parenthesize?*
- *Taking Shortcuts*
- *Quoting*
- *Extended Regular Expressions*
- *A Word Of Warning*
- *Grab Bag*

Odd Corners

The place through which he made his way at leisure was one of those receptacles for old and curious things which seem to crouch in odd corners of this town...

Charles Dickens, *The Old Curiosity Shop*

Perl is a powerful and complex language. As with many languages, the expressions you write may be simple or complicated, verbose or terse. You may write scripts that are elegant and carefully crafted, or scripts that "just get the job done". There really is More Than One Way To Do It.

So far, we've presented a subset of Perl – a subset we think you can use to create many useful programs. We hope that we've also provided you with a solid base on which you can build. You should be well equipped to learn more about Perl as you find new areas to explore and new problems to solve.

Along the way, we've touched on a number of special constructs that make Perl (and MacPerl) powerful, interesting, and often unique. Perl is full of interesting idioms, programming paradigms, curious constructions, and odd corners. In this chapter, we will focus on these special constructs, pulling them together into one place and discussing them in more detail.

We don't expect everyone to use all of the features we discuss in this chapter (we even recommend against one or two of them!). Everything here is part of the language, however, and sooner or later you're liable to run across some of these "odd corners"; we think it's best if you're properly prepared.

$_

The global scalar variable, $_, represents the default input and pattern searching space. There are many places in Perl where, if you don't specify a variable to use, Perl will assume $_.[1] These include

- all of the file test operators (except for -s, which defaults to STDIN)

- various functions, such as chomp(), print(), unlink(), and int()

- pattern matching operations: m//, s///, and tr/// (if you leave out the =~)

- foreach loops, if no other iteration variable is specified

- while loops, when the sole condition of the while is to read input records from a <> or <FILEHANDLE>

For example

```
while (<>) {            # read input line into $_
  chomp;                # chomp($_)
  if (/^#/) {           # if ($_ =~ m/^#/)
    print;              # print "$_"
  }
}
```

When you see Perl statements that don't appear to be acting upon a variable, they are most likely acting upon $_.

use English

If the symbol soup of the special variables begins to get too confusing, an alternative is available. Simply begin your program with the directive

```
use English;
```

and you will be able to use longer (and theoretically more mnemonic) names. Some variables have both a medium and a long name. The medium-length name is usually reminiscent of a similar variable in another language, such as awk or C. For example, here are some of the global special variables and their longer "English" names:[2]

---

[1] If you like, you can always *specify* $_. But Perl will understand if you don't.

[2] See Chapter 21, *Special Variables*, for caveats and a definitive list.

```
$_       $ARG
$.       $NR          $INPUT_LINE_NUMBER
$/       $RS          $INPUT_RECORD_SEPARATOR
$\       $ORS         $OUTPUT_RECORD_SEPARATOR
$0                    $PROGRAM_NAME
$]                    $PERL_VERSION
$^O      $OSNAME
```

MacPerl Oddities – Portability Issues

In many ways, MacPerl is no different from "regular" (that is, Unix) Perl. In some ways, however, it is vastly different. Recognizing those differences will help you to understand why scripts you might pick up from the CPAN or other sites may not work without some effort on your part. Understanding the differences may also help you to write programs that are more portable to other platforms.

`#!perl`

We've said that MacPerl programs can (and should) begin with the string

```
#!perl
```

optionally followed by switches, such as -w. On Unix systems, the #! line is magical – it provides a directive to the Unix kernel, giving it the path to the program that should be used to run the script, as if that command were given on the command line. On a Macintosh, the #! line is **emulated**. Mac-Perl itself reads the #!perl line and any switches that may be included on it. Because of the way #! is implemented, many Perl switches cannot be included in it when using MacPerl. If you try, you'll get an error message:

```
# Can't emulate -x on #! line.
```

\n and \r

On Unix systems, the line-ending character (record separator) is the line feed (ASCII \012). On Mac OS, it's the carriage return (\015). On MS-DOS and Windows systems, it's the sequence "carriage return/line feed" (\012 \015). Perl uses \n to represent a **newline**, which Unix systems interpret as a line feed character. For portability, the newline character in MacPerl outputs a carriage return (the Mac OS newline character).

This can cause some difficulties if you share files (or scripts!) between Mac OS and Unix systems. You'll need to be sure to **translate** the newline characters to avoid problems. Smart text editors such as BBEdit or Alpha, and many file transfer programs such as Fetch will make the proper translations for you. The debate over whether MacPerl should recognize and translate various line-endings frequently rages hot and heavy in some circles. For now, however, accept the fact that there is a difference to be handled.

You should also note that, although \n produces a carriage return under MacPerl, \r (which produces a return without a newline under Unix Perl), produces a line feed under MacPerl. Programs that use \r to back up to the beginning of a line (without moving to the next line) will not exhibit the expected behavior under MacPerl. Beware.

Running commands: `system()` and backquoted commands

Unless you are using ToolServer and MPW, the `system()` command is not available under MacPerl. A few backquoted commands, such as `` `pwd` ``, are emulated, but the number available is small. Even with ToolServer, the only commands you will be able to use will be MPW commands.

Unfortunately, if you start picking up Perl scripts from the Net, you will find that many of them make use of `system()` and backquoted commands. The good news is that many of these scripts can be modified to run under MacPerl (by rewriting these calls in native Perl code). You may have to do a little research, and you may need to get creative, but give it a try before you give up.

Here are some common Unix commands that may be found in `system()` statements, along with their Perl equivalents:

```
system("mv...")        rename(...)
system("rm...")        unlink(...)
system("date...")      localtime(...) # must be parsed
system("cp...")        use File::Copy; copy(...)
system("find...")      use File::Find; find(...)
system("echo...")      open(...); print...
system("mkdir...")     mkdir(...)
```

Processes: `fork, exec, wait...`

Unfortunately, the Mac OS is not designed to fork and execute processes in the same way that a Unix system does. These commands are not implemented, and there are no good workarounds available. If you pick up a Perl script that `forks` subprocesses, you're probably in for a difficult porting effort. You may want to try to find some other way to solve the problem ...

Time

Both Unix and the Mac OS view time as the number of seconds since the **epoch**. However, the two operating systems have vastly different ideas of when the epoch began! Unix, and Unix Perl, count time from January 1, 1970. In contrast, Mac OS and MacPerl count time from January 1, 1904.

The various time functions, such as `localtime()`, have been modified to take this difference into account. However, if you work with raw time values, such as those returned by `time()`, or port your code to another operating system, be wary.

Filename Globbing

Under Unix, the `glob()` function (and the shorthand globbing operator, `<>`) invoke the C shell to handle filename expansions. Under Mac OS, the C shell is not available, so MacPerl implements filename globbing itself. Unix Perl has a few extra metacharacters available for glob patterns, such as character classes (e.g., `[a-f]*`). MacPerl currently supports only two metacharacters: * matches any number of characters; ? matches a single character.

Pathnames

If you pick up Perl scripts from the net, read other books on Perl, or move a script from Mac OS to a Unix machine, sooner or later you will run into differences in pathnames. On Unix systems, pathnames are relatively common; it's difficult to spend very much time entering commands from a command line without using pathnames! However, because of the Macintosh's point and click, drag and drop interface, Mac OS users can go for a long time without knowing about pathnames, much less getting used to employing them.

Not only are pathnames unfamiliar to many Mac OS users, but Mac OS pathnames and Unix pathnames are only superficially similar. Users of both operating systems can specify either absolute (full) or relative paths, where the last element of the path can be a file or a directory (folder) and the elements leading to it are directories. Now for the differences...

Unix pathname elements are separated by a slash, `/`. An absolute pathname always starts with a `/`. A relative pathname always starts with the name of a directory, except, of course, in the minimal case of naming a single file. The current directory is specified by **.** ("dot"); the parent directory is specified by **..** ("dot dot"). The file tree can be traversed upwards by adding additional parents, **..**, always separating path elements by **/**.

```
/usr/local/bin/perl        # absolute pathname
../local/bin/perl          # relative pathname
../../bin/perl             # relative pathname
bin/perl                   # relative pathname
perl                       # relative pathname (file)
```

Mac OS pathname elements, in contrast, are separated by a colon, **:**. An absolute pathname always starts with the name of a volume. A relative pathname starts with a colon, **:**, followed by the name of either a folder or a file (except in the minimal case of naming a single file, in which case the colon is optional). The current directory is specified by **:**; the parent directory by **::**. The file tree can be traversed upwards by adding additional parents, **:**, but no additional separators.

```
HD:MacPerl ƒ:MacPerl        # absolute pathname
::MacPerl ƒ:MacPerl         # relative pathname
:MacPerl ƒ:MacPerl          # relative pathname
:MacPerl                    # relative pathname (file)
MacPerl                     # relative pathname (file)
```

To Parenthesize Or Not To Parenthesize

Throughout Part II of this book, we have made very liberal use of parentheses. As we have pointed out, "if it looks like a function, it is a function", and in Part II our examples have cast most of the Perl named operators and list operators as functions.

In the "real world" of Perl code, however, this is not always the norm. In particular, `print`, `die`, and `warn` statements are often seen without parentheses. This is especially useful in cases where you want to mix strings to print with expressions to be evaluated.

```
print '10**3 is ', 10**3, ".\n";

die "Something went wrong: $!";
```

In Part III, you will see many more statements without parentheses. Keep in mind, however, that you can always parenthesize if it makes the meaning clearer, or helps determine precedence. (Just be careful to get it right!)

Taking Shortcuts

According to Larry Wall, the three great virtues of a programmer are **laziness**, **impatience**, and **hubris**. Perl gives you ample opportunity to develop these virtues. One of the ways it does this is by providing ways to create shortcuts in your code; why write several statements where one will serve?

We saw a little of this back in Chapter 5, *Building Blocks*, with the shortcut assignment operators:

```
$x = $x +1;
$x += 1;
$x ++;
```

But there are many other (and sometimes very interesting) ways to create shortcuts. For example, here's a popular idiom; instead of

```
$a = $b;
$a =~ s/^/#/;
```

why not make the assignment and the substitution at the same time?

```
($a = $b) =~ s/^/#/;
```

Note that $b is unchanged.

The ?: Conditional Operator

The ?: conditional operator can provide a shortcut for the simple if ... else ... statement. Recall this code from *Building Blocks*:

```
if ($count == 1) {
  print("My Mac has 1 mouse.\n")
} else {
  print("My Mac has $count mice.\n")
}
```

Using the ?: operator, we can rewrite this as

```
print "My Mac has $count ",
  ($count == 1) ? "mouse.\n" : "mice.\n";
```

As shown here, the second line handles the conditional. The part before the ? is the `if` part (the condition). If the condition is true, the expression following the ? is executed. Otherwise, (`else`), the expression following the : is executed.

Shortcut Subroutine Returns

Recall the `min2sec` function from Chapter 8, *Curious Constructions*:

```
sub min2sec {
  $minutes = shift(@_);
  return($minutes * 60);
}
```

If we take advantage of the fact that, by default, `shift()` will shift the `@_` array in a subroutine, we can write a very short subroutine indeed

```
sub min2sec{ return(shift() * 60); }
```

Here's part of the code from the `hms` subroutine from *Curious Constructions:*

```
if (wantarray()) {
  return($hr, $min, $sec);
} else {
  return(sprintf("%02d:%02d:%02d",
    $hr, $min, $sec));
}
```

we could rewrite this as

```
@list = ($hr, $min, $sec);
$scalar = sprintf("%02d:%02d:%02d", $hr, $min, $sec);
return (wantarray() ? @list : $scalar);
```

We use the `?:` conditional operator to determine which value to return. Or, we could get even more clever and not set any variables at all!

```
return (wantarray()
  ? ($hr, $min, $sec)
  : sprintf("%02d:%02d:%02d", $hr, $min, $sec)
);
```

A Forever Loop

Here's a quick shortcut for setting up an **infinite loop** (a **forever** loop), that is, a loop that never exits:

```
for (;;) {
  # body of the loop goes here
}
```

The initial expression, the condition, and the followup expression are all null. While you might have thought this would make the loop exit immediately (considering that the condition seems to be met already), instead, this loop will repeat forever.[3] Just remember to include a `last` statement somewhere within the loop or your program will never exit!

Changing Defaults

Perl has many defaults, and you may not like all of them, or the current default may be inappropriate for your program and data. So, you may be pleased to learn that many of these defaults can be changed. We suggest that you exercise caution, however; some of the defaults are there for what Perl's authors considered good reasons.

If you get tired of printing newlines all of the time, consider changing the output record separator. By default, when you use `print()`, Perl just prints the list you specify, with no newline or other record separator attached. However, if you prefer, you can specify that Perl include a newline (or just about anything else) as the output record separator.

The `$\` variable contains the current output record separator. By setting this to `\n`, you can force Perl to print a `\n` after every output line.

You can also use the `-l` switch on the `#!perl` line (or on the `perl` command line, under MPW) to enable automatic line-end processing. You may (optionally) specify an octal number following the `-l`; if you do, it represents the ASCII value of the character you want to use as the record separator. If you specify the `-l` switch without an octal number, Perl will use the current value of the **input record separator**; the default is newline.

As you may be guessing, you can also change the input record separator, either by setting the global special variable, `$/`, or by using the `-0` switch on the `#!perl` line. If you change the input record separator *after* you enable line-end processing with `-l`, the output record separator will be

---

[3] The `for` and `while` constructs regard an empty test clause as true; `if`, `unless`, and `until` regard it as a syntax error. Yoicks!

unaffected (it acquired its value before you made the change to the input separator).

You can change other defaults. See the chapters on *Operators* and *Special Variables* in Part IV, or the online help under *Predefined Variables*.

When you change a default, take care to save the original value, in case you need to restore it later. For example, let's say that you are reading several input files. One file is to be read in "paragraph" mode, while the rest are to be read a line at a time.

Before reading in the "paragraph" mode file, save the current value of the input record separator, then set it to null for paragraph mode.

```
$slash = $/;
$/ = '';
```

After you have processed the file, you can restore the previous value of the input record separator

```
$/ = $slash;
```

Quoting

We've said many times that in Perl, There Is More Than One Way To Do It. This applies as much to quoting techniques as to anything else. Perl provides the customary (single, double, and back-) quotes we've mentioned above, and there are also quite a few alternative quoting choices.

In Perl, the difference between quotes and operators is somewhat fuzzy (in fact, we've included quoting in our *Operators* chapter). The parentheses in a list and the slashes in a pattern match or substitution are, in fact, forms of quoting. (That is, they affect the interpretation of the enclosed characters).

Perl also provides a set of operators (with names starting with the letter q) that replace many of the customary quote characters:

Customary	"Generic"	Description
'single quotes'	q/.../	literal; no interpolation
"double quotes"	qq/.../	literal; variable interpolation
`backquotes`	qx/.../	command; variable interpolation
(list)	qw/.../	word list; no interpolation

Use the generic quoting operators if you need to enclose quote characters in the quoted string and prefer not to use backslash ("escape") characters:

```
$message =   q/Don't type that!/;
$error   = qq/The file "myfile" could not be found./;
@days    = qw/Monday Wednesday Friday/;
```

Wait, There's More!

If this doesn't seem flexible enough, the delimiter can be (just about) any-thing;[4] The slash, /, is only a suggestion. Again, the reason is to let you avoid including so many backslashes (and simply because TMTOWTDI :-). As mentioned in a previous chapter, the delimiter character can also be changed in pattern matches, substitutions, and translations.

```
$the_date = q#Saturday, 3/21/98#;
$line =~ s,^,#,;
```

If the opening delimiter is a character that is considered part of a bracket-ing pair, such as (, {, [, or <, the closing delimiter is the matching charac-ter; embedded delimiters must match in pairs.

```
$message = q[Don't type that!];
```

For the substitution and translation operators, which normally have three delimiters, if you use a bracketing pair for the first two delimiters, the last delimiter gets its own starting quote character as well. The two pairs of bracketing delimiters do not need to be identical. For example:

```
$var =~ tr[a-z][A-Z];
$line =~ s(^)<#>;
```

Implicit Quoting

To prevent variable interpolation from acting upon the wrong string of characters, you can wrap the "variable" part of the string within braces.

```
$var = 'butter';
print "${var}fly\n";
```

This causes Perl to separate the variable identifier string from any alpha-numeric (or underscore!) characters that follow. Also, the identifier within

---

[4] Any non-alphanumeric, non-whitespace character, that is.

the braces is forced to be a string (as long as it is a single identifier, and not an expression); thus, the braces provide some implicit quoting of their own.

```
$days{'Monday'}
```

could be written (though we don't recommend it!) as

```
$days{Monday}
```

Extended Regular Expressions

Regular expression patterns can become complex very rapidly. For example, here is a code fragment that validates its input data by matching the input fields to expected patterns:

```
($record !~ m/^g\d+\d\t\w+\.?\w+\t[\w\s]+[35]\'/) or
    die "bad input data";
```

We could make this seem less complex by breaking up the pattern and commenting it, which we can do if we use the /x modifier for **extended regular expressions**. By including an x after the final pattern delimiter, we can put any desired whitespace and comments into our pattern.

> **Note**: If the pattern itself contains whitespace, be sure to specify it with the appropriate escape character (e.g., \s), rather than with literal blanks and tabs, because the blanks and tabs are interpreted as "organizational" spacing rather than literal parts of the pattern!

```
($record !~ m{          # check for a "clean" record
  (^g\d+\d\t)           # g1281914
  (\w+\.?\w+\t)         # mb45a01.r1
  ([\w\s]+[35]\')       # prime value 5'.
}x) or die 'bad input data';
```

Note how each piece of the pattern can be commented with a sample of what an actual valid field might contain. We've changed the delimiters to braces because the pattern looks like a block of code (although it's not what Perl thinks of as a **block**).

Here's an example we have adapted from Chapter 2 of *Programming Perl*, second edition. In this example, the authors used comments to explain the higher level algorithm used (in this case, for finding duplicate words in paragraphs):

```
$/ = '';                    # paragraph mode
while (<>) {
  while (m{
                \b          # start at a word boundary
                (\w\S+)     # find a wordish chunk
                (
                  \s+       # separated by some whitespace
                  \1        # and that chunk again
                )           # repeat ad lib
                \b          # until another word boundary
             }xig
         )
  {
     print "dup word '$1' at paragraph $..\n";
  }
}
```

Again, you should note the difference between the {} delimiters in the pattern and the {} that surround the code block of the while statements. Similarly, you should recognize the difference between the required parentheses around the while conditions and the parentheses used to group parts of the pattern space.

As explained above, the construct

```
$/ = '';
```

is used to put Perl into "paragraph mode". The special global variable, $/, defines the input record separator. By setting it to the null string, '', you cause Perl's input operator, <>, to read in paragraphs (terminated by an empty line) rather than individual lines (terminated by a newline).

A Word Of Warning

With all the idioms, shortcuts, and multiple ways to do things, Perl gives you plenty of opportunity to get into trouble. Don't despair, though; Perl also tries to reduce your chances of doing something you might regret.

If you include the -w switch on the #!perl line (or the MPW command line), or check Compiler Warnings item in the Script menu, Perl will warn you about certain risky kinds of behavior. These include variables that are used before they are set, identifiers mentioned only once (possible misspellings), redefined subroutines, attempts to write to a filehandle that was opened as read-only, and many other possibilities for error. For a complete list, see the online help for Diagnostic Messages under Troubleshooting.

If you plan to use the -w switch, you should take care when writing certain statements, to avoid warnings. For example, when using the <> loop to read in your input data, check explicitly to ensure that the value you read is not undefined:

```
if (defined(<IN>)) {
   # code goes here...
}
```

Also, be sure to initialize (write to) your variables before you read from them. Perl guarantees that all variables which have not been specifically initialized to a value will have an initial value of null, but you will get a warning if you take advantage of this and attempt to use a variable which has not previously been set.

Many authors recommend that you use -w while you are learning Perl, and we have tried to ensure that all of the examples in this book will run correctly with Compiler Warnings turned on. After you have been programming in Perl for a while, it will be your decision whether to leave -w set for "production" code.

For even more assistance, you may want to use the strict pragmas which restrict certain constructs deemed as unsafe. You can include the line

```
use strict;
```

at the top of your script, to apply all restrictions, or specify only a few. At present, there are three areas of restrictions defined as part of the strict pragmas.

```
use strict 'vars';
use strict 'refs';
use strict 'subs';
```

These impose the following restrictions

- 'vars' generates an error if you access a variable that wasn't fully qualified, imported from a module, or declared with my().

- 'refs' generates an error if you use any symbolic references.

- `'subs'` generates an error if you try to use any bareword (unquoted) strings.

Grab Bag

This section covers a few idioms and odd corners that we didn't feel fit well anywhere else in the chapter.

Using a List in Scalar Context

If you use an array variable in a scalar context, you get a scalar result. Specifically, the number of elements in the array. This can be very convenient. For example, the following code fragment evaluates the input argument array, @ARGV, in a scalar context and stores the result (the number of input arguments) in a scalar variable.

```
$argc = @ARGV;
```

or or ||

The operators or and and were created to give Perl programmers more choice when writing statements such as

```
open(IN, 'myfile') or die 'Oops!';
```

In previous versions of Perl, only the || and && operators were available. The or and and operators were created because they are more readable and because they have very low precedence (allowing programmers to choose to use fewer parentheses).

"Funny Characters" vs. Octal Notation

When you're writing a script, there may be times when you need to work with characters that are not part of the "standard" set of alphanumeric or punctuation characters, that is, the Mac OS "option" characters. For example:

```
$line =~ tr/'/'/;      # replace curly single quote
$line =~ tr/"/"/;      # replace curly double quote

if ($line =~ /^•/) {    # match on bullet character
```

You may decide to specify these characters literally or to use their numeric (octal, decimal, or hexadecimal) ASCII equivalents.The latter may be more portable (some systems do not support 8-bit character sets!). Recall from chapter 6 that, in pattern specification, a backslashed two- or three-digit octal number matches the character with the specified value.

```
$line =~ tr/\325/'/;     # replace curly single quote
```

Similarly, a backslashed x followed by one or two hexadecimal digits matches the character with that (hexadecimal) value.

```
$line =~ tr/\xD2/"/;     # replace curly double quote
```

Several font utilities are available to help you determine the ASCII encoding of a given character, as well as various other useful information. We have included one such, FontView, on the MacPerl CD-ROM.[5]

```
1;
```

Perl modules are required to return a true status. To guarantee this, a common idiom is for the last line of the module to be written as:

```
1;                          # return(1);
```

Simple, but effective.

_____

[5] FontView is shareware. If you keep using it, please respect the shareware license.

Chapter 10:

- *Start With A Good Editor*
- *Good Habits Cost No More*
- *Debugging Techniques*
- *RTFM*
- *Recommended Reading*
- *The Perl Community*

Help!

Humpty Dumpty sat on a wall,
Humpty Dumpty had a great fall.
All the kings horses and all the king's men
had scrambled eggs for breakfast again.

– Anonymous, variation on an old English nursery rhyme

A book like this one can only take you so far. Sooner or later (probably sooner!), you'll want to start writing scripts of your own, rather than just trying out our examples. Inevitably, something will go wrong (we hope it's something small) and you'll need to know where to turn to get help, answers to your questions, and more information. This chapter gives advice on what to do and where to look if anything should go worng [sic :-].

Start With A Good Editor

Before you go too far, we recommend that you start using a good text editor. Although MacPerl comes with an editor of its own, you'll probably exceed its range of capabilities fairly soon. The MacPerl internal editor is based on TextEdit, the same engine Apple used first in TeachText and later in SimpleText. A simple (perhaps too simple) editor for creating README files (its original purpose) and small MacPerl scripts, it has several limitations.

The MacPerl text editor cannot open, or edit, files with more than 32 KB of text (typically less than a thousand lines of Perl code). It doesn't show tabs or character spacing consistently, so indentation is very difficult to get right. Most critically, it has no special features to support programming.

Fortunately, several text editors are available which have excellent support for writing code in general and MacPerl in particular. Their features include language-sensitive text coloration, advanced search-and-replace functionality, regular expressions, split-screen capability (letting you view a function and the code which calls it simultaneously), indentation (and exdentation) as well as entabbing and detabbing, and much, much more.

The authors use BBEdit, from BareBones Software. The Alpha editor (from Pete Keleher) is also highly recommended by many MacPerl users. Versions of both editors are included on the MacPerl CD-ROM. MPW users may simply want to use the MPW shell editor, but should be sure to upgrade to the latest version if need be. It has many excellent code editing features, including text coloring.

AlphaLite and Alpha are both shareware; AlphaLite has fewer features than Alpha. If you continue to use Alpha or AlphaLite, please respect the shareware license (and the author's willingness to allow us to distribute his programs) and pay for it!

BBEdit Lite is a freeware derivative of the current commercial version of BBEdit. The Lite version has fewer capabilities, but is still a powerful editor. BBEdit is a commercial product; we have included the demonstration version on the CD. The demo is fully featured, except that saving documents is disabled and printed documents are given a "BBEdit Demo" watermark. Information on purchasing the commercial version of BBEdit is included.

Good Habits Cost No More

One of the best things you can do to keep yourself out of trouble is to develop a good Perl programming style and practice until it becomes habit. The code in this book is, in all modesty, a good example to follow. By and large, we follow the style guidelines set forth by Perl's author and documented in the Perl style guide (under the topic, Various, in the Help menu).

On occasion, we'll break one of these style rules, usually because of the constraints inherent in fitting examples into a 6 by 7 inch printed page! Please bear with us, understanding why we formatted the code that way. In any case, we will still try to keep our code as clear and easy to read as possible.

The easier your code is to read, the easier it will be to understand (we hope) and to maintain. Use whitespace for readability. Use parentheses for clarity. Use comments. Eschew obfuscation. Avoid unnecessary "cuteness". On the other hand, try not to go overboard on any of these recommendations.

> **Fable:** One day, a programmer picked up a program that he had written a while back and found he had *no idea* how it worked. He studied and worked for hours, tracing each statement until at last he understood the code again. At that point, he realized that the logic was obvious and thus didn't need comments.

> **Moral:** Will you remember how your code works in 6 months? How "obvious" do you think it will appear to you?

Check the syntax of your script before attempting to run it. Use the Syntax Check ... menu item or the -c command line option (in MPW).

Make sure that your code runs with Compiler Warnings checked, or using the -w switch. Run your code under the use strict pragma. Do not assume that code written by other people, *even modules in the MacPerl distribution,* are necessarily "strict clean", however, or that such code will run without compiler warnings. Rather than trying to prevent all warnings, be sure you know what they mean (and whether they pose a real problem).

Always check the return status of system calls such as open(). These calls return success or failure for a reason. Handle error conditions. Print error messages to STDERR; don't mix them with the normal output. A good error message says what went wrong, and, if appropriate, includes the system error message (e.g., $!) as well.

Check your input data for validity. Check the arguments to your script. Bulletproof your code. Develop an attitude of cynical paranoia toward the users of your script (including yourself). To paraphrase one of Henry Spencer's *Ten Commandments for C Programmers:*

> ... for surely where thou typest "foo" someone someday shall type "supercalifragilisticexpialidocious".

Read this book. Read the online documentation. Read other books. Read the example scripts in the MacPerl distribution, on our CD-ROM, and on the CPAN site. Find and read scripts from other sources. Learn to distinguish good scripts from not so good scripts. Rewrite the not so good ones and make them better. Write your own scripts, then rewrite them when you learn something new. Practice, practice, practice, but be sure to have fun doing it!

Debugging Techniques

Even with all the care in the world, eventually something will go wrong. You should plan for this occasion, so that you won't be caught unprepared.

There are two major types of errors that you will encounter: syntax errors and logic errors. For each, there are various debugging techniques that you can use to help you figure out what went wrong, fix it, and get on with the fun of writing and running your program.

What Broke?

First of all, it's important to figure out what broke. For example, consider the following code fragment

```
if ($a > 0) {
  print "greater\n;
}
elsif ($a < 0) {
  print "less than\n";
}
else {
  print "equal to\n";
}
```

When MacPerl syntax-checks this code, it produces 18 lines of diagnostics:

```
# Bareword found where operator expected, near "print "less"
#    (Might be a runaway multi-line "" string starting on line 2)
File 'Untitled #3'; Line 5
#        (Do you need to predeclare print?)
# syntax error, near "print "less than"
File 'Untitled #3'; Line 5
# String found where operator expected, near "print ""
...
```

Wow! All that noise from such a little piece of code? Syntax-checking code frequently produces **cascading errors**. A small error produces more and more error messages as the interpreter tries to recover from the initial problem.

The best debugging technique is to look at the first error message first. Find the problem, fix it, and run the script again. In this case, the first error was

```
# Bareword found where operator expected, near "print "less"
#    (Might be a runaway multi-line "" string starting on line 2)
File 'Untitled #3'; Line 5
```

If you're using an editor such as BBEdit or Alpha, be sure to turn on the line number display feature; it will make your programming life much easier. If you're using the MacPerl editor, select the error message line (in the MacPerl window) that includes the file name and line number

```
File 'Untitled #3'; Line 5
```

then select Jump to ... from the MacPerl Edit menu.

```
print "less than\n";
```

Hmmm. That line looks just fine. What broke?

If you look at the code for a little while and nothing appears to be wrong, don't spend too much time trying to figure out what happened. The problem may be earlier in the code and this is only the point where MacPerl figured out that there *was* as problem. Take a look at the preceding code, keeping in mind the complete text of the error message as you do so.

```
# Bareword found where operator expected, near "print "less"
#    (Might be a runaway multi-line "" string starting on line 2)
```

Ah yes, line 2. The closing double quote is missing.

```
print "greater\n;
```

Insert the quote and run the code again. What do you know? It works!

Traces And Other Debugging Tools

Once you have the syntax right, your script should work perfectly. Well, maybe not. The errors that arise from code that is syntactically correct, but still (often subtly) wrong, are called **logic errors**. The following example looks at some simple logic errors.

This script reads an input file, printing the data to standard output. Each input line consists of an ID field and some additional data; as long as the ID field doesn't change, we just keep reading and printing lines. When the ID field changes, we print some summary information before proceeding to the next ID. (At least, that's what we had in mind!)

Given this input data:

```
X12344      diamond
X12345      apple
X12345      banana
```

Here's the output we want:

```
X12344 diamond
X12344 = 1 entry
X12345 apple
X12345 banana
X12345 = 2 entries
```

The code:

```perl
#!perl
open (ID, ":Data:IDs.dat");

$count = 0;
while(<ID>) {
  chomp();
  ($id, $entry) = split('\t');

  if ($id = $last_id) {
    print;
    $count++;
  } else {
    print "$last_id = $count ",
      ($count > 1) ? 'entries' : 'entry', "\n";
    $last_id = $id;
    $count = 0;
  }
}
```

The results:

```
= 0 entry
= 0 entry
= 0 entry
```

Oh dear; that's not right.

If you can't figure out what went wrong after a little study, try adding some trace statements. Traces can be as simple as a few `print` statements, or you might design a `trace()` function for more flexibility.[1]

Let's add a `print` statement to display the interesting variables:

---

[1] An example of a trace routine is included on the CD-ROM.

```
while (<ID>) {
  ($id, $entry) = split('\t');
   print("\$id=$id, \$entry=$entry, ",
     "\$last_id=$last_id, \$count=$count\n");
```

We've placed the variables within angle brackets to make it easier to see if they have null values, or contain whitespace. Here's the output:

```
$id=X12344, $entry=diamond, $last_id=, $count=0
 = 0 entry
$id=X12345, $entry=apple, $last_id=, $count=0
 = 0 entry
$id=X12345, $entry=banana, $last_id=, $count=0
 = 0 entry
```

There's the problem; `$last_id` is never initialized! We'll add a line to set `$last_id` to `$id` on the first line of input.

```
. . .
while (<ID>) {
  ($id, $entry) = split('\t');
  $last_id = $id if ($. == 1);
. . .
```

Here's the output

```
$id=X12344, $entry=diamond, $last_id=, $count=0
X12344      diamond
$id=X12345, $entry=apple, $last_id=X12344, $count=1
X12345      apple
$id=X12345, $entry=banana, $last_id=X12344, $count=2
X12345      banana
```

Still not right. The count just keeps increasing; we never enter the `else` block. Take another look at the code ... Oops; we're using an assignment instead of a comparison![2]

```
    if ($id = $last_id) {
```

Since `$last_id` hasn't been set yet, it defaults to 0. So, `$id` is assigned to `$last_id`; the resulting value, 0, is false, so Perl executes the `else` block! Let's change that and run the script again.

---

[2] A common error.

```
    if ($id == $last_id) {
```

Now the output is

```
$id=X12344, $entry=diamond, $last_id=, $count=0
X12344 diamond
$id=X12345, $entry=apple, $last_id=X12344, $count=1
X12345 apple
$id=X12345, $entry=banana, $last_id=X12344, $count=2
X12345 banana
```

That's still not right. We need to examine the data a little more closely to realize that we're misusing a *numeric* comparison operator on *string* data.[3] (The IDs begin with letters.) Let's fix the line (again) and re-run the script.

```
    if ($id eq $last_id) {
```

Let's try it again

```
$id=X12344, $entry=diamond, $last_id=, $count=0
X12344 diamond
$id=X12345, $entry=apple, $last_id=X12344, $count=1
X12344 = 1 entry
$id=X12345, $entry=banana, $last_id=X12345, $count=0
X12345 banana
```

That looks pretty good; let's turn off the traces and see what happens.

```
X12344 diamond
X12344 = 1 entry
X12345 banana
```

OK, the numbers add up now. Funny thing, though, there's no summary after banana. And ... wait a minute! Where's the entry for `apple`?

Even when the output looks good, it's important to check it against the data and the expected results. In this case, even though the numbers appear to add up (i.e., the results are **plausible**), we still have a bug in the code. We've forgotten to count the first line in each new set (when $id is new), and we're not printing the summary information for the final set of entries.

Here's the final code, all tested, debugged, and working, with the traces removed:

---

[3] Another common error.

```perl
#!perl
open (ID, ":Data:chapter10.dat");

$count = 0;
while (<ID>) {
  chomp();
  ($id, $entry) = split('\t');
  $last_id = $id if ($. == 1);

  if ($id eq $last_id) {
    print "$_\n";
    $count++;
  } else {
    print "$last_id = $count ",
      ($count > 1) ? 'entries' : 'entry', "\n";
    $last_id = $id;
    print "$_\n";
    $count = 1;
  }
}
print "$last_id = $count ",
  ($count > 1) ? 'entries' : 'entry', "\n";
```

Now, that wasn't so hard, was it?

The important thing to remember when testing and debugging a Perl script is to take your time and keep calm. If you find yourself **thrashing** (trying something new just "because", with no real plan or thought), stop and take a deep breath. If you can't find the bug by looking at it, add some `print` statements. If you get too much output, make the `print`s conditional.

Or, call someone else over and ask them to help you look for the bug. Walk your friend through the script, explaining what it's (supposed to be) doing, line by line. Typically, without your friend saying a word, you'll suddenly realize that something you just said does *not* match the code you're seeing. You'll be back on your way to fixing the bug and finishing your script!

The Perl Debugger

If you prefer not to insert `print` statements, you may be pleased to learn that Perl has a fully-functioned source code debugger (just like the fancy compiled languages :-). Invoke your script with the -d switch, or check the Perl Debugger item in the Script menu, to activate the Perl debugger.

The Perl debugger is actually a special version of the standard Perl "Run Script" environment.[4] When you work with the debugger, you're working inside an interactive Perl environment that knows all about your code. It also knows how to step through code one line at a time, set breakpoints, print stack traces, change variable values dynamically, and much more.

Here are a few of the basic debugger commands, to get you started. For complete details, examples, etc., see the Debugging item under Troubleshooting in the MacPerl Help menu.

Command	What it does
h	print a help message
s	single step through the code; enters subroutines
n	skip over a subroutine call without going into it
r	return from the current subroutine
V Foo	display all variables in package Foo
V Foo var	display only variables *var in package Foo
X var	same as V, assumes current package
x $var	show the value of $var
x @var	show the value of @var
t	toggle trace mode
command	execute the given command as a Perl statement
q	quit the debugger

RTFM[5]

MacPerl comes with extensive online help. Over fifty help files in POD (Plain Ol' Documentation) format are readily available from the MacPerl Help menu. These files are best viewed with the Shuck application; the Lookup and Find menu items are very handy for locating desired topics.

We recommend that you spend some time familiarizing yourself with the online help. The top-level categories include:

- MacPerl Overview
- Macintosh-specific features
- Perl FAQ
- Table of Contents
- Macintosh Toolbox Modules
- Syntax

---

[4] Specifically, the -d switch (or the menu item) tells Perl to insert information about your program's source code into the parse trees it gives to the interpreter.

[5] Read The Fine Manual

- Operators and Precedence
- Built-in functions
- Data structures
- Troubleshooting

- Regular expressions
- Predefined variables
- Advanced Topics
- Various

Recommended Reading

Although we've tried to make this book self-contained, we couldn't tell you everything there is to know about Perl in one volume. We've concentrated, instead, on getting you started using (Mac-)Perl. We've covered a subset of Perl, enough to provide you with a sound basis for learning how to program and a solid framework for adding more detailed knowledge.

Parts III and IV delve deeper into MacPerl-specific areas, covering topics that you might not be able to find elsewhere: Mac Toolbox modules, Data Storage, Mac OS GUI interfaces, etc. As a result, we've had to leave some things out to make room for other information we thought you should have.

We don't feel too badly about this, however, because we know that this material is well covered by other books (particularly O'Reilly's fine set of Perl books). Take another look at our chart in the *Introduction* and consider investing in some of these books. Also, consider getting some of the other books on Perl and related topics that we list in Chapter 23, *Books, Etc.*

Periodical Publications

More articles and columns about Perl are being written every day. Randal Schwartz, co-author of *Programming Perl* , has regular columns in *UNIX Review* and *Web Techniques.* Other periodical publications (e.g., *SunExpert*) also feature regular or irregular articles on Perl.

The Perl Journal (`www.tpj.com`) is entirely devoted to the topic of Perl. Recent articles have included a restrospective account of the creation of MacPerl, by Matthias Neeracher, and a tutorial discussion of using Apple Events, by Chris Nandor.

The Perl Community

The Web

You can find many resources and a lot of helpful information on the World Wide Web. In particular, the primary Perl site (`www.perl.com`) contains recent news bulletins, pointers to the CPAN and the latest version of Perl,

FAQs, Support, and Bug Reporting areas, a searchable Perl Reference, and more. You should also visit The Perl Institute (`www.perl.org`), a "non-profit organization dedicated to making Perl more useful for everyone".

Finally, there are a number of Web sites becoming available for MacPerl. The MacPerl Homepage (Matthias Neeracher) and the MacPerl Pages (Prime Time Freeware) are available via the MacPerl Help menu. Both sites contain links to other MacPerl-related pages.

The USENET and the MacPerl Mailing List

The Internet provides plenty of opportunity for you to interact with fellow Perl (and MacPerl) users. On USENET, the `comp.lang.perl.misc` newsgroup covers myriad Perl topics, up to several hundred messages a day!

The MacPerl mailing list, specializing in MacPerl-specific discussions, has much lower traffic. To join the mailing list, send email to

```
mac-perl-request@iis.ee.ethz.ch
```

with only the word

```
subscribe
```

in the body of the message. (The subject will be ignored.) You should receive a confirmation message by return email.

Before posting a question to either `comp.lang.perl.misc` or the MacPerl mailing list, take some time to research the question and check the online documentation. Your fellow Perl programmers will thank you (and be more willing to help :-) if your question is interesting, novel, and topical.

The Annual Perl Conference

The first annual Perl conference, sponsored by O'Reilly & Associates, was held in August 1997, in San Jose, California. Attended by over one thousand people, the first conference was a huge success. At this writing, the second conference is planned for August 1998. We believe that this conference will become a regular, and highly respected, annual event.

The Perl conference is a great opportunity to meet and interact with other Perl programmers, at all levels. It's also a fantastic opportunity to meet and hear from some of the leading lights of the Perl community, such as Larry Wall himself! For more information on upcoming Perl conferences, visit the conference web site at `conference.perl.com`.

Part III

Advanced Topics

In traveling, a man must carry knowledge with him,
if he would bring home knowledge.

– Samuel Johnson, quoted in Boswell's *Life of Samuel Johnson*, 1778

A man should keep his little brain attic stocked with all the
furniture that he is likely to use,
and the rest he can put away in the lumber-room of his library,
where he can get at it if he wants it.

– Sir Arthur Conan Doyle, "Five Orange Pips",
The Adventures of Sherlock Holmes, 1891

Chapter 11:

- *Packages, Modules, Extensions (Oh My!)*
- *Understanding Modules*
- *Getting Modules*
- *Installing Modules*
- *use-ing Modules*
- *Object-Oriented Programming*

Extensibility And Re-use

> *This freedom we shall observe ourselves,*
> *and desire to be observed in good faith*
> *by our heirs in perpetuity.*
>
> *– Magna Carta, 1215 A.D.*

Perl's extensibility and ability to reuse code are among its most important features. A Perl programmer can ease maintenance by separating auxiliary code from the main program and/or reusing code from other programmers. If the task requires it (and few do!), a Perl programmer can change or expand the code of MacPerl itself.

Packages, Modules, Extensions (Oh My!)

Packages were discussed briefly in the introductory chapters and are covered more fully below. For now, just think of a package as a grouping of related code and data: code blocks, subroutines, variables, etc.

A **module** is a file that contains the Perl code for a package. For consistency and simplicity, the names of modules are based on the names of the corresponding packages. For instance, the module file CGI.pm contains the CGI package.[1] This allows a package's code to be stored and loaded as a unit.

Modules are the primary method of importing external code into programs. The Internet-based **CPAN** (Comprehensive Perl Archive Network) contains a large number of modules, covering a wide variety of capabilities.

---

[1] Pieces of the CGI package can be kept elsewhere, and other packages can be in the CGI.pm file, but the main pieces of the package are in the module file.

If you plan to create substantial pieces of Perl software, you will want to become comfortable with the ins and outs of package and module construction.[2] If you merely plan to *use* packages and modules, however, our introductory coverage should suffice.

Extensions can be very powerful, because they directly affect the code of MacPerl itself. They are difficult to implement, however, as they are not even written in Perl! Consequently, we will not cover them in any detail.

An extension is accessed through a corresponding module; the fact that a module loads or accesses an extension is entirely invisible to the user of the module. Nonetheless, some understanding of the basic nature of extensions may serve to keep you out of trouble.

Normally, a module's documentation will note the fact that an extension is being used. Nonetheless, keep your eyes out for files with the .xs suffix. Most extensions are written for use with Unix and will need to be **ported** (edited, compiled, etc.) to the Macintosh before you can make use of them.[3]

If an extension is required for a module, you probably should forget about using it with MacPerl. But, if you are feeling brave and/or confident, don't let us stop you. The `perlxstut` documentation and *Advanced Perl Programming* are good places to start learning what you'll need to know.

Libraries are collections of related subroutines that are grouped together in single files. Perl libraries usually have the suffix .pl and were primarily written for Perl version 4.[4] During the past few years, libraries have been mostly replaced by modules. Modules do not work under Perl version 4, but libraries do work under Perl version 5.

Finally, remember that the purpose of all of these forms of code encapsulation is to make *your* life easier. Rather than writing the same code over and over again or – worse – spending time duplicating the functionality of code someone else has already written, code reuse allows you to spend your time and brainpower more efficiently.

---

[2] See the `perlref`, `perldsc`, `perllol`, `perltoot`, `perlobj`, and `perlbot` manual pages, as well as *Modules: Creation, Use and Abuse* in the `perlmodlib` manual page and, as always, *Programming Perl*.

[3] See Chapter 23, *Building MacPerl And Extensions*, for more information.

[4] Many people use the .pl suffix for general Perl scripts, too, not just for Perl libraries.

Note: Installation and use of modules requires substantial understanding of Perl. If much of this chapter seems incomprehensible, get help from an experienced Perl user the first time you install or use a module.

Understanding Modules

In order to understand the structure of a module, it is necessary to understand the concepts of **namespaces** and **packages**. A namespace is a specifiable context in which a name has meaning. By giving a namespace a unique label, ambiguous interpretations can be avoided. The name "Chris", for instance, is very meaningful within the Nandor home, but quite ambiguous outside it. As such, it must be tied to a unique namespace (i.e., "Nandor").

If Chris has an unmarried sister named Jennifer, and then marries a woman named Jennifer who takes his family name, a **name clash** will occur with the names of the two ladies. The name clash may be alleviated by changing one of the ladies' names (unlikely), removing one of them from existence (usually illegal), or by moving one of them to another namespace (i.e., marrying off the sister). If the name clash is not alleviated, we might find the ladies opening each other's gifts at Christmas.

Similarly, Perl's packages implement namespaces for variable names, subroutines, etc. Within a given package, care must be taken that all variables and subroutines have unique names, to avoid name clashes.

If a piece of external code needs to access data within a package, the external code must make the context clear to MacPerl. In other words, the program must somehow tell MacPerl where a particular variable or subroutine resides. This is done by using the "double-colon" syntax[5], as:

```
Package::subroutine()
```

If the package name is omitted, MacPerl will assume that the current package is meant. The starting package is always called `main`. Thus, the two `print` statements below are exactly equivalent:

```
$x = "Hello world.\n";
print $x;
print $main::x;
```

---

[5] You may see older code that uses the single-tick syntax (e.g., `Package'variable`), but this has been officially deprecated and should be avoided.

If the current package is main, the variable $x can be accessed as either $x or, more specifically, as $main::x. The current package can be changed at any time within a program, using the package declaration:

```
$v = 'foo';

package A;
$v = 'bar';
sub myprint { print $_[0] || $v }

package main;
print $v;            # prints 'foo'
print $A::v;         # prints 'bar'
A::myprint();        # prints 'bar'
A::myprint($v);      # prints 'foo'
```

There are two different variables here, $main::v and $A::v. Because myprint() is in package A, when it looks for $v, it finds $A::v. In the main package, however, $v corresponds to $main::v. And, when code in the main package wants to access myprint(), it must ask specifically for it as A::myprint(). (That is, perl will not "guess" what is meant.)

As we discussed in Chapter 8, *Curious Constructions*, global variables can be "seen" from any part of the program. Package variables are visible in the same way. In fact, Perl considers global variables to be a special case of package variables, with main as the default package.

A couple of cautions are in order, however. Accesses from other packages must, in general, be qualified with the variable's package name.[6] Also, the effects of a package declaration are limited to the enclosing block; thus:

```
$i = 1;
print "$i\n";        # prints '1'
if ($i == 1) {
  package A;
  $i = 2;
  print "$i\n";      # prints '2'
}
print "$i\n";        # prints '1'
```

---

[6] Some special global variables, such as $], belong to package main but do not need to be qualified with the package name when accessed from other packages.

Getting Modules

Modules of all shapes and sizes are available from many places; finding, understanding, and using them is, of course, your responsibility. The module information on our CD-ROM is a very good starting point. We also recommend the module reference books in O'Reilly's *Perl Resource Kit*.

The best place to find modules is in the MacPerl distribution. The modules that come with MacPerl have, in general, been tested and (if need be) modified for use with MacPerl. The distribution includes a slew of modules for doing CGI, text manipulation, database access, benchmarking, networking, and other fun things all developers should keep in their bag o' tricks.

If, however, you do not see what you need in the distribution, you will have to start hunting around. The first stop on your treasure hunt should be the MacPerl Pages (`www.ptf.com/macperl`). Drop into the Online Support area, look through the MacPerl FAQ-O-Matic, and see if someone has left a trail of crumbs for you to follow.

While you are there, be sure to join the MacPerl mailing list. The list is a great resource for MacPerl users; if you have a question about MacPerl that *isn't* answered in this book or on the MacPerl Pages, the MacPerl list is a very good place to ask. Specifically, if you need a module that works under MacPerl, these folks can probably find one for you.

Before asking the list, however, you might want to check the Comprehensive Perl Archive Network. The CPAN (`www.perl.com/CPAN/CPAN .html`) is the authoritative repository for Perl-related materials. It is a world-wide, distributed network of archive sites, providing fast and reliable access in many parts of the world. It is also, unfortunately, strongly oriented towards Unix-based Perl and its organization is imperfect.

The CPAN includes the source code for Perl, ports to non-Unix platforms (including the Macintosh), assorted Perl scripts, documentation, and many hundreds of modules. Although the CPAN includes a fair amount of indexing, it is a large repository and can be a bit confusing. Relax and take your time; eventually, you'll (probably :-) find something you can use.

We have included an indexed snapshot of the CPAN on the enclosed CD-ROM. We have expanded and unpacked many of the archives of Perl source code and documentation. The CPAN is very active, however, so you may want to look for (and perhaps retrieve) updated or new modules.

Installing Modules

Be sure to examine modules before you attempt to install them. Some of the CPAN's modules are accessed via extensions; in general, you can't use these with MacPerl. Other modules may be platform-specific, which usually means "specific to Unix", but a substantial number of modules are also specific to other platforms, such as Microsoft Windows 95/NT.

Most modules, however, require only pure Perl. These are usually safe for use with MacPerl, as long as their authors followed the guidelines for good cross-platform Perl (see Chapter 9, *Odd Corners*). There are also some modules on the CPAN that are specific to MacPerl. You will usually find these in the area `CPAN/modules/by-module/Mac`.

Even assuming these constraints, modules from the CPAN require certain steps to be followed before they can be used with MacPerl. This process is not substantially different from the mostly automated process followed on Unix, but you will need to perform some manual steps:

- Decompress and extract the file from any archive
- Check the contents
- Move the files to an appropriate location
- Handle line breaks
- Check for AutoSplit

We'll cover these steps in detail below.

1. Decompress and extract from archive

Many modules are "tarred and gzipped", and have the double suffix .tar.gz or .tgz. **tar** is a program that archives (bundles together) any number of files and directory structures into a single file. It does not compress the files at all, however; it simply archives them. So, module developers then use the **gzip** (GNU zip) program to compress the archive.

In order to use a tarred and gzipped file, the process must be reversed; the file must be "gunzipped and untarred". There are, of course, versions of tar and gzip for Mac. **MacGzip** and **suntar** are freeware programs (included on the CD-ROM) that can create and extract from tar and gzip files.

If there is no need to create tar or gzip archives, but only to extract from them, the most common and probably easiest solution is Aladdin Systems'

StuffIt Expander and **DropStuff with Expander Enhancer**.[7] The Expander Enhancer that comes with DropStuff (shareware) allows StuffIt Expander (freeware) to extract from many UNIX formats, including tar and gzip.

2.   Check the contents

Untarring the archive should create a folder containing all the files in the module's distribution, including documentation. Start by looking over the documentation files, often called README and INSTALL.

The module's usage documentation may be embedded in the module itself, using Perl's POD (plain old documentation) format (see `perlpod`). You can read it with any text editor, as the markup is reasonably simple and unobtrusive, but it is meant to be viewed with a POD viewer. **Shuck**, bundled with MacPerl, is probably the best tool to use for viewing POD on a Mac.

If the documentation mentions any files with an .xs suffix, or you see such files in the unpacked directory, the module is probably based on a Perl extension. If so, you should probably forget about using it with MacPerl.

In general, notes or directions having to do with "make", "Makefile", or "MakeMaker" can be ignored. Make is a Unix facility that can compile and install extensions, install the modules themselves, and more. Unfortunately, the installation under MacPerl will have to be done manually.

3.   Move the files to an appropriate location

When MacPerl looks for a module, it looks in the folders specified in the **Libraries** Preferences (found under the **Edit** menu). Specifically, it examines the folders in the specified order, checking for the requested module. Naming conflicts are not an issue for MacPerl (it just grabs the first match it finds), but programmers must keep them in mind.

Create a new folder (conventionally named site_perl) for storing locally-added modules. Then, in the **Preferences** dialog, add the folder to MacPerl's search list by clicking on **Add Path** and selecting the directory.[8]

---

[7] Both Stuffit Expander and DropStuff are available at `www.aladdinsys.com`.

[8] If you name the folder **site_perl** and put it in the MacPerl folder, you do not need to add it to your preferences, as that folder name is specially added for you. But, when you upgrade your version of MacPerl, don't forget to retain a copy of the folder!

Note: No part of any path added to the preferences can have a comma in it, including the names of the folders enclosing the target folder.

MacPerl needs to know the complete path of the module file, including its position in the folder hierarchy. Consequently, you must tell MacPerl the module file's complete **path name**, including the entire series of folders that leads from the hard disk to the file.

Because of the Finder's interactive user interface, Mac OS users don't deal very often with path names, so a short review may be appropriate. Let's say that your hard disk is named HD, that you have installed the MacPerl distribution in a top-level folder named MacPerl *f*, and that you have created a folder named site_perl within the MacPerl *f* folder, as:

```
HD
    MacPerl f
        site_perl
```

In Mac OS file naming syntax, the location of the site_perl folder is:

```
HD:MacPerl f:site_perl:
```

This name specifies the **full path** from the top of the file tree (the hard disk volume) down to the site_perl folder. Assuming that the CGI module were installed in site_perl, its full path name would be:

```
HD:MacPerl f:site_perl:CGI.pm
```

Fortunately, MacPerl doesn't need to know the complete path when finding modules referenced by your program. It is capable of using a **relative path**, starting from the directories specified in your Libraries preferences.

In the example above, the directive use CGI would cause MacPerl to look for a file named CGI.pm, installed directly within site_perl. If the module is installed at a lower level, however, more complicated syntax would be needed. Let's say that we need to use the module:

```
HD
    MacPerl f
        site_perl
            Mac
                Apps
                    Anarchie.pm
```

Recall that the package separator for Perl is the double colon (: :). When a package is in a module, the double colon also represents a certain directory structure. Thus, our Perl code would ask for `Mac::Apps::Anarchie`, causing MacPerl to look for a file named:

HD:MacPerl *f*:site_perl:Mac:Apps:Anarchie.pm

Note: MacPerl packages and Mac OS paths use similar, but different syntax (i.e., double colons, rather than single colons). The fact that similar symbols are used to represent these slightly different concepts is purely coincidental. *Remember the difference, however!*

Sometimes, there are many modules in one archive, as is the case with LWP (also known as **libwww-perl**), a set of modules providing World Wide Web access (see Chapter 17, *Network Programming*). It is imperative that each file with the .pm suffix get installed in its proper directory. Otherwise, MacPerl will not be able to find (and load) the required module code.

4. Handle breaks

Computers use certain characters – usually invisible – to represent line breaks. Mac OS uses the octal character \015 for line breaks (sometimes called carriage return, or CR). Unix uses \012 (line feed, or LF). DOS and Windows use the sequence \015\012. (Aren't standards wonderful? :-)

Most of the time, the decompression and extraction process will automatically convert the line breaks for you. But, if you need to fix them yourself, there are innumerable ways to do it. Advanced text editors (e.g., BBEdit) and many utilities can do the conversion. You can also do the conversion with Perl. Drop any file on the droplet called `lf2cr4mac` (included on the CD-ROM) and any line breaks will be converted automagically.

Note: If you open a file in MacPerl and it shows as one long line, the file is probably using \012 as its line break character. If every line is preceded by a tall rectangle or other funny-looking symbol, then \015\012 is probably being used. In either case, you will need to fix the file.

5. Check for AutoSplit

During the automated process Unix uses to install modules, some modules are automatically split up (**autosplit**) into smaller files. The `AutoSplit` module can be used with MacPerl, but it must be invoked explicitly, as described below. Alternatively, you can simply avoid using this feature.

The basic idea behind `AutoSplit` (using the `AutoLoader` module to do all the real work) is this: if a part of a module is not used, it is a waste of coputing power to interpret and compile that part. So, some modules are designed to have subroutines moved to separate files.

We don't need to discuss the intricacies of `AutoSplit` here, except to say that there are two easy ways to help MacPerl deal with modules that need to be autosplit. One is to comment out the __END__ line in the module. The subroutines to be split out are stored after that line, so MacPerl will be able to find and compile them (regardless of whether they are needed).

The other way is a bit more complicated, but allows the `AutoSplit` optimization to be used. After putting the module in the proper directory, use `AutoSplit` to do the work for you. Keep in mind that you must redefine `$dir` and complete the full path to the module to be autosplit:

```
#!perl -w
use AutoSplit;
my $dir = "$ENV{MACPERL}site_perl";
autosplit("$dir:Mac:Apps:Anarchie.pm",
  "$dir:auto", 0, 1, 1);
```

This will split any subroutines after __END__ into separate files (named <subname>.al), and will put the files in the specified folder:[9]

HD:MacPerl *f*:site_perl:auto:Mac:Apps:Anarchie:

Nothing bad happens, by the way, if this script is run on a module that isn't meant to be autosplit. So, if you aren't sure whether a module needs to be autosplit, feel free to run autosplit on it as a precautionary measure.

use-ing Modules

A module file can be included in your program with either the **use** or **require** directive; use is more typical, however. The differences are both syntactic and functional. Syntactically, `require` is usually given a filename, while use must be given a package name (which MacPerl then translates into a filename).[10]

---

[9] The auto directory will be created automatically if it does not exist already.

[10] Since libraries are not packages, as modules are, they are called with `require`.

The functional differences are twofold. First, `use` preloads and executes the requested module at compile time; `require` loads the module at runtime. Second, if the module tries to export any symbols (such as subroutines or variables) into the current package, `use` will import the symbols automatically and `require` will not.[11] The following code snippets are equivalent:

```
use Some::Module;                # package name,
...                              # auto-imports symbols

BEGIN {
   require ':Some:Module.pm';    # relative path name
   Some::Module->import();       # force import symbols
}
...
```

The special `BEGIN` block tells perl to execute a given block of code at compile time. If `require` is not enclosed in a `BEGIN` block, its execution will be delayed until runtime.

What Next?

At this point, your actions will be dependent upon the specifics of the module itself. The documentation – usually embedded POD in the module – will dictate how you should continue. Read the documentation, then start writing code that will use the module. However, if the module is object-oriented, then you will need to be familiar with a few more concepts.

Object-Oriented Programming

As with libraries, the primary purpose of modules is to define a collection of subroutines. But, in many of the available modules, a collection of subroutines or data is accessed through an **object**, bringing the wonders of **Object-Oriented Programming** (**OOP**) to Perl.[12]

OOP techniques are useful because they hide the implementation details of objects behind well-documented access methods. This enables a very useful

---

[11] If `require` is called with a package name instead of a filename (e.g., `require Some::Module`), then it, too, will preload the module at compile time, like `use`. However, it will not import the exported data as `use` does.

[12] We cannot possibly teach OOP here in this book, or even sufficiently cover OOP as it relates to Perl. Hopefully, this will help you understand a little bit more about what some modules are doing, and frame OOP terms in Perl terms for you.

bargain to be made: the programmer that is using a module promises not to make use of the implementation details; the programmer that creates the module promises not to modify the interfaces to the access methods.

Many modern programming languages, such as C++ and Java, include support for OOP. With the advent of Perl version 5 and modules, Perl does too. Many of the modules in the CPAN are written using OOP concepts and syntax, so you will need to learn a bit about OOP in order to get by.

Let's start with a discussion of some OOP concepts and terminology, as used in the Perl community. Don't feel that you have to memorize these terms; we won't be depending on them much, except in the Toolbox Module chapters. You may encounter them, however, as you read literature on Perl.

An **object** is a **reference** that knows which class it belongs to. A **class** is a package that provides for working with objects. A **method** is a subroutine that is accessed via objects or classes. That's it. Really!

The bottom line is that in OOP, all of the information and interactions related to an item are accessed through an object. We touched on this in Chapter 1, with Rachel's "egg" object and its `get()` and `put()` methods.

A module that implements OOP style defines how each new **instance** of an object is to be created. For example, an egg is an object; each individual egg is an *instance* of the egg object: very alike, but distinct.

If the client code wants a new egg object, it asks the appropriate module to create one, passing back a reference. The creation is done by a special type of method, often called a **constructor** (conventionally named **new**).

The reference to the object can then be used to invoke methods that are defined for the object's class. **Virtual** methods are called through the object reference; **static** methods are called through the class.

```
use Carton::Eggs;
$cart = new Carton::Eggs;      # construct a carton
print $cart->count();          # should print "12"
$egg  = $cart->getEgg();       # get an "egg" object
print $cart->count();          # should print "11"
```

For more information on OOP theory, check your local bookstore. Many books on OOP theory and programming are available. Alternatively, read *Advanced Perl Programming*, which covers OOP in a Perlish context.

Chapter 12:

- *Volumes, Paths, And File Specifications*
- *File Information*
- *Answer, Ask, Pick*
- *Quit*
- *$Version*
- *LoadExternals*
- *DoAppleScript*
- *Reply*

The MacPerl Package

"Several large, artificial constructions are approaching us,"
ZORAC announced after a short pause.
"The designs are not familiar,
but they are obviously the products of intelligence.
Implications: we have been intercepted deliberately
by a means unknown, for a purpose unknown,
and transferred to a place unknown by a form of intelligence unknown.
Apart from the unknowns, everything is obvious."

– James P. Hogan, *Giants Star*

Because MacPerl runs on Mac OS, it has some different requirements than do Perl versions for other platforms. Some of the differences have to do with the filesystem, others with processes, inter-application communication, or built-in OS scripting. Because of these differences, special functionality has been included in MacPerl that is not found on other platforms.

Matthias Neeracher, the author of MacPerl, has written many MacPerl-specific modules and functions for the MacPerl distribution. These functions vary in complexity and utility, but they all have one main purpose: to make your Mac OS scripting easier and more powerful.

> **Note:** The first time we introduce a function, we will list its expected arguments using single, fully capitalized words, with square brackets enclosing optional arguments, as: `FooBar(ABC [, DEF])`, where function `FooBar()` takes the required parameter `ABC` and the optional parameter `DEF`.

MacPerl's built-in functions and variables are accessible just like any Perl function or special variable, with one caveat: they must be accessed via the `MacPerl` package.[1,2] So, you must use the `package MacPerl` directive before referencing these items or access them (from outside that package) with the double-colon syntax.[3]

Volumes, Paths, And File Specifications

Probably the most noticeable difference between MacPerl and other forms of Perl is in the specification of **pathnames** (see the previous chapter). Mac OS syntax uses colons, rather than (back-)slashes, to separate the elements of the name. Also, there is no overall "root" for the file tree as a whole.

Complicating the situation still further, Mac OS programs are able to use an alternate form of specifying a file: the **file system specification record** (**filespec**). A filespec is a special encoding of the path name which is guaranteed to be unique for every file. These lines could specify the same file:

```
$path = 'HD:MacPerl ƒ:Shuck Manual';
$fss  = ' FFFF000114B7:Shuck Manual';
```

As used by MacPerl, a filespec starts with a character (possibly invisible, depending on your font) whose high (i.e., sign) bit is set. It continues with a series of letters and numbers, followed by a colon and a filename.

> **Note:** The "series of letters and numbers" encodes a unique identifier for the hard disk partition and folder that contain the file. Unlike a path name, the identifier will continue to "point to" the folder as long as the folder exists (even if the folder is moved a different location).
>
> If the file is removed and replaced by a file with the same name, the identifier will also continue to work. If the folder is removed, how-

---

[1] MacPerl also includes modules which are useful for dealing with the Mac OS Toolbox. We will introduce these modules in the next chapter.

[2] Actually, we lied. They can also be exported into the current package by the `MacPerl` module if asked for explicitly:

```
use MacPerl qw(Ask Answer Pick); $x = Answer('Hello');
```

[3] Interesting note: a package's symbol table is a hash. To see every symbol available in a given package, try:

```
foreach (keys(%MacPerl::)) {print "$_ => $MacPerl::{$_}\n"}
```

ever, the identifer will not "find" a new folder with the same name. In short, the semantics of filespecs is *not* the same as that of path names.

In many situations, either a path name or a filespec can be used; `open()`, for instance, will accept either one. In some cases, however, a function may require a filespec instead of a path. Also, some functions *return* filespecs; if your program isn't ready for a filespec, it won't know what to do with it.

Luckily, the `MacPerl` package provides these translation functions:

```
MakeFSSpec(PATH)    # convert path to filespec
MakePath(FSSPEC)    # convert filespec to path
```

`Volumes()` is a good way to practice with filespecs and paths. In a scalar context, this function returns the filespec of the startup volume. In a list context, it returns the filespecs of all available volumes, in the order that they were mounted (the startup volume is always first). The script below uses `Volumes()` to display these filespecs, sorted by volume name:

```
$svol = MacPerl::Volumes();
print "The path name of the startup volume is:\n";
printf("  %s\n", MacPerl::MakePath($svol));

print "The filespecs of the other volumes are:\n";
@vols = MacPerl::Volumes();
foreach $vol (sort(@vols)) {
  printf("  %s\n", MacPerl::MakeFSSpec($vol))
    if ($vol ne $svol);
}
```

Note that we called `MakeFSSpec()` on the volumes, even though they already are filespecs. This works because `MakeFSSpec()` and `MakePath()` return the right thing whether they receive a filespec or a path. If you aren't sure which one you have in your variable, feel free to pass it through either function to ensure that you will get what you need.

File Information

Each Mac OS files has a **creator** and a **type**. A document's creator (application ID) is the same as that of its assigned application. The type encodes the type of document (e.g., text or graphic file).

For instance, script files that "belong" to MacPerl have the creator `McPL` and the type `TEXT`.[4] Files created by MacPerl's `open()` function have, by default, the creator `'MPS '` (MPW's application ID) and type `TEXT`.[5]

`SetFileInfo(CREATOR, TYPE, FILES)` applies the specified creator and type to a list of files. `GetFileInfo(FILE)` returns either the file type (in a scalar context) or an array of the creator and type (in a list context).

This short script opens a directory and looks through all of the files. If a file is of type `TEXT`, the script changes the file's creator to `R*ch` (BBEdit's application ID).

```perl
#!perl -w
my($dir, $file, @files);
$dir = 'HD:Desktop Folder:Text Files';

chdir($dir);
opendir(D, $dir) or die($!);

foreach $file (readdir(D)) {
  if (-f $file &&
      MacPerl::GetFileInfo($file) eq 'TEXT') {
    push(@files, $file);
  }
}
MacPerl::SetFileInfo('R*ch', 'TEXT', @files);
```

Answer, Ask, Pick

These three basic dialog functions are extremely useful for putting a quick **Graphical User Interface (GUI)** on top of an otherwise text-based script. They are normally the best way to get simple user input.[6]

`Answer(PROMPT [, BUTTON1, BUTTON2, BUTTON3])` puts up a dialog box with a message (`PROMPT`) and a choice of buttons for the user to click.

---

[4] MacPerl itself has type APPL (as all applications do) and, of course, creator McPL. For more about creator IDs, see Chapter 13, *The Toolbox Modules*.

[5] If you know how to use ResEdit, you can change the default in MacPerl's GUΣI resource ID 12040. Do not attempt this if you do not know what you are doing.

[6] There are also several GUI modules for more advanced interaction; these are discussed in Chapter 14, *GUI Toolbox Modules*.

If BUTTON1 is unspecified, it will be given the label OK. Thus, the calls Answer('Wake Up') and Answer('Wake Up', 'OK') do exactly the same thing. Both return a dialog box that says Wake Up and has a single, highlighted button that reads OK.

The buttons are displayed in reverse order. The first button passed to the function – which is the last button displayed on the screen – is always highlighted. So, the following call will print a dialog box with three buttons – Yes, No, and Maybe, in that order – with Maybe highlighted:

```
$ans = MacPerl::Answer('Are you awake?',
   'Maybe', 'No', 'Yes');
```

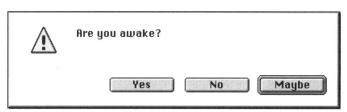

Then, of course, you want to get a value back to find out what the user has clicked. The first button *on the screen* always returns a 0. Since the last button passed to the variable is always first in the dialog box, clicking on OK in the following examples always returns 0:

```
$an1 = MacPerl::Answer('Delete?', 'Huh?', 'No', 'OK');
$an2 = MacPerl::Answer('Delete?', 'No', 'OK');
$an3 = MacPerl::Answer('Delete?', 'OK');
$an4 = MacPerl::Answer('Delete?');
```

Ask(PROMPT [, DEFAULT]) is similar, but instead of having buttons to return a value, it has a text input box. Like Answer(), the first argument is the prompt. The second argument, which is optional, allows you to put some default text into the box for the user.

The value returned by the function is the text that is in the box when the user clicks OK. If the user clicks Cancel, the function returns undef.

> **Note:** User-supplied data should always be considered tainted, and is usually tainted under Unix Perl. However, the special MacPerl routines generally do not taint this data. You might want to consider using the Taint module from the CPAN, with which you can intentionally taint

any data you have. See Chapter 16, *CGI Scripting*, and `perlsec` for more details on tainting.

```
$name  = MacPerl::Ask('What is your name?');
$quest = MacPerl::Ask('What is your Quest?',
  'I seek the Holy Grail');
```

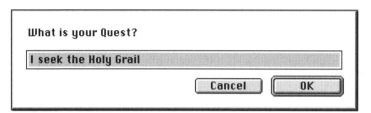

`Pick(PROMPT, VALUES)` allows you to put up a scrolling list of items. Again, the first argument is the text prompt for the dialog box. But here, the number of following arguments is limited only by memory, and each argument will be a value in the list. Again, the selected value will be returned if the user clicks OK, and `undef` will be returned on Cancel.

```
$suit = MacPerl::Pick('Pick a Suit',
  qw(Hearts Spades Diamonds Clubs));
$card = MacPerl::Pick('Pick a Card',
  ('A', 2..10, 'J', 'Q', 'K'));
```

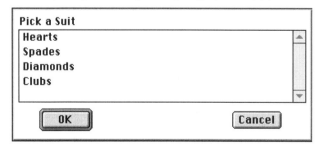

You can also have `MacPerl::Pick` allow the picking of multiple items by assigning it in a list context, as in:

```
@major = MacPerl::Pick('Your college major(s)',
  qw(Psychology Sociology Journalism));
```

Quit

`Quit(LEVEL)` sets a flag that tells MacPerl whether or not to quit after the current script has finished execution. It does not quit until the script is finished, if at all. `LEVEL` defines under what conditions this happens, as:

0   Do not quit.
1   Only quit if this is a "runtime" script.
2   Always quit.
3   Only quit if this is the first script run since MacPerl was launched.

```
MacPerl::Quit(2);
MacPerl::Quit(0) if MacPerl::Answer(
  'Should I stay or should I go?', 'Stay', 'Go'
);
```

$Version

`$Version` is the one item in the `MacPerl` package that is not a function. It is a read-only scalar variable that holds the MacPerl version information. This differs from the special Perl variable **$]**, which holds the version of the Perl sources from which MacPerl is built.

`$Version` always changes when a new MacPerl is released, but often those releases are based on the same Perl sources, so `$]` doesn't always change.

```
print "MacPerl $MacPerl::Version, Perl version $]";
```

Displays a line of the form:

```
MacPerl 5.1.9r4 Application, Perl version 5.004
```

LoadExternals

One really nifty feature of MacPerl is its ability to use other Mac OS languages. `LoadExternals()` is a way to use XFCN and XCMD extensions, which are commonly used in HyperCard scripting. The argument passed is a library file, with the same path rules as `require`.

Dartmouth College has developed some useful XFCNs and XCMDs. One of them, for Clipboard access, is on our CD-ROM. Copy Clipboard.XFCN to your site_perl folder. This file contains an XFCN that can copy information to and from the Mac OS clipboard, by means of the `Clipboard()` function.

If an argument is passed, LoadExternals puts it on the Mac OS clipboard. Otherwise, it returns the contents of the Clipboard. Note that, because LoadExternals() brings functions directly into the current package, many people prefer to call the function from a separate package.

```
package Dartmouth;
MacPerl::LoadExternals("Clipboard.XFCN");

package main;
Dartmouth::Clipboard("D'oh!");
print Dartmouth::Clipboard(), "\n";
```

If everything has worked properly, the specified text should land on the Clipboard (D'oh!). You can go to the Finder and select Show Clipboard from the Edit menu to prove it to yourself, if you like, or just paste it somewhere.

DoAppleScript

DoAppleScript(SCRIPT) takes the text of an AppleScript as its argument. We'll cover this more in Chapter 18, *AppleScript, Etc*.

```
$script = <<EOS;
tell application "MacPerl"
  make new window
  copy "MacPerl: Power and Ease" to character 1 of front
window
end tell
EOS
MacPerl::DoAppleScript($script);
```

Reply

Reply(REPLY) is used primarily for returning data to programs that call MacPerl. For example, AppleScript can call MacPerl as follows:[7]

```
tell application "MacPerl"
  Do Script "MacPerl::Reply('Hello')"
end tell
```

If run from Script Editor, Apple's AppleScript editor, this will return the text "Hello". We will see more of this in Chapter 18, *AppleScript, Etc*.

---

[7] Remember, this is AppleScript code and will not run as-is in MacPerl.

Chapter 13:

The Toolbox Modules

> *Everybody knows a little bit of something.*
>
> – King's X, *Gretchen Goes to Nebraska*

The previous chapter covered the Mac-specific built-in functions that are contained in the `MacPerl` package. This chapter covers a set of MacPerl-specific modules, known as the Toolbox Modules. These modules cover all manner of Mac OS programming needs, from getting file information to process control, interapplication communication, graphics, speech recognition, QuickTime movies, and the Earth's revolution around the Sun.[1]

> **Note**: Some functionality in the Perl core modules (e.g., File::Copy) is implemented via the Toolbox Modules. These modules are not installed by default on 68K Macintoshes. If you use a 68K Macintosh, make sure that either CFM-68K MacPerl or BigMacPerl is installed.

There is a lot of stuff here. We suggest that you start by skimming through the chapter. After you have become familiar with the general purposes of the modules, you can go back and try one of them out. In short, you don't need to understand it all; you only need to understand the parts that you use.

One more note: these modules have been used to varying degrees and are at various levels of maturity. It is possible that some functions will not work as expected; if something does not work properly, report it to the MacPerl mailing list. Also, though the interfaces seem to be stable, they are subject to change. As always, let the programmer beware.

---

[1] Assuming that the Earth does, indeed, revolve around the Sun.

The **toolbox modules** access the Mac OS Toolbox,[2] a set of instructions for controlling various Mac OS functions. Mac OS has thousands of toolbox calls; these modules attempt to provide MacPerl with a useful subset.

Inside Macintosh provides useful information on the toolbox calls; the documentation that comes with each module provides detailed information on the module and any module-specific issues that may be involved. The Mac-Perl folder contains some examples of module use, in the folder :ext:Mac:.

> **Note:** *Inside Macintosh* (available from Apple Computer) details the Macintosh system software. The books are freely available on the Internet in various electronic forms, and the most important books to MacPerl programming are on the MacPerl CD-ROM. In some cases, the cross reference and other books could be out of date. Check the Apple site periodically for updates.

This chapter is an introduction and supplement to, not a replacement for, the detailed documentation listed above. As the descriptions for the toolbox modules state:

> Access to *Inside Macintosh* is essential for proper use of these functions. Explanations of terms, processes and procedures are provided there. Any attempt to use these functions without guidance can cause severe errors in your machine, including corruption of data. **You have been warned.**

With luck, we will give enough guidance to allow you to use some modules successfully. Nonetheless, you will be directly accessing Mac OS toolbox calls through MacPerl, and you are running a risk if you do not know what you are doing. The authors of this book will **not** be held responsible if you unknowingly alter the Earth's orbit.

The good news is that if you know Mac OS programming, the documentation included here and with the toolbox modules is sufficient to get you going. If not, you should read the relevant sections of *Inside Macintosh* anyway.

Inside Macintosh has a cross reference which includes every toolbox routine name. If you will be using the toolbox modules extensively, spend some time familiarizing yourself with the cross references and general layout of the books. This will help you to find what you need quickly and painlessly.

---

[2] Also called the Mac OS **API** (Application Program Interface).

Using The Toolbox Modules

The MacPerl toolbox functions have the same names and take their input arguments in basically the same order as their Mac OS toolbox counterparts. Output from the functions is always returned as either a single value or as a list (if multiple arguments are returned). If an error occurs, the function returns `undef` for scalar context or `()` for list context; the error code is available in the special variable **$^E**.[3]

Complex data structures are put into **objects** (as discussed in chapter 11). The data fields are made available through methods which normally return the value of the field when called without an argument, changing the value of the field when called with an argument:

```
$object = someFunction();
$data   = $object->dataField(); # get data
$object->dataField('somedata'); # set data
```

Functions and constants are exported into the namespace of the package that is current when the module is called with `use`.[4] Constants are represented as functions that return a constant value,[5] so they normally should be followed by parentheses (i.e., `$Data{someConstant()}`). Other data structures (e.g., hashes) may be exported, as well.[6]

Mac::AppleEvents, Mac::OSA

The `Mac::AppleEvents` and `Mac::OSA` modules, along with `MacPerl::DoAppleScript()`, are the primary means of doing **interapplication communication** with MacPerl (that is, communicating with other programs on your Macintosh).

This is such a rich and important topic that we have given it given it a whole chapter, *AppleScript, Etc.* If you have not used any of the toolbox modules, however, you might want to read further here before moving on.

---

[3] `$^E` is similar to **$!** (which contains the current error), but is for platform-specific errors. MacPerl uses `$^E` only for its toolbox modules.

[4] Because they are explicitly exported, the toolbox functions and constants do not need to be prefixed with `Mac::` before each use. Note the examples throughout this chapter.

[5] Perl has constants, but they are currently implemented as subroutines.

[6] Also see Toolbox.pod in the MacPerl distribution, available under the Help menu under Macintosh Toolbox Modules / Overview.

Mac::Files

The `Mac::Files` module is not, ironically, used for dealing with files, *per se*. Instead, it contains functions for moving, renaming, creating, finding, modifying, and getting information about files and folders on your machine.

`FSpCreate(FILE, CREATOR, TYPE)` creates a file with a specified creator and type. The Perl `open()` function creates files, but with MacPerl's default creator and type. You can also use `MacPerl::SetFileInfo()` to change the creator and type, as discussed in the previous chapter.

In the course of your toolbox usage – especially in Apple Event programming – you might need access to an alias handle for a file. `NewAliasMinimal(FILE)` returns the needed alias handle.

You can also use toolbox calls to lock files. `FSpSetFLock(FILE)` and `FSpRstLock(FILE)` set and reset (release) a lock on a specified `FILE`. This is **not** the same as Perl's `flock()` function, which is not implemented in Mac-Perl, but it is similar.

Locking a file with `FSpSetFLock` makes all new access paths to that file read-only. If a file is already opened by an application when the file is locked, that application can write to the file as before. For this reason, the first `open()` below succeeds, while the second `open()` fails.

```
#!perl -w
use Mac::Files;
my($f) = 'myfile';

open(F, ">>$f") or warn($!);
FSpSetFLock($f);
print F "some text\n";
close(F);

open(F, ">>$f") or warn($!);
FSpRstFLock($f);
```

`Mac::Files` also has a function for finding the path to a particular folder (usually on the startup volume). `FindFolder()` is passed a volume and a type to look for. (Hint: to specify the startup volume, pass the parameter `kOnSystemDisk()`.) As the second argument, pass a **constant** specifying the type of the item to be found. Acceptable constants are:

```
kAppleMenuFolderType          kShutdownFolderType
kControlPanelFolderType       kStartupFolderType
kDesktopFolderType            kSystemFolderType
kExtensionFolderType          kTemporaryFolderType
kFontsFolderType              kTrashFolderType
kPreferencesFolderType
```

Here is a portable way to open a preference file (e.g., "myprefs") on any Macintosh, regardless of the name of the startup volume or system folder:

```
#!perl -w
use Mac::Files;
my($prefsDir, $mpp);

$prefsDir = FindFolder(kOnSystemDisk(),
  kPreferencesFolderType()
);
$mpp = "$prefsDir:MacPerl 5 Preferences";
```

Mac::Files also provides a way of getting information about files, though it can be a bit cryptic to use. FSpGetCatInfo(FILE [, INDEX]) and FSpSetCatInfo(FILE, INFO) deal with objects in the CatInfo class. See *Inside Macintosh* for in-depth information, but here is an overview.

After passing a file to FSpGetCatInfo() and retrieving an object of the class CatInfo, you can call various methods that will return either scalar values or objects of other classes.

```
#!perl -w
use Mac::Files;
my($file, $fileCat, $fileInfo);

$file     = 'HD:Desktop Folder:Untitled';
$fileCat  = FSpGetCatInfo($file)     or die($^E);
$fileInfo = $fileCat->ioFlFndrInfo() or die($^E);
print  $fileCat->ioNamePtr(), "\n";
print $fileInfo->fdCreator(), "\n";

$fileInfo->fdCreator('R*ch')         or die($^E);
print $fileInfo->fdCreator(), "\n";

$fileCat->ioFlFndrInfo($fileInfo)    or die($^E);
FSpSetCatInfo($file, $fileCat)       or die($^E);
```

Displays:

```
Untitled
McPL
R*ch
```

In this code, `ioNamePtr()` returns the file name and `ioFlFndrInfo()` returns an object (belonging to class `FInfo`) through which more file information can be retrieved. Note that, after we change the creator in the `FInfo` object to `R*ch`, we need to copy it back to the `CatInfo` object, then set it with `FSpSetCatInfo()`.

As we already know, we can find out this same information with other routines. But sometimes, as with the `Mac::StandardFile` module, we will have to use these methods to get our file information. Also, if you need some slightly more obscure information about a file, such as flags, these methods are the ones to use.[7]

Mac::StandardFile

The Mac OS standard file dialogs are found in the `Mac::StandardFile` module. The four basic functions – standard open and save dialogs, custom open and save dialogs – are all that are needed to do the majority of GUI file system interaction that programs need to do.

Note that these functions do not actually open or save files; they only let the user interact with a GUI to tell your program which file he wants to access. Your program must do the work of saving and opening the file.

Let's start with the basic `StandardGetFile(FILEFILTER, TYPELIST)` function. When called, it opens a standard dialog box in the directory specified in the Mac OS General Controls Control Panel. It will only show files that match file types specified in `TYPELIST`. (If `TYPELIST` is null, all files will be shown.)

The function returns a `StandardFileReply` object. This object has a set of methods that return information about the file. The `sfType()` method, for example, returns the file type of the selected file. `sfFile()` contains the

---

[7] Perl's -s file test gives the size of a file's data fork only. To get the full size of a file, including the resource fork, get the `CatInfo` object for the file; the size is `$fileCat->ioFlLgLen() + $fileCat->ioFlRLgLen()`.

full file name. sfGood() is a Boolean value that is true if a file was selected, false if the user cancelled the operation.

This example looks for TEXT and clpt (clipping) files; note that the types are concatenated ('TEXTclpt') without intervening spaces.

```
#!perl -w
use Mac::StandardFile;
my($file);

$file = StandardGetFile(0, 'TEXTclpt');
if ($file->sfGood()) {
  printf("You chose %s, of type %s.\n",
    $file->sfFile(), $file->sfType()
  );
} else {
  print "You cancelled the operation.\n";
}
```

Displays:

```
You chose HD:Desktop Folder:Hello.pl, of type TEXT.
```

When the file is selected, an object is passed back. We check to see if the user actually selected a file (with sfGood()), and if so, print out information about that file. Now that we have the name in $file->sfFile(), we can open the file with open() and do what we want with it.

The FILEFILTER parameter allows you to filter candidate files. If you pass a null value, no filtering takes place. You can pass a reference to a function, however, and filter files in any desired manner.

Your filter function will be passed a CatInfo object (from the Mac::Files module) for each file that the dialog box encounters. Most filters have to do with file name, file type, or creator type.

The filter function checks each file that gets passed to it. In the example below, we check the file name to see if it ends in .pl, then check to make sure this is a MacPerl text file. We can let the filter check the file type; however, in practice, it is faster to let StandardGetFile() take care of that. The filter function can only filter files that `StandardGetFile()` passes to it.[8]

Note that the `FILEFILTER` returns *true* for a file that should not be shown, and *false* for a file that should be shown. We are checking for characteristics of files that we *do* want to show, so we negate the return value.

```perl
#!perl -w
use Mac::StandardFile;
use Mac::Files;
my($file);

$file = StandardGetFile(\&myFilter, 0);
if ($file->sfGood()) {
  printf("You chose %s\n", $file->sfFile());
} else {
  print "You cancelled operation\n";
}

sub myFilter {
  my($fileCat, $fileInfo);

  $fileCat  = $_[0];
  $fileInfo = $fileCat->ioFlFndrInfo() or die($^E);
  return !(
    $fileInfo->fdCreator() eq 'McPL' &&
    $fileInfo->fdType()    eq 'TEXT' &&
    $fileCat->ioNamePtr()  =~ /\.pl$/
  );
}
```

Displays:

```
You chose HD:Desktop Folder:Hello.pl.
```

Our call to `StandardGetFile(0, 0)` specifies no filter function or file types, so all files are shown.

`Mac::StandardFile` also provides a `StandardPutFile(PROMPT, DEFAULTNAME)` function. This puts up a **Save As** dialog with a message

---

[8] The Mac OS **Easy Open** Control Panel can cause problems with recognizing the file types you specify in `TYPELIST`. Checking the file type in the filter will take care of this.

prompt for the user and an optional default name for the file. This time,
sfReplacing() returns true if this file is replacing another file, false
otherwise. If the file already exists, the script below double-checks and
asks the user if he really wants to erase the existing file.

```perl
#!perl -w
use Mac::StandardFile;
my($answer, $file);

$file = StandardPutFile('Filename:', 'myfile.txt');
if ($file->sfGood()) {
  $answer = (
    MacPerl::Answer('Erase existing file?',
      'No', 'OK')
  ) if ($file->sfReplacing());
  if ($answer) {
    printf("%s exists; cancelled.\n",
      $file->sfFile());
    exit();
  }
  open(FILE, '>' . $file->sfFile()) or die($!);
  print FILE "Here is some text.\n";
  close(FILE);
  printf("File created: %s\n", $file->sfFile());
} else {
  print "User cancelled operation.\n";
}
```

If these dialog boxes are insufficient for your needs, feel free to create your
own. This will require an intimate understanding of dialog resources, however, and some extensive use of *Inside Macintosh*. See Chapter 14, *GUI Toolbox Modules*, for some introductory material.

Here's a quick example, using a dialog resource that is already available in
the MacPerl application. The standard MacPerl **Save As...** dialog is in ID
192. We use the Mac::QuickDraw module and its Point class to position
the window (the given values center the dialog on the screen).

```perl
#!perl -w
use Mac::StandardFile;
use Mac::Files;
use Mac::QuickDraw;
my($file, $x);
```

```
$x    = new Point (-1, -1);
$file = CustomPutFile('Filename:', 'file.txt', 192,
  $x);
if ($file->sfGood()) {
  printf("File selected: %s\n", $file->sfFile());
} else {
  print "User cancelled operation.\n";
}
```

Mac::MoreFiles

`Mac::MoreFiles` offers several file and directory access routines that complement the ones in `Mac::Files`.

`FSpCreateMinimum(FILE)` creates a file from a given path or filespec, like `FSpCreate()`, but gives the file no creator or type. `FSpShare(FILE)` and `FSpUnshare(FILE)` take a directory or volume filespec and turn file sharing on or off for it. `FSpDirectoryCopy(SRC, DEST, PREFLIGHT)` copies a directory to another location. (It does not rename the directory.)

```
#!perl -w
use Mac::MoreFiles;
my($dir)  = 'HD:MacPerl ƒ:macscripts';
my($dest) = 'HD:Desktop Folder';

FSpDirectoryCopy($dir, $dest, 0) or die($^E);
```

`FSpDTGetAPPL(VOLUME, CREATOR)` returns the full path to an application with the specified creator ID. The time it takes may vary, based on the condition of your desktop database and the size of your filesystem.

Because you might not know the application's volume, `Mac::MoreFiles` exports a tied hash (using `FSpDTGetAPPL()`) called `%Application`. Using an application ID as the key, the hash returns the path to the application. The two `print` statements below will display exactly the same information, if your MacPerl application is on your startup volume:

```
use Mac::MoreFiles;
print FSpDTGetAPPL(0, 'McPL');
print $Application{'McPL'};
```

On most Mac OS filesystems, the Finder gives access to file comments by means of the Get Info item in the File menu. `FSpDTSetComment(SPEC,`

COMMENT) sets a filespec comment to a text string. FSpDTGetComment
(SPEC) returns the comment; FSpDTCopyComment(SRCSPEC, DSTSPEC)
copies a comment from one file to another.

Here we set the comment for the MacPerl application, then copy its comment to another file:

```perl
#!perl -w
use Mac::MoreFiles;
my($file1, $file2);

$file1 = MacPerl::MakeFSSpec($Application{'McPL'});
$file2 = MacPerl::MakeFSSpec('HD:Files:file.txt');
FSpDTSetComment($file1, 'Power and Ease');
FSpDTCopyComment($file1, $file2);
print FSpDTGetComment($file2), "\n";
```

Displays:

```
Power and Ease
```

FSpDTGetAPPL() and %Application return paths, but the comment-
handling functions need filespecs. So, we use MacPerl::MakeFSSpec() to
convert the paths above into filespecs.

Mac::Processes

A **process** is a program that is running on a computer. This might be, among
other things, an application or a desk accessory.

Mac::Processes exports a hash called %Process. Each key of the hash
is a **process number**. The values are objects that allow access to methods for
getting more information about a specific process, including its name, type,
and more. By iterating over the hash, you can get information on all active
processes. The script below prints a sorted list of application names:

```perl
#!perl -w
use Mac::Processes;
my($psn);

foreach $psn (keys(%Process)) {
  push(@names, $Process{$psn}->processName());
}
print map("$_\n", sort(@names));
```

Displays:

```
BBEdit 4.5
File Sharing Extension
Finder
MacPerl
Shuck
```

The objects in `%Process` have access to the following methods:

processActiveTime	processName
processAppSpec	processNumber
processLaunchDate	processSignature
processLauncher	processSize
processLocation	processType
processMode	

The `%Process` hash is implemented throughthe `GetNextProcess(PSN)` and `GetProcessInformation(PSN)` functions.

`GetNextProcess()` returns the process whose number follows `PSN` (even if `PSN` is not a valid process number). If `PSN` is `0`, the function returns the lowest-numbered process. `GetProcessInformation()` retrieves information about a given process, returning the process object described above.

Two other functions return process numbers. `GetCurrentProcess()` returns the number of the process that is using the CPU. Because of the way Mac-Perl works, this will always be the process number of MacPerl. `GetFront-Process()` returns the number of the process that is "in front" on the screen. `SetFrontProcess(PSN)` moves the specified process to the front.

`Mac::Processes` also gives MacPerl scripts the ability to launch other applications. It isn't as simple as it is in Unix, where an `open()`, `exec()`, or similar call can open a process.[9] Instead, you have to use the `Launch-Application()` function.

The implementation of this function changed in MacPerl 5.1.4r4, so older code might not work. First, we call `new()` in the `LaunchParam` package. This constructor accepts a hash of parameters describing the process to be launched. See *Inside Macintosh* for complete details.

---

[9] If you have MPW and ToolServer, you can call an external program from a MacPerl program with `system()`, however.

The new() constructor requires the launchAppSpec parameter, which is the filespec of the application to launch. We can get the filespec by using the %Application hash from Mac::MoreFiles. We also want to set the launchControlFlags parameter to launchContinue(). Without this, MacPerl would quit after launching the application.

```
#!perl -w
use Mac::MoreFiles;
use Mac::Processes;
my($app);

$app = new LaunchParam(
    'launchControlFlags' => launchContinue(),
    'launchAppSpec'      => $Application{'R*ch'}
) or die($^E);
LaunchApplication($app) or die($^E);
```

Mac::Gestalt

Mac::Gestalt returns information about the operating environment. It exports the tied hash %Gestalt, which returns codes for a (large!) set of constants. *Inside Macintosh* gives a complete list of the constants and their meanings. Here is an example to get you started:

```
#!perl -w
use Mac::Gestalt;
my($arch, %archs, $mac);

$arch  = $Gestalt{gestaltSysArchitecture()};
%archs = (gestaltPowerPC() => 'a PPC',
          gestalt68k()     => 'a 68k');
$mac   = (defined($archs{$arch}) ?
                  $archs{$arch}  : 'an unknown');
MacPerl::Answer('You are using a Macintosh with ' .
    "$mac architecture.");
```

To print the complete list of constants, try:

```
...
my($key);

foreach $key (sort(keys(%Mac::Gestalt::))) {
    print "$key\n" if ($key =~ /^gestalt/);
}
```

Mac::Types

There are basically two functions in this module, `MacPack(CODE, DATA)` and `MacUnpack(CODE, DATA)`. `MacPack()` is similar to (and implemented via) Perl's `pack()` function. It puts a value (or a list of values) into the specified Mac OS data type.

For instance, with Apple Events, every parameter must be of a certain type (e.g., keyword, TEXT). To make sure that you are passing the correct type, you can filter the value through `MacPack()` first. And, when you receive values, you can filter them through `MacUnpack()`. Here is an example of packing and unpacking a short integer:

```perl
#!perl -w
use Mac::Types;
my($x);

$x = MacPack('shor', 9874.70);
print MacUnpack('shor', $x), "\n";
```

Displays:

```
9874
```

`Mac::Types` can pack and unpack many different data types:

`'bool'`	A boolean (true/false) value
`'doub'`	A double-precision floating-point number
`'enum'`	An enumerated type
`'fss '`	A file specification record
`'keyw'`	A 4-byte ("keyword") string
`'long'`	A long integer
`'magn'`	An unsigned long integer ("magnitude")
`'qdrt'`	A QuickDraw Rect
`'shor'`	A short integer
`'sing'`	A single-precision floating-point number
`'STR '`	A Pascal-style string
`'STR#'`	A string list
`'TEXT'`	text

Mac::Memory

`Mac::Memory` provides an interface to the Mac OS memory manager and access to special data manipulation in memory.

In general, Perl programmers do not need to worry about memory. Perl has no memory limitations aside from those imposed by your system and it automatically adjusts allocated memory for data structures as needed. However, Mac OS programs are assigned a certain amount of memory in which to work. If you are dealing with enough data, you could easily use up all of MacPerl's allocated memory.[10]

The following script snippet shows the current amount of free space that is available in the MacPerl application. It can be useful for identifying memory leaks, which MacPerl is prone to due to occasional bugs in the Perl core and the nature of the toolbox modules, which sometimes require manual deallocation of memory.

The general concept is that the toolbox module calls in MacPerl do not automatically dispose of memory that a C programmer would dispose of manually. We'll see more of this in Chapter 18, *AppleScript, Etc.*

`FreeMem()` returns the amount of free memory that is available in the application. `MaxMem()` compacts and purges the current memory zone, returning an array of two values: the amount of memory that is available and the amount by which the memory can grow.[11]

```perl
#!perl -w
use Mac::Memory;

printf("Free Memory: %0.2f MB\n",
  mbytes(FreeMem()));
printf("Max  Memory: %0.2f MB\n",
  mbytes((MaxMem())[0]));

sub mbytes { $_[0] / (1024**2) }
```

---

[10] You can give any application (including MacPerl) more memory by selecting it in the Finder, choosing **Get Info** from the **File** menu, and changing the value of **Preferred Size**. Note that this can only be done when the application is not running.

[11] The syntax around `MaxMem()` puts the function into a reference to an anonymous array and pulls out the first value.

Displays:

```
Free Memory: 6.37 MB
Max  Memory: 6.34 MB
```

`Mac::Memory` can also be used as a way to manipulate data in memory. We will see an example of this below, in `Mac::Resources`, where the data of a resource is stored in an object from the `Handle` class in `Mac::Memory`.

Mac::Resources

`Mac::Resources` allows you to access the Mac OS Resource Manager. Normally, this will involve searching through, reading, and editing existing resources, as well as creating new resources. The following example demonstrates some basic routines.

This example droplet takes a MacPerl file saved as a CGI script and sets the default number of minutes it stays open (5) to any value from 1 to 127 (a value of 0 keeps the CGI script open indefinitely).

We first use `Mac::Types` to pack the number into the correct format. The script then opens each file that is dropped on it as a resource file, using `OpenResFile(FILE)`. This sets the current resource file, which is returned at any time by `CurResFile()`. We ask for the `time` resource ID 128; if it exists, an object of the `Handle` class from `Mac::Memory` is returned. We set its value with the `set(OFFSET, LENGTH, DATA)` method.

Now the changed resource is in memory, but needs to be saved back to disk. We mark the resource as changed, using `ChangedResource(HANDLE)`, update the file, then close it.

We have to release the memory, because while MacPerl handles memory allocation for us, the toolbox does not. So we call `ReleaseResource()` when we are done with the resource handle.[12]

```
#!perl -w
use Mac::Resources;
use Mac::Memory;
use Mac::Types;
my($min, $pmin, $file, $res);
```

---

[12] This droplet, with a GUI interface, is stored on the CD-ROM as setCGImins.drop.

```
$min  = 15;  # any value 1..127, or 0
$pmin = substr(MacPack('long', $min), 3, 1);
foreach $file (@ARGV) {
  OpenResFile($file)                  or die($^E);
  $res = Get1Resource('time', 128);
  if ($res) {
    $res->set(0, 1, $pmin)            or die($^E);
    ChangedResource($res)             or die($^E);
    UpdateResFile(CurResFile())       or die($^E);
    ReleaseResource($res)             or die($^E);
  } else { warn($^E) }
  CloseResFile(CurResFile());
}
```

Note that we can *get* the current value of the `Handle` object with the `get()` method, and that there are several other functions for getting and updating resources. All of these are thoroughly documented in *Inside Macintosh* and the `Mac::Resources` documentation.

Mac::InternetConfig

A freeware configuration system called **Internet Config** has surfaced because of the need to keep Internet-related preferences in a central location. It is so handy that it has become a standard on Mac OS.

`InternetConfig` provides a basic interface to the preferences. The module is normally used to retrieve and set the values stored by Internet Config. It exports a tied hash for this purpose, named `%InternetConfig`. A list of all possible constants is given in the documentation, but this script displays of the more some useful ones:

```
#!perl
use Mac::InternetConfig;

print $InternetConfig{kICRealName()},    "\n";
print $InternetConfig{kICEmail()},       "\n";
print $InternetConfig{kICWWWHomePage()}, "\n";
```

Displays:

```
Joe Smith
joe@company.com
http://www.company.com/
```

These values can also be set, using the same interface:

```
$InternetConfig{kICEmail()} = 'jsmith@company.com';
```

`ICLaunchURL(INST, HINT, DATA)` is another useful Internet Config routine. The example below starts a connection to the Internet Config system, using `ICStart()`, returning an **instance**.

The instance is configured, then used to launch a URL. In this case, the URL we specify is the user's home page (already set in Internet Config). We then close the link to the Internet Config system, using `ICStop(INSTANCE)`.

```perl
#!perl -w
use Mac::InternetConfig;
my($icInst);

$icInst = ICStart();
ICGeneralFindConfigFile($icInst);
ICLaunchURL($icInst, 0,
  $InternetConfig{kICWWWHomePage()});
ICStop($icInst);
```

`Mac::InternetConfig` also (as of MacPerl 5.1.6r4) provides access to the file mappings database in MacPerl. By passing the tied hash `%Internet ConfigMap` a filename with an extension in the database, or a reference to an array containing a file type and creator, you get back an object whose methods return information about that entry in the IC database.

```perl
use Mac::InternetConfig;
$map1 = $InternetConfigMap{'myscript.pl'};
$map2 = $InternetConfigMap{['TEXT', 'R*ch']};
print $map1->file_type(),  "\n";
print $map2->entry_name(), "\n";
```

Several methods are available to each object, as:

```
creator_app_name   extension       file_type
entry_name         file_creator    MIME_type
```

If more than one entry fits the key passed to the hash, the hash returns the first one it finds. You probably have a single entry for the .pl extension, but you are likely to have multiple entries for `TEXT/R*ch` if you use BBEdit.

Chapter 14:

- *Windows*
- *Window Definitions*
- *Drawing And Text*
- *Events*
- *Controls*
- *Menus*
- *Dialogs*
- *Roll Your Own*

GUI Toolbox Modules

> *The medium is the metaphor.*
>
> – Neil Postman

Possibly the biggest reason people use Mac OS is for its renowned ease of use. This manifests itself in every aspect of the Macintosh, both hardware and software, but software is the most profound part of this ease-of-use experience for most users.

The Mac OS, due in no small part to the tremendous work Apple has done in human interface research, has a nicer Graphical User Interface (GUI) than its Microsoft Windows or X11[1] counterparts. The widgets are easier on the eye and the menus and dialog boxes are more intuitive. Overall, the entire experience is more integrated.

Thanks to several of MacPerl's toolbox modules, this aspect of Mac OS programming can be extended to your MacPerl programs as well. And, if you program Mac applications in C or Pascal, these modules help turn MacPerl into a powerful prototyping tool.

There are volumes of information in the *Inside Macintosh* series detailing how to use windows, menus, dialogs, and other GUI features of Mac OS. We can't cover all of this information here. Consequently, this chapter will function primarily as a "cookbook", introducing some common tasks and

---

[1] X11 is a windowing system that is common on Unix systems.

concepts that can be used directly, reworked into other programs, or built upon for more complex tasks.

The standard toolbox module disclaimers apply: these operations should not be used without access to *Inside Macintosh*. In addition, these modules are not as well-tested as some of the others; if you are venturing into more obscure portions of the modules, bugs and misfeatures become more likely.

We recommend that you read *Macintosh Human Interface Guidelines* (a part of *Inside Macintosh*), which is designed to help "link the philosophy behind the Macintosh interface to the actual implementation of interface elements."[2]

Windows

GUI programming in MacPerl often requires multiple modules for simple tasks. For example, `Mac::Windows` must be used to create a window, `Mac::QuickDraw` to place it, `Mac::Fonts` to put some text in it, and `Mac::Events` to respond to mouse clicks on it.

The basic building block of the window, and many other GUI elements, is the **rectangle**, which is accessed via the `Rect` class.[3] It is comprised of four numbers, which comprise two (X, Y) coordinate sets. X is a horizontal offset in pixels (picture elements, i.e., dots on the screen); Y is a vertical offset.

The first coordinate set defines the top left corner of the rectangle (e.g., 50, 50), which is the starting point of the rectangle in the frame (which is, for a window, your screen). The second set (e.g., 300, 100) defines the bottom right corner of the rectangle. The other two corners are extrapolated automatically.[4]

50,50   300, 50

50, 100   300, 100

---

[2] For the sake of example, we may break one or more of the guidelines proffered there.

[3] From `Mac::QuickDraw`.

[4] The created rectangle's four elements can be accessed via `$rect->left()`, `$rect->top()`, `$rect->right()`, and `$rect->bottom()`.

The MacWindow class (from Mac::Windows), with its new() constructor, does all of the background magic behind window handling. It accepts five primary arguments to create a window: a boundary (a rectangle), title bar text, a visibility boolean, a window style, and a close-box boolean.[5]

The script below will stay open until the window's close box is clicked. WaitNextEvent() waits for a new event to come; then the loop continues. If the window is gone after the event arrives (e.g., the close box is clicked), $win->window() evaluates to false and the while loop ends.

If the window is still open when the script ends, the END block will remove it. Normally this would be the result of a premature ending to the script, because of an error or a **Command-.** key sequence.[6]

```perl
#!perl
use strict;
use Mac::Windows;
use Mac::QuickDraw;
use Mac::Events;
my($style, $title, $win, $winr);

$style = floatProc();
$title = 'Welcome to MacPerl';
$winr = Rect->new(75, 75, 425, 250);
$win = MacWindow->new(
  $winr, $title, 1, $style, 1
);
$win->sethook('redraw' => \&draw_it);

while ($win->window()) {
  WaitNextEvent();
}

END {
  $win->dispose() if (defined($win));
}

sub draw_it {}
```

---

[5] If no close box can be used with a given style, this parameter has no effect.

[6] We'll see how to handle keyboard and mouse events, later in the chapter.

Of course, this window is not very interesting. It should display items, respond to other events beyond clicking on the close box, etc. Nonetheless, it does contain the basic framework for the window; the additional functionality can be written into the routine `draw_it()`.

Note that, instead of calling `draw_it()` directly, the program sets a **hook** with `$win->sethook()`. This attaches the subroutine to the window.[7]

Window Definitions

There are many different styles of windows,[8] as you probably know if you have used Mac OS much. `floatProc()` is just one that we decided to use. Before we add more complexity to our example window, though, we should explore the features and characteristics of the available window styles.

Some windows have the title bar on the side (or no title bar at all), some zoom, some are resizable, and some have no close box. Pick the style of window that best suits the task at hand. Don't forget that the rectangle defines the usable area of a window, not including any borders or title bar. So, a window with no title bar might fit in a place that the same-sized window with a title bar might not.[9]

There are three basic types of windows: dialog windows, standard windows, and floating windows. The tables below give information about each window style. The styles are accessed via subroutines that return integers representing that style (the integers given in the table can be used in place of the subroutines, of course).

Also given in the tables are five characteristics of the window. A bullet (•) or a dash (-) is used to indicate whether the window does or does not have a title bar (**T**), a drag bar (**D**), a close box (**C**), or a grow box (**G**).[10]

---

[7] This is an example of setting an event handler.

[8] The toolbox modules even allow custom windows, but we won't discuss that here. There is an example of custom windows in the MacPerl distribution.

[9] Windows may appear differently on different versions of Mac OS or if extensions such as Kaleidoscope are installed. The windows shown here are the Mac OS 8 windows, and are 130 pixels wide by 40 pixels tall.

[10] You can put a grow box on a window that cannot use it, and it will be non-functional. To remove a non-functional grow box, use `$win->sethook ('drawgrowicon' => sub{})`.

If the window has a zoom box (**Z**), then the zoom box's behavior is noted. It either toggles between the current size/position and full screen (**A**), or the last size/position and the default size/position (**B**).

All of the windows have borders (**B**), using one of four types: the normal Mac OS border (**N**), a chiseled border (**C**), a simple shadowed border (**S**), or a one-pixel border (**P**).

Dialog Windows

Dialog windows have no zoom, grow, or close box, and only the movable DBoxProc is movable. Dialog windows are used primarily for **dialog box** functions, discussed later in this chapter.

Because these windows do not have **close boxes**, they must be closed in some other fashion. If there is a call in the END block to $win->dispose(), it can be closed with Command-., but normally some sort of **event** will close the window, such as a click on a button, which sends a signal to the program that can trigger a function. This is also discussed later in the chapter.

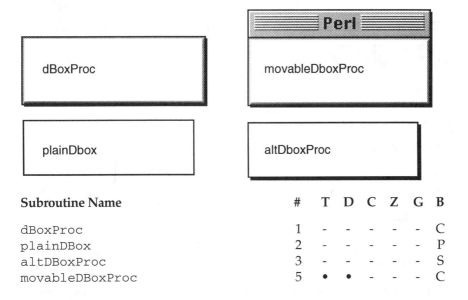

Subroutine Name	#	T	D	C	Z	G	B
dBoxProc	1	-	-	-	-	-	C
plainDBox	2	-	-	-	-	-	P
altDBoxProc	3	-	-	-	-	-	S
movableDBoxProc	5	•	•	-	-	-	C

Standard Windows

These windows are the standard ones that are used by most non-dialog Mac OS window functions. Which one is used is determined by whether or not the window needs a **grow** or **zoom** function. The fifth window in this table, `rDoc Proc`, is a special window that used to be used primarily by desk accessories. It is rarely used anymore.

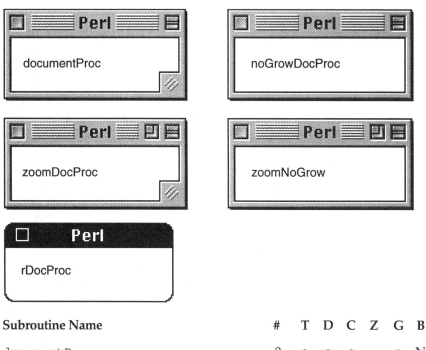

Subroutine Name	#	T	D	C	Z	G	B
documentProc	0	•	•	•	-	•	N
noGrowDocProc	4	•	•	•	-	-	N
zoomDocProc	8	•	•	•	A	•	N
zoomNoGrow	12	•	•	•	A	-	N
rBoxProc	16	•	•	•	-	-	P

Floating Windows

Floating windows are used primarily for special functions (e.g., palettes, status, and help windows), that normally "float" on top of the other windows in an application. The "side" floating windows don't have a title bar, as such; instead, they have a **drag bar** on the left-hand side.

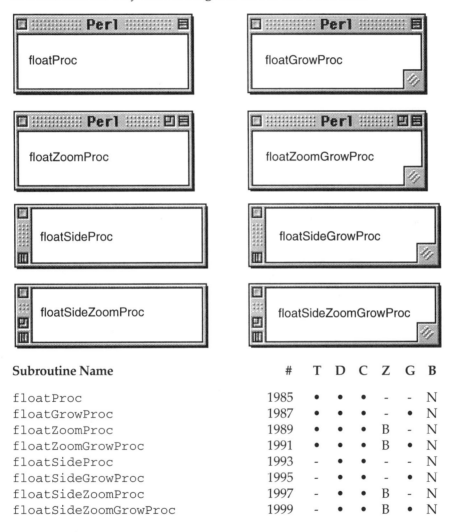

Subroutine Name	#	T	D	C	Z	G	B
floatProc	1985	•	•	•	-	-	N
floatGrowProc	1987	•	•	•	-	•	N
floatZoomProc	1989	•	•	•	B	-	N
floatZoomGrowProc	1991	•	•	•	B	•	N
floatSideProc	1993	-	•	•	-	-	N
floatSideGrowProc	1995	-	•	•	-	•	N
floatSideZoomProc	1997	-	•	•	B	-	N
floatSideZoomGrowProc	1999	-	•	•	B	•	N

Drawing And Text

The Mac::QuickDraw module can be used for drawing things, not just for placing them with rectangles. There are all sorts of functions in the module for drawing lines and shapes and for manipulating images.

Go Ahead, Draw Something

To draw a shape, we only need to add functionality to the draw_it() routine. Let's draw an oval in the window.

```
sub draw_it {
  PaintOval(
    Rect->new(105, 15, 245, 90)
  );
}
```

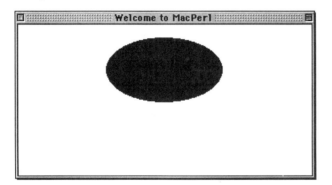

Whenever the redraw event happens for the window – such as when the window is moved or another window passes in front of it – the routine draw _it() is executed, because that is the routine we attached to the redraw event for this window.

PaintOval() paints an oval that is bounded by a specified rectangle. We use Rect->new() again, defining a rectangle relative to the enclosing window (not to the screen, as was the case with the "window" rectangle).

Not all drawing requires rectangles, though. Lines just require a start and end point. MoveTo() and LineTo() are used, respectively, to move the "pen" to a specified point and to draw a line to another point. MoveTo()

can also be used to make a starting point for drawing text,[11] in conjunction with `DrawString()`. So, let's rewrite the `draw_it()` function.

```
sub draw_it {
  MoveTo(120, 65);
  LineTo(223, 65);

  MoveTo(130, 55);
  TextSize(20);
  DrawString('MacPerl');
}
```

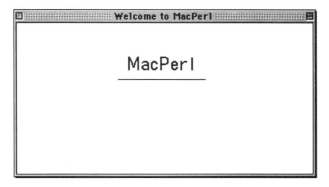

A Dash of Color

Let's put the oval back into the `draw_it()` function, but in another color, so that the drawings on top of it can be seen. In order to use color in the window (more than just the 8 default colors), our window must be created with `NewC Window()`. This routine uses the same arguments, so the change is minor.

```
$win = MacWindow->new(
  NewCWindow($winr, $title, 1, $style, 1)
);
```

There are two color characteristics of the window that we work with: the background color and the foreground color. By default, the background is white and the foreground is black. Before we can draw something in a given color, however, we need to specify the color.

---

[11] To change the font, use the functions in Mac::Fonts.

Color specifications are composed of three colors – red, green, and blue – ranging from 0 (off) to 65535 (full on). The values are packed into a single value. For convenience, we will use a function to create the value and bless it into the RGBColor class:[12]

```perl
sub new_color {
  bless(\pack('SSS', @_[0..2]), 'RGBColor');
}
```

Calls to SetForeColor() then change the color for us as needed:

```perl
sub draw_it {
  RGBForeColor(new_color(0, 50000, 50000));   # aqua
  PaintOval(
    Rect->new(105, 15, 245, 90)               # oval
  );

  RGBForeColor(
    new_color(16384, 16384, 16384));          # grey
  MoveTo(120, 65);
  LineTo(223, 65);                            # line

  RGBForeColor(new_color(0, 0, 0));           # black
  MoveTo(130, 55);
  TextSize(20);
  DrawString('MacPerl');                      # text
}
```

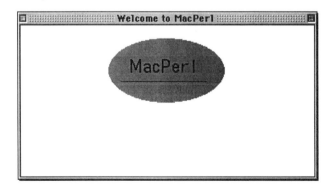

---

[12] RGBColor->new() may soon be added to Mac::QuickDraw, to do this task.

Now For An Image ...

Using `GetPicture()`, the program can import a PICT resource from the open resource file (by default, the resource fork of MacPerl). Resource 128 is the main image in MacPerl's about box (the word "MacPerl", in black).[13]

`DrawPicture()` is used to draw the pictures in the window. It is passed the picture and a rectangle that gives the coordinates of the picture, which happen to be saved in the picture's `picFrame()` method.

> **Note:** PICT rectangles do not always start at (0, 0); they may start at something completely different. `OffsetRect()` changes the starting location; it is passed the rectangle and a starting (X,Y) offset.

```
sub draw_it {
  RGBForeColor(new_color(0, 50000, 50000));
  PaintOval(
    Rect->new(105, 15, 245, 90)
  );

  RGBForeColor(new_color(16384, 16384, 16384));
  MoveTo(120, 65);
  LineTo(223, 65);

  RGBForeColor(new_color(0, 0, 0));
  MoveTo(120, 55);
  TextSize(20);
  DrawString('Welcome to');

  my($p, $r);
  $p = GetPicture(128);
  $r = $p->picFrame();
  DrawPicture($p, OffsetRect($r,
    (30 - $r->left()), (100 - $r->top())
  ));
}
```

---

[13] A PICT *file* can be opened and made into a picture object, too. Just `open()` the file and skip the first 512 bytes of the file and pass the rest of the data as a scalar to `PicHandle->new(DATA)`.

Events

If a window always stays "in front", it will never need to be redrawn. Users have a nasty habit of moving things around, however, so provision must be made for the fact that all or part of a window may be temporarily obscured, then exposed to view.

The previous example used **events** to redraw the screen as necessary. The MacWindow class took care of *when* to redraw the window and the redraw event handler took care of *what* to draw in the window.

An **event handler** is a function that is called whenever a particular event is detected. So, when the window needs to be redrawn, the redraw event handler is called. If a key is pressed, the key event handler is called. Mac OS windows normally close when a Command-w key sequence is detected. This might be passed to the application's key event handler.

Event handlers are passed two parameters; the event's object (such as our window object) and a value. If a user types the w key, the key event handler gets the decimal value of w in ASCII (119, as returned by ord('w')).

The event handler should return true if it handles the key.

```
sub handle_keys {
   my($my, $v) = @_;
   my($mod) = $Mac::Events::CurrentEvent->modifiers();
   if ($v == ord('w') &&
      ($mod & cmdKey()) == cmdKey()) {
      $my->dispose();      # handle Command-w
```

```
    return(1);              # note that key was handled
  }
}
```

Modifier keys (command, option, control, shift, and caps lock) do not trigger the `key` event handler by themselves, but are stored in `$Mac::Events::CurrentEvent->modifiers()`. At the moment of the event, this value can be examined to see if a particular modifier key has been pressed. Each modifier key is assigned a unique bit in the value, so we can use a **bitmask** to find out whether a given key is pressed.

And as you might guess, the event handler would be set beneath the similar call to the `redraw` handler, and would look like this:

```
$win->sethook('key' => \&handle_keys);
```

Controls

`Mac::Controls` provides access to all of the extra widgets that sometimes are provided in windows, including radio buttons, check boxes, scroll bars, popup menus,[14] and push buttons.

There are three steps to using a control. First, it must be created. Second, it should be given one or two event handlers. Third, its events must be handled. The best way to create a control is with the `new_control()` method of the window object, which accepts seven parameters (enumerated below).

There are two event handlers that can be set for a control; the primary one is `click`, which is activated when the control is clicked, returning the value of what was clicked. The other handler is `track`, which returns the mouse's coordinates as of the time when it was clicked on the control.

Push Button

A push button needs no value, so those three parameters can be 0. The title is the label on the button.

```
$con = $win->new_control(
  Rect->new(20, 20, 100, 40),     # rectangle
```

---

[14] Popup menus work similarly to the others, but they must be defined in a resource file. An example is included with MacPerl, but we don't cover it here.

```
  'Hit Me',              # title
  1,                     # visibility boolean
  0, 0, 0,               # default, min., and max. values
  pushButProc()          # type
);
$con->sethook('hit' => \&hit_me);
```

The value that is passed to `hit_me()` normally isn't important, but it can be retrieved from `kControlButtonPart()`.

```
sub hit_me {
  if ($_[1] == kControlButtonPart()) {
    MacPerl::Answer('Ouch!');
    return(1);
  }
}
```

Radio Button / Check Box

Radio buttons and check boxes are created in the same way, differing only in what they look like and how they are used. Radio buttons are used if only one value can exist for a given group of choices; check boxes are used when multiple values can exist. Here are some sample images:

○ Off   ● On   ⊖ Mixed

☐ Off   ☑ On   ⊟ Mixed

Button and box values can be 0 (off), 1 (on), or 2 (mixed). Mixed is almost never used for radio buttons, but is sometimes used for check boxes.

```
$con0 = $win->new_control(
  Rect->new(20, 20, 100, 40),
  'Off', 1, 0, 0, 1, radioButProc()
);
$con1 = $win->new_control(
  Rect->new(20, 40, 100, 60),
  'On' , 1, 1, 0, 1, radioButProc()
);
```

```
$con0->sethook('hit' => \&hit_off);
$con1->sethook('hit' => \&hit_on);
```

This create a vertically-arranged pair of radio buttons. $con0 starts with a default value of 0, $con1 with 1. Whichever button is clicked is turned "on"; the other button is turned "off".

```
sub hit_off {
   SetControlValue($con0->{control}, 1);
   SetControlValue($con1->{control}, 0);
   $val = 'Off';
   return 1;
}
sub hit_on {
   SetControlValue($con0->{control}, 0);
   SetControlValue($con1->{control}, 1);
   $val = 'On';
   return(1);
}
```

Because we saved the value of which button was on in $val, we can print out the final selection when the main `while` loop ends.

```
print "You selected: $val\n";
```

Scroll Bar

A scroll bar has no title. It has two "direction" buttons, a position indicator, and two bar segments, running between the indicator and the buttons. A user can click on any of these, returning one of five values to the event handler:

```
kControlUpButtonPart      kControlDownButtonPart
kControlPageUpPart        kControlPageDownPart
         kControlIndicatorPart
```

The value of the control is the indicator's position on the bar, ranging from the minimum (top/left) to the maximum (bottom/right).

The narrow dimension of the scroll bar's rectangle should be 16 pixels. The enclosing rectangle should be spaced away by one pixel on all sides, so that the borders will overlap. The rectangle below places the scroll bar along the bottom of a 350 by 175 pixel window , as in the first example.

```
$con = $win->new_control(
  Rect->new(-1, 160, 351, 176),
  0, 1, 0, 0, 1, scrollBarProc()
);
$con->sethook('hit' => \&hit_me);
```

By examinig the return values, we can determine whether the user hit one of the buttons, hit a position within one of the bars, or clicked and dragged the indicator, letting go at a new position.

```
sub hit_me {
  my($my, $v)  = @_;
  my($cv) = GetControlValue($my->{control});
  if ($v == kControlUpButtonPart()    ||
      $v == kControlPageUpPart()       ||
     ($v == kControlIndicatorPart() && $cv == 0)) {
    SetControlValue($my->{control}, 0);
    return(1);
  } elsif ($v == kControlDownButtonPart()  ||
           $v == kControlPageDownPart()     ||
     ($v == kControlIndicatorPart() && $cv == 1)) {
    SetControlValue($my->{control}, 1);
    return(1);
  }
}
```

Menus

Menus, supported by `Mac::Menus`, are comparatively simple to create, primarily because no coordinates are involved. A menu is constructed with `MacMenu->new()`. Every menu gets an ID and a title, and can include any number of anonymous arrays, each representing an item in the menu.

It is important to use an ID that is not already taken by the MacPerl application. Menus must be installed with `insert()` and, like windows, must be disposed of after use.

Each menu item can have several characteristics. Titles are required, as are event handlers (except in the case of submenus, described below). Keyboard shortcuts are optional, as are icons and marks to put next to the items.

```
$m1 = MacMenu->new(2048, 'Test Menu', (
   [ 'Submenu',        # title
     undef,            # event handler (null)
     chr(27),          # shortcut keystroke
     chr(221)],        # ID of $m2 sub-menu
   [],                 # adds divider line
   [ 'Quit',           # title
     \&menu_hit,       # event handler
     'W'],             # shortcut keystroke
));
$m2 = MacHierMenu->new(221, 'Submenu', (
   [ 'Hit me',         # title
     \&menu_hit,       # event handler
     'M'],             # shortcut keystroke
));
$m1->insert();
$m2->insert();
WaitNextEvent while (1);

END {
   $m1->dispose() if (defined($m1));
   $m2->dispose() if (defined($m2));
}
```

Hierarchical Menus

A submenu, or **hierarchical menu**, can be added into a menu. A hierarchical menu is created in the same manner as a normal menu, except that its class is MacHierMenu and its ID number must be in the range 1-255. The item where the submenu is to be inserted should have a key of hMenuCmd() [15] and a mark of chr(ID), where ID is the submenu's ID number.

Instead of the menu object, the (sub-)menu event handler is passed the menu ID. This allows a single handler to respond properly to any of several menus. The value passed is the item number, where 1 is the first menu item.

```
sub menu_hit {
   my($m, $v) = @_;
```

---

[15] In older versions of MacPerl, where this function is not exported by Mac::Menus, chr(27) can be used instead.

```
    if ($m == $m1->{id} && $v == 3) {
      exit;
    } elsif ($m == $m2->{id} && $v == 1) {
      MacPerl::Answer('Ouch!');
      return(1);
    }
  }
```

Dialogs

Dialog boxes are similar to windows, but normally serve different functions, as in the case of an **Open…** dialog box. They can have controls, but use their own kind of control routines, not the ones provided by `Mac::Controls`.

Window items are drawn, then controls are attached via calls to `new_con trol()`. In dialog boxes, items are stored in an item list and accessed via an item number.[16] A dialog item has three parameters: type, rectangle, and a title / value.

In this example,[17] a list of dialog items is added to the call to `MacDialog ->new()`. **OK** and **Cancel** buttons are created, followed by some static text, a checkbox, and an editable text box.[18]

```
$dlg = MacDialog->new(
  Rect->new(50, 50, 450, 155),    # dialog rectangle
  'Welcome to MacPerl',           # dialog title
  1,                              # is visible?
  movableDBoxProc(),              # window style
  0,                              # has go away box?
  [ kButtonDialogItem(),
      Rect->new(300, 30, 380, 50), 'Cancel'],
  [ kButtonDialogItem(),
      Rect->new(300, 70, 380, 90), 'OK'],
  [ kStaticTextDialogItem(),
      Rect->new(10, 10, 220, 30),
```

---

[16] See the `Mac::Dialogs` documentation for a list of different items that can be used.

[17] Don't forget to declare your variables with `my()` and `use strict`, `Mac::Windows`, `Mac::Events`, and `Mac::Dialogs`.

[18] Note that the checkbox comes before the edit box in the list, but is placed below it in the dialog box itself. Placement in the box has nothing to do with order in the list.

```
              'How do you like MacPerl?'],
       [ kCheckBoxDialogItem(),
           Rect->new(15, 80, 180, 95),
           'First time user?'],
       [ kEditTextDialogItem(),
           Rect->new(15, 50, 180, 65), ''],
   );
```

Using some standard calls, the OK and Cancel buttons can be attached to the associated key sequences (e.g., return, enter, escape, Command-.) and the text box can be selected so that typed text will go there by default. These calls access the items by their order in the list. The Cancel button is first, the OK button second, and the text box fifth.

```
   SetDialogCancelItem ($dlg->window(), 1);
   SetDialogDefaultItem($dlg->window(), 2);
   SelectDialogItemText($dlg->window(), 5);
```

Hint: You may prefer to set up a hash for these button numbers, such as
%dlgh = (cancel=>1, ok=>2, ..., edit=>5), so that you can
use $dlgh{ok} instead of trying to remember that its value is 2.

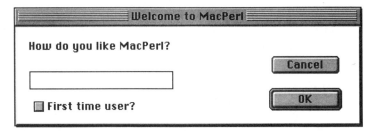

Then, of course, event handlers must be set. This dialog box needs three: one each for the OK and Cancel buttons and the checkbox.

```
   $dlg->item_hit(1 => \&d1);
   $dlg->item_hit(2 => \&d2);
   $dlg->item_hit(4 => \&d4);
```

Because d4() should toggle, its checkbox value needs to be set to the opposite of the value it had at the time it was clicked (0 becomes 1; 1 becomes 0). Note that the dialog box object and the item number that is hit are passed as the two arguments to the handler.

```
sub d4 {
  my($dlg, $item) = @_;
  if ($dlg->item_value($item) == 0) {
    $dlg->item_value($item, 1);
    return(1);
  } elsif ($dlg->item_value($item) == 1) {
    $dlg->item_value($item, 0);
    return(1);
  }
}
```

Or, more tersely:

```
sub d4 {
  my($dlg, $item) = @_;
  $dlg->item_value($item, 1-$dlg->item_value($item));
  return(1);
}
```

d1() prints a message and closes the box, ending the main loop.

```
sub d1 {
  my($dlg) = @_;
  print "You clicked Cancel\n";
  $dlg->dispose();
  return(1);
}
```

d2() also prints a message and closes the box, but its message is the text
that was typed and an indication of whether the box was checked.

```
sub d2 {
  my($dlg) = @_;
  printf "You typed: %s\n", $dlg->item_text(5);
  printf "You are %s first time user\n",
    $dlg->item_value(4) ? 'a' : 'not a';
  $dlg->dispose();
  return(1);
}
```

If the script ends prematurely, the dialog box should be disposed of.

```
END { $dlg->dispose() if (defined($dlg)) }
```

Now all that's left is to determine the behavior of the dialog box while it waits.

There are two major types of dialog boxes, **modal** and **nonmodal**. The difference lies in how they are used, not in how they are created.[19] A modal dialog box allows no other actions to take place while it is open. It forces the user to deal with the dialog box in some way. A nonmodal dialog box acts more like a regular window, allowing the user to perform other actions not related to the dialog box (e.g., creating new windows).

The `while` loops are similar, except that the modal version will call `$dlg ->modal()` in the loop, and the nonmodal one will perform the same type of action as a regular window (e.g., calling `WaitNext- Event()`).

Modal:

```
while ($dlg->window()) {
   $dlg->modal();
}
```

Nonmodal:

```
while ($dlg->window()) {
   WaitNextEvent();
}
```

Roll Your Own

There is much about the GUI toolbox modules that we did not cover. By now, however, you should be able to learn more on your own and understand new concepts that build on this foundation, such as adding lists with the `Mac::Lists` module, or creating text edit boxes with `Mac::TextEdit`.

Put together your own examples and play around. The point of providing all of this flexibility is that application programmers, and now MacPerl programmers, can customize their user interfaces to meet specific needs of the application and its users.

---

[19] Sometimes they will differ in style (e.g., nonmodal dialogs might have a close box).

Chapter 15:

- *Database Basics*
- *Delimited Text*
- *DBM*
- *Database Servers*
- *Data Formats*

Data Storage

> *"Where is the wisdom? Lost in the knowledge.*
> *Where is the knowledge? Lost in the information."*
>
> – T.S. Eliot

> *"Where is the information? Lost in the data.*
> *Where is the data? Lost in the #@$%?!& database."*
>
> – Joe Celko

Perl has enough kinds of internal data structures to accomodate almost any needs a progammer might have. Similarly, it offers a variety of ways to access external ("persistent") data storage:

- `close, getc, open, print, printf, read, seek, <>, ...`

  These routines allow files to be written (read, etc.) in a buffered manner, as by the Unix `stdio` (standard I/O) library.

- `format, formline, write, ...`

  These routines also do buffered I/O, but use a controlling format specification. They have several features that make them handy for creating multi-page business reports, etc.

- `tie, untie, ...`

  These routines allow Perl data elements (e.g., scalars, lists, hashes) to be "tied" to arbitrary routines. They are often used to deal with access methods such as **DBM** (Data Base Management) or **ISAM** (Indexed Sequential Access Method).

- `dbmopen, dbmclose, ...`

  These routines allow hashes to be tied to Unix-style `dbm(3)` data files. When the program exits, the files (and thus the hashes) persist. The Camel book deprecates these calls (in favor of using `tie()` / `untie()` with DBM modules), but we find them to be simple and convenient.

- `sysclose, sysopen, sysread, syswrite, ...`

  These routines, which are seldom needed, allow the use of unbuffered ("raw") I/O, as by the Unix `read(2)` system call.

Any of these forms of storage may be used to create a **database** (a grouping of related information in a computer-readable format). An arbitrary file, however, does not qualify as a database unless it is organized in a manner that assists the computer in using its contents.

Most of the time, for instance, an article from the New York Times could not be considered a database. Even if the article contained a list of facts, the computer (for the most part) could not read those facts and use them in an organized fashion. A file containing several articles could be a database, however, if the articles were indexed by author, topic, etc.

As the size and complexity of databases grow, hand-crafted solutions can become unwieldy. At some point, a programmer may decide to turn to a **data base management system** (**DBMS**). Alternatively, it may be necessary to interact with a DBMS for other reasons. For instance, the database may already be stored under FileMaker or Oracle. Fortunately, Perl is very good at dealing with data base management systems, of whatever type:

- big, expensive servers (e.g., Oracle and Sybase)
- smaller-scale SQL servers (e.g., mSQL)
- end-user solutions (e.g., 4D and FileMaker)

We won't get into the differences between these systems, which are many and detailed, but we can and will discuss some of their common features.

Database Basics

Databases tend to have certain things in common. Most databases are organized into **records** (collections of data describing a given entity). Each record may have one or more **fields** (single data values).

Let's consider a database of information on pets.[1] Each pet's name occupies a field, of course, but we also want to know the pet's type, breed, and weight (in pounds). So, we add three more fields:

```
Name     Type   Breed              Weight
----------------------------------------
Banjo    dog    Labrador              110
Fester   cat    Abyssinian             12
Iris     dog    Retriever              45
```

In many databases, you must select a **key** for the database. A key is a special field that must always be unique; no two records can have the same value for that field.[2] Key choice can be tricky: if we use the `Name` field as the key, we can't allow more than one pet to have the same name.

Let's add a field for details regarding each type of pet. Putting this information into each pet's record would be a waste of space, but we can add another **table** to the database, or create a new database entirely.[3]

```
Type     Food          Designation
----------------------------------------
dog      dog food      Canis familiaris
cat      cat food      Felis domestica
```

In Perl, these tables might be represented as multi-dimensional hashes:

```perl
$by_name{'Banjo'}{'Type'}       = 'dog';
$by_type{'dog'}{'Designation'} = 'Canis familiaris';
...
$type = $by_name{'Banjo'}{'Type'};
print "$by_type{$type}{'Designation'}\n";
```

Displays:

```
Canis familiaris
```

---

[1] This is only a representation of a database, not necessarily an example of what a database file might look like internally.

[2] The resemblance to a Perl hash is not coincidental. In fact, hashes may be tied to DBM files, yielding a simple form of database.

[3] Some databases allow multiple tables in one database. Simpler databases, like text files and DBMs, do not. But then, you can always have multiple files (TMTOWTDI :-).

That is, `%by_name` is a hash whose indices are pet names and whose elements are also (references to) hashes. We can thus index one of these elements by the text string `'Type'`, storing `'dog'` in that position. Using similar techniques, we can store and retrieve other related data.[4]

But how does this data get saved to or read from a file? More to the point, how can we get it into a DBMS? As it happens, that is our next topic.

Delimited Text

Different programs store their databases in different (often proprietary and/or undocumented) formats. Consequently, it is seldom advisable for a Perl program to read from (let alone write to) one of these databases.

Data exchange is a fact of life, however, so DBMS vendors tend to provide ways to **export** and **import** data. This requires a file format which clearly delineates the database's records and fields. By choosing **delimiters** (e.g., commas, newlines, and tabs) that are not found in the data, vendors can provide a format for export files, while keeping their own formats private.

If it were exported into **delimited text**, our pet database might look like:

```
Banjo,Dog,Labrador,110
Fester,Cat,Abyssinian,12
Iris,Dog,Retriever,45
```

This format is easy for Perl scripts to read and parse:

```
while (defined($line = <FILE>)) {
  chomp($line);
  @line = split(/,/, $line);
  printf("My %s %s, a %s, weighs %s lbs.\n",
    $line[1], $line[0], $line[2], $line[3]);
}
```

Displays:

```
My dog Banjo, a Labrador, weighs 110 lbs.
...
```

---

[4] See the `perlref`, `perldsc`, and `perllol` manual pages for more information on multi-dimensional data structures.

Because text fields might themselves contain delimiters, many export formats use single or double quotes to enclose text fields, as:

```
"Banjo","Dog","Labrador",110
"Fester","Cat","Abyssinian",12
"Iris","Dog","Retriever",45
```

This solves a data representation problem, but it creates a programming problem: our simple `split()` no longer works. Fortunately, MacPerl comes with a `quotewords` function (in `Text::ParseWords`) that splits text on a specified delimiter, stripping out any quote marks. Using this function, we can write something similar to what we used before:[5]

```
use Text::ParseWords;
while (defined($line = <FILE>)) {
  chomp($line);
  @line = quotewords(',', 0, $line);
  printf("My %s %s, a %s, weighs %s lbs.\n",
     $line[1], $line[0], $line[2], $line[3]);
}
```

Array numbers aren't particularly memorable, however. Fortunately, this is Perl, so There's More Than One Way To Do It:

```
($name, $type, $breed, $weight) =
  quotewords(',', 0, $line);
printf("My %s %s, a %s, weighs %s lbs.\n",
  $type, $name, $breed, $weight);
```

If you really need to keep the values in an array, there are still ways to resolve the problem. Just create a named item – a scalar, subroutine, or hash key – that corresponds to the array index:

```
sub name { return 0 }       # set up a function
$type = 1;                  # set up a scalar
$pet{'breed'} = 2;          # set up a hash
printf(
  "My %s %s is a %s.\n",
  $line[$type],             # index by a scalar
  $line[name()],            # index by a function
```

---

[5] If the fields were delimited by tabs instead of commas, we would pass `"\t"` to `quotewords()` instead of a comma.

```
    $line[$pet{'breed'}]          # index by a hash
);
```

Creating a comma-delimited text file is a simple matter:

```
printf NEWFILE ("%s,%s,%s,%s\n", @line);
```

Or, if we need embedded quotes:

```
printf NEWFILE (qq{"%s","%s","%s","%s"\n}, @line);
```

This type of database has a very flexible structure. You can choose any key you want, multiple keys, or no keys at all. You can have any number of records and fields, and any amount of data (limited only by your storage). Most proprietary databases can export to this type of database format, and it is portable and free to use.

Unfortunately, it is also slow and a bit awkward to use. So, for larger databases that will be accessed frequently, we recommend the use of other database types.

DBM

Data Base Management (DBM) routines are very efficient at finding a given record in a database. Typically, they use only two disk accesses to find a given key, no matter how large the DBM file.

DBM files are more restrictive than delimited text files, however. Like hashes, they allow only two fields per record: a key and a value.

> **Note:** The two-field limitation is not as severe as it might seem. You can open more than one DBM, if you wish, and you can also encode multiple scalars into each "value":
>
> ```
> $hash{'Banjo'} = '"Dog","Labrador",110';
> @fields = quotewords(',', 0, $hash{'Banjo'});
> ```

Some types of DBM files put restrictions on assorted (e.g., field, record, or file) sizes. The material below, however, concentrates on the DB_File module, which does not impose size restrictions outside of those imposed by your system.[6]

---

[6] DBM access is always fast, but creating large DBMs with MacPerl can be slow.

AnyDBM_File

Only two DBM modules come with MacPerl: DB_File and NDBM_File. NDBM_File in MacPerl is an emulation layer on top of the same routines DB_File is based on, but the two modules have different capabilities. Since they use the same underlying routines, however, the files are compatible with each other.

Not all versions of Perl have every DBM module. All Unix versions of Perl come with SDBM_File, and many come with ODBM_File and GDBM_File. MacPerl has none of these, however, and not all Unix versions of Perl have DB_File or NDBM_File. So, how does one assure portability?

If a program depends on certain features of a given DBM type (such as arbitrarily large sizes), portability cannot be ensured. But for many cases, your program can remain agnostic about the type of DBM being used.

AnyDBM_File offers a true virtual base class, with no methods or data of its own. It attempts to inherit from other DBM modules: NDBM_File is tried first (for compatibility with dbmopen() in Perl 4), then DB_File, then by the others. If you use AnyDBM_File, your code should work no matter which DBM modules are present on a given machine. The search order can be changed; see the pod documentation for details.

> **Note:** This allows portability of code, but not of files produced by the code. DBM files are not necessarily portable between machines!

tie()

Perl supplies a mechanism, called tie(), that can hide complex data routines behind a data structure.[7] For example, the Mac::MoreFiles module provides a tied hash called %Application. When the hash is accessed, Perl automatically (and invisibly) calls the FSpDTGetAPPL() function to find the path to the given application in the filesystem. So, the calling program doesn't need to know about the function.

DBM files are accessed in a similar way. A hash is tied to a database file via a DBM module. First, you have to use the module. Then, tie() is passed the hash, the name of the module, the filename, the database

---

[7] Read perltie for more information.

flags,[8] and the mode (Unix-style file permissions) value.[9] When we want to close the file, we just `untie()` the hash.

```perl
#!perl -w
use DB_File;
my(%hash1, %hash2);

tie(%hash1, 'DB_File', ':my_dbm', O_RDWR|O_CREAT,
    0644);
$hash1{'key'} = 'value1';
untie(%hash1);

tie(%hash2, 'DB_File', ':my_dbm', O_RDONLY, 0644);
$hash2{'key'} = 'value2';
print $hash2{'key'};
untie(%hash2);
```

Displays:

```
value1
```

We are planning on writing to the database file for `%hash1`, so we use flags that direct MacPerl to open it in read/write mode, creating the file if necessary. Because we opened the file for `%hash2` in read-only mode, we cannot assign any values to `%hash2`. So, when we try to assign a value to `$hash2{'key'}`, it fails (silently, unlike the behavior of most other DBMs).

Database Servers

High performance databases are usually implemented as servers. This lets multiple users log in and perform functions on the data. Oracle might well be the most popular database server; Informix, Ingres, Postgres, Sybase, and others are also very popular.

Most of these servers use **SQL (Structured Query Language)** to perform operations on the data. Many databases, usually for Windows, also support **ODBC** (Open Data Base Connectivity) to interact with external programs.

---

[8] These flags (e.g., O_RDWR) are implemented as function calls, but common practice for constant usage is to leave the parentheses (e.g., O_RDWR()) off, except when necessary.

[9] Because Macs do not use file permissions, we can use 0 as the mode. If you want the program to be portable to Unix machines, you should supply an appropriate value.

Most of this functionality is provided by a single module and set of drivers known as **DBI** (**Data Base Interface**).[10] DBI is a standardized **API** (**Application Programming Interface**) for accessing databases. Using driver modules called **DBDs** (**Data Base Drivers**) , a programmer can connect with all kinds of SQL and ODBC database servers.

If we are using **mysql**, a freely available SQL database server, we would connect to it using DBI and DBD::mysql. If we decide to upgrade to an Oracle server later, we could change a few lines of code to use DBD::Oracle, and need few (or possibly no) other code changes.

DBI makes accessing databases of all kinds quite simple. Unfortunately, DBI is not presently available for MacPerl. A client library has to be ported to Mac OS, in order to access the server on another machine, then the corresponding DBD has to be ported to MacPerl, as well.

Client libraries for several databases do exist on Mac OS, including Oracle and mSQL. A port of DBI and some DBDs might be coming soon. Until then, there is no easy way with MacPerl to interact with database servers on other machines. (TCP/IP and sockets are, however, a possibility …)

If the server is on the same machine as MacPerl, you might be able to communicate with it using Apple Events. Oracle supports this capability.

Data Formats

Although database export formats are considerably easier to parse than internal database formats, they can still contain some peculiarities. Worse, these peculiarities are seldom documented in the database system's user documentation. Here are some notes on FileMaker Pro, by way of example.

FileMaker Pro's export files use carriage returns and tabs to delimit records and fields. So, the basic parsing code is pretty straightforward:

```
while (defined($line = <FILE>)) {
  chomp($line);
  @fields = split(/\t/, $line);
}
```

---

[10] For more information about DBI, see www.hermetica.com/technologia/DBI/.

If a field holds multiple values, however, a special delimiter (\035) is used. Also, text fields may use some oddball characters (e.g., curly apostrophes) which don't work well with other applications or systems (e.g., HTML), so you may want to edit them out.

There are far too many Macintosh (and other!) applications, however, for us to have any chance of covering them all. So, here's some general advice:

- Examine the application's documentation. Although many programs do not document their export formats, some do, and you could get lucky.

- Contact the vendor. The vendor may have developed a technical note that describes their export format; it certainly can't hurt to ask.

- Ask around. If there is a USENET newsgroup or email list for the application, someone on it may have the information you need. Don't forget to ask the MacPerl list, while you're at it.

- Export a file and examine it. BBEdit is surprisingly useful on arbitrary binary files. Alternatively, a small Perl script can tell you quite a lot.

Here is a sample file analysis script; tweak it to fit your needs:

```perl
#!perl
$/ = ''; $text = <>;
foreach $ord (unpack('C*', $text)) { $m[$ord]++; }

print("occurs  oct  dec\n");
foreach $ord (0 .. 31, 127 .. 255) {
  printf("%6d  %03o  %3d\n", $m[$ord], $ord, $ord)
    if ($m[$ord] != 0);
}
```

Displays:

```
occurs  oct  dec
 24984  011    9
    52  013   11
. . .
```

Just remember, we cannot stress it enough (especially when dealing with data storage): There's More Than One Way To Do It.

Chapter 16:

- *Web Servers*
- *The CGI Script Extension*
- *CGI vs. ACGI*
- *Taint Checking*
- *Environment Variables*
- *CGI.pm*

CGI Scripting

Perl is the duct tape of the Internet.

– Hassan Schroeder (Sun Microsystems' first webmaster)

The advent of the World Wide Web and Perl's natural fit into web server programs have provided a tremendous boost to Perl's popularity. Perl has what most web server programs need: quick development time, superior text and data manipulation, cross-platform availability, interprocess communication, and comprehensive operating system interaction.

The majority of web server programs use the **Common Gateway Interface** (**CGI**). CGI programs can be written in any language, not just Perl. In fact, many Mac-based web sites never employ Perl at all (a situation we hope to remedy! :-). Remember, in any case, that there is more to Perl than CGI, and more to CGI than Perl.

This is not a chapter on how to write CGIs;[1] please consult a book on CGI programming for that. This chapter covers only the use of MacPerl for CGI programming, and assumes a prior familiarity with CGI programming. See Part V, *Resources*, for several good books on CGI programming.

Web Servers

If you want to serve CGIs from your Mac OS computer, you will need a web server. Even if you plan to use MacPerl only for developing CGIs for use on other servers, you should still install a local web server for testing. Just

---

[1] "CGI programs" are often called, simply, "CGIs".

remember that a Mac-based server will act differently in some respects than a Unix- or Windows-based server:

- The Mac is case-preserving, but not case-sensitive in handling file names (it sees `readme`, `Readme`, and `README` as the same file). Unix is case-sensitive.

- The Mac allows almost any character (including ones with the high order bit set) in file names. Unix does not deal well with the presence of spaces and/or "wild card" characters (e.g., `*` and `?`) in file names, though any USASCII (7-bit ASCII) character (except `/`) is allowed. Microsoft Windows defines a large set of illegal characters.

- The Mac uses carriage returns to terminate lines of text. Unix uses line feeds; Windows uses the sequence "carriage return / line feed". Most Web browsers are willing to accept any reasonable line termination, but the issue may come up when a MacPerl script attempts to read a file that was generated on another machine.

Not all web servers support CGI, though most do.[2] We will not advocate the use of any server over another, though we do suggest that you look over the servers which we have included on the CD-ROM. For instructions on how to use a given server and for complete details of CGI support administration for each server, please refer to the server's documentation.

> **Note:** Check with your local network administrator before you put up a web page. This may prevent a wide range of unwanted technical and/or political problems. For instance, your company may not want its telephone directory visible to outside parties.

The choice of a server can be tricky. Some good servers may not work on your machine or may not provide the performance you need. Some servers may not support CGI, opting instead to provide other interfaces.[3] For our purposes, of course, Perl support is mandatory. Here are some popular servers that work under Mac OS:

---

[2] CGIs on Mac OS are normally implemented through the WebStar CGI specification, and MacPerl CGIs are no exception. When we discuss Mac OS CGIs or server capabilities, we mean the WebStar specification unless otherwise stated.

[3] If a server's limitations on CGIs are too severe, it might be necessary to write WWW programs using a server's own API, such as WebStar's W*API.

Server Name	Current Version	Supports CGIs
AppleShare IP	5.0	√
Apple Personal Web Sharing	1.1	√
MacHTTP	2.2.2	√
MS Personal Web Server	1.0c	√
NetPresenz	4.1	√
Pictorius Net Servers	1.17	√
QuidProQuo	2.0	√
WebSTAR	2.1	√
WebTen[4]	1.1	NA

If you are testing your CGIs on an unconnected computer, feel free to use the string `localhost` in place of an Internet address in your web browser's URL line (`http://localhost/test.html`).

If your machine is not connected to other machines on a permanent basis, it probably does not have an assigned **IP (Internet Protocol)** address or **DNS (Domain Name Service)** name. The lack of an assigned IP address (let alone the lack of a permanent network connection) will prevent other machines from "finding" your web pages.

We cannot hope to give you sufficient information to understand the operation of a web server here, let alone HTML, CGI, or web server administration style and technique. Read your server documentation thoroughly and consult books, web resources, your ISP, and your network administrator about CGI support, DNS, HTML, web and Mac OS security issues, etc.

The CGI Script Extension

MacPerl comes with a file called CGI Script which resides in the MacPerl Extensions folder. This appears in the popup menu in MacPerl's Save As ... dialog box, and saves your program in a CGI format.

A MacPerl CGI script is actually an application of its own. The web server passes data to the script, which runs under MacPerl. The script processes the data and generates results which are sent back to the server. All of the communication in the Macintosh is handled through Apple Events.

---

[4] WebTen comes with its own version of Perl integrated into the server's environment, and does not use MacPerl for CGIs.

After getting your server software set up, try a sample script, such as:

```
#!perl -w
print "Content-type: text/html\n\n";
print "Hello, world!\n";
```

The first `print` statement generates the content type, followed by two line breaks. This is the first output that all CGIs must make. MacPerl CGIs do not require this line; if it is omitted, it is assumed, using `text/html` as the content type. You should include it, however, for clarity and portability.

Now save this script to your server's CGI directory (usually called cgi-bin[5]) as a CGI script and access it through a web browser. You should see the text `Hello, world!` in the browser.

If you want to see exactly what Apple Events are being sent where, bring the CGI script to the front once it has been run (you can select it under the Mac OS application menu) and hit the Command-L key sequence on your keyboard. This will create a text file called MPCGI Log on your desktop.

Because your CGI script communicates via Apple Events, it has the same limitations that all Apple Events have. Prior to Mac OS 7.6, an Apple Event could only contain a limited amount of data (64 KB or less). Fortunately, this limitation has been lifted in Mac OS 7.6 and 8.0.

The CGI script application stays open for five minutes of inactivity, then closes automatically. If some user calls the CGI at least once every five minutes, the script will never close. This eliminates a significant amount of overhead (in launching the MacPerl application). If the script stays open, it can respond more quickly to subsequent requests.

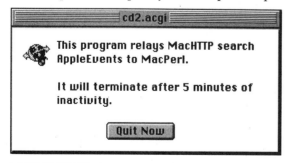

---

[5] See your server's documentation.

If you are proficient with ResEdit, you might want to edit the amount of time the CGI script stays open. The resource will revert to the five-minute default any time the CGI script is opened and saved again from MacPerl; however, if you make the ResEdit change to the CGI Script extension itself, the new value will replace five minutes as the default time-out period.[6]

To make the change, open the file you want to change (either the saved script or the CGI Script extension) with ResEdit. Open the time resource (ID 128). The middle column will contain the current time-out, in minutes. If it has not been edited before, this value will be 05, the hexademical representation of the decimal numeral 5. Change this to any hexademical number from 01 to 7F (one minute to 127 minutes). A value of 00 will keep the script open indefinitely (until a reboot or some manual close takes place).

There is also a droplet on the CD-ROM (setCGImins.dp),[7] which can make this change for you, without having to use ResEdit (but the same disclaimers apply). The droplet will take files that are dropped on it and set the time resource of each file to the number of minutes (0 to 127) specified.

CGI vs. ACGI

Most advanced web servers have the ability to respond to more than one request simultaneously. Unfortunately, most Mac OS web servers will wait for a CGI to finish running before responding to any other requests, whether for an HTML page, an image, or another CGI. CGIs can take a while to run, so a CGI can appear to slow down the entire server significantly.

This is where **Asynchronous CGI** (**ACGI**) comes in. Web servers that can use ACGIs (most do!) will respond to other requests while the ACGI is processing, instead of waiting for it to finish.

Making a CGI into an ACGI is very simple: instead of using the suffix .cgi, use .acgi. Actually, you should always use the .acgi suffix for your CGIs, as there is really no reason not to (unless you *want* to slow down the server :-).

> **Note:** ACGI has nothing to do with how many simultaneous requests MacPerl can handle. A given instance of MacPerl can only execute one script at a time. So, if you are running MacPerl for your own purposes,

---

[6] As always, use ResEdit at your own risk. Make backups!

[7] Part of the code for the script is in Ch. 12, under `Mac::Resources`.

you may well get in the way of your CGIs (and vice versa!). Running multiple copies of MacPerl is, however, a possible workaround.

Taint Checking

Perl has an advanced security framework that allows the programmer to check for possibly "tainted" data. Basically, this is data that is imported into the program from an outside source, and is explicitly untrusted.[8]

Tainted data can still be used for most purposes; you can print it, use it for addition, and whatnot. What you cannot do with tainted data, if taint checks are on, is use it in any sort of system interaction. For instance, taint checks will prevent you from opening a file whose name was typed into a web page (the user might have specified a file that you do not want him to see and/or overwrite).

```
my $data = get_form_data();     # tainted!
open(F, ">$data") or die($!);
```

If the contents of $data happened to be "::index.html", then your CGI would go to the directory above the one containing the CGI and create a file called index.html, deleting any existing file that might have been there. With taint checking on, MacPerl would have quit with an error, which is exactly what we would have wanted it to do.

As of Perl version 5.004, taint checks can only be turned on with the command-line argument **-T**. That is, if a script called myscript.pl has a first line #!/usr/bin/perl -T and is executed by its name on the Unix command line, taint checks will be enabled. But, if the same script is executed from the Unix command line as perl myscript.pl, the script will generate an error, because the -T switch was not on the command line that called the script. It must be called with perl -T myscript.pl.

This causes problems for MacPerl, because the first line of a script does not actually call the Perl program as it does on Unix. So, trying to enable taint checks by putting #!perl -T in a script will always generate an error.

At present, there are only two methods of turning on taint checking in Mac-Perl. The primary way is with the menu option Taint Checks, under the

---

[8] Taint checks are not exclusive to CGI programming, but they are especially useful for CGIs, so we are discussing them here. For more detailed information about taint checks and Perl security, including how to deal with tainted data, see the perlsec man page.

Script menu. This causes problems, however, because generally you won't want taint checks on for all your scripts.

The other way is only used when sending a script to MacPerl from an outside source using the Do Script Apple Event.[9] The parameter TAIN with a true value will turn taint checks on for that event.

Because CGI Scripts also execute their contents via the Do Script mechanism, it is possible to send the same TAIN parameter via the CGI Script. There is a special version of the CGI Script extension called CGI Script (Taint Check) on the CD-ROM. This version does the same things as the regular version, save that it has MacPerl do the taint checks.

If you are using modules or required files that depend on your library preferences, you will have to take another MacPerl difference into account. The library paths are hard-coded into the Unix Perl binary, but they are not hard-coded into MacPerl.

Taint checks – for security's sake – wipe out your path preferences, so you will have to restore them. Put the following at the top of your script:[10]

```
BEGIN {                      # restore lib paths
  $ENV{MACPERL} =~ /^(.+)$/;
  my($f) = $1;
  unshift(@INC,
    "${f}lib:$MacPerl::Architecture:",
    "${f}lib:");
}
```

It is a bit cumbersome to put this at the top of any CGI Script that will use taint checks, but it is probably worth it. Considering the inherent differences (security, processes, etc.) between Mac OS and Unix, there could be changes to the MacPerl security model to make it different (and more usable) in the future.

We recommend that you always use the taint checking version of the CGI Script extension, unless you have a specific reason not to, and can complete-

---

[9] See Chapter 18, *AppleScript, Etc.*

[10] This only works in MacPerl 5.1.6 or later, as $MacPerl::Architecture was introduced in that release.

ly trust the incoming data.[11] Finally, remember that these taint checks are only as secure as your computer and related files; the taint checks are useless to protect against anyone who has physical access to your computer.

Environment Variables

CGIs make heavy use of environment variables, which are accessed through %ENV. MacPerl provides basically all the same variables provided through any other CGI.

One primary difference is in $ENV{PATH_INFO}. Consider this call to a Unix CGI:

```
http://www.host.com/cgi-bin/my.cgi/path/info?foo=bar
```

The CGI my.cgi would be called, with an $ENV{PATH_INFO} of /path/info and an $ENV{QUERY_STRING} of foo=bar. But, in order for this to work with a Mac OS CGI, a $ must be addded immediately after the CGI name, so the server can know exactly where the CGI is:

```
http://www.host.com/cgi-bin/my.cgi$/path/info?foo=bar
```

Different web clients supply different environment variables, too. All good CGI books contain a list of CGI environment variables, but if you want to see exactly what environment variables are available to your CGI, try the following CGI:

```
#!perl -w
my($key);

print "Content-type: text/plain\n\n";
foreach $key (keys(%ENV)) {
  print "$key => $ENV{$key}\n";
}
```

CGI.pm

CGI.pm has become the *de facto* standard module for writing CGIs with Perl. It is so widely used that it has been included in the standard distribution and is the recommended method for writing CGIs in Perl.

---

[11] You might think that you have all your bases covered and have no need for taint checking; remember, though, that some crackers out there are often smarter than you are (or at least very persistent!). No offense.

CGI.pm eases much of the "grunt work" of doing CGIs, including entity translation, input processing, address redirection, and header manipulation. It also includes methods for producing HTML and forms more easily.[12]

There are no known significant differences between CGI.pm on MacPerl and on any other web server, with one exception: the file upload feature that some browsers support. CGI.pm could likely be modified to work with MacPerl in this regard, but as of this writing it does not.

CGI.pm includes a convenient facility for debugging without a web server. When the script is run without the web server (from the MPW command line or with the Run Script menu command), it will open up the MacPerl window and ask for user input. You can then type in your parameters as name/value pairs, as below, hitting return after each one. After you input all the pairs, hit Control-D on your keyboard.

```
#!perl -w
use CGI;
my($cgi) = new CGI;

print $cgi->header();
printf("'%s'<BR>\n", $cgi->param('foo'));
printf("'%s'<BR>\n", $cgi->param('bar'));
```

Displays:

```
(offline mode: enter name=value pairs on the keyboard)
foo=fooval
bar=barval
Content-type: text/html

 'fooval'<BR>
'barval'<BR>
```

Note the apparent extra space before 'fooval'. This is not really a space. Networking applications normally use CRLF (\015\012) as new lines, and that is what CGI.pm returns. The MacPerl application renders the CR to a line break and the LF as a character that looks like a space (or some funny

---

[12] The HTML modules on CPAN may be more appropriate for advanced HTML production, and they can complement CGI.pm nicely.

character, depending on your font). Since this output is only used for debugging puposes, you can ignore it here.

`CGI.pm` is a very large module, and has a ton of features available. Read its documentation to find out more about it.

Chapter 17:

- *Sockets*
- *libnet*
- *LWP*
- *AppleTalk*
- *Debugging*

Network Programming

> *Life in a great society,*
> *or for that matter in a small,*
> *is a web of tangled relations of all sorts,*
> *whose adjustment so that it may be endurable*
> *is an extraordinarily troublesome matter.*

> – Learned Hand, *The Spirit of Liberty*

Today, no programmer can avoid network programming, even if he wants to. Most of the time, it seems, this is really Internet programming; transferring files via FTP, getting information from the World Wide Web, or checking the current time on a remote machine.

Perl supports all of these activities and so, by and large, does MacPerl. A few similarities and differences are, however, worth noting:

- Both Perl and MacPerl support the TCP and UDP[1] protocols.

- MacPerl has not implemented the ICMP protocol, used by the Unix `ping` program. The Mac interface is incompatible with that of the Unix protocol; it would be possible to write an extension for MacPerl to add ICMP functionality, but at present none exists.

- MacPerl supports AppleTalk, which Unix systems generally do not.[2]

---

[1] TCP (**Transmission Control Protocol**) is wrapped around the Internet Protocol (IP) to form TCP/IP, the basis of reliable Internet communications. UDP (**User Datagram Protocol**) is an alternate protocol used for situations (e.g., broadcast messages) where guaranteed reception of ordered information is not required.

[2] A freeware package for Unix, `netatalk`, fills this need quite admirably.

For more complete information than is presented here, see `perlipc` and the documentation for the specific modules mentioned.

Sockets

A socket is a bi-directional interface for network communication between two processes. One process writes to the socket; the other reads from it (and vice-versa). A socket is thus something like a pair of Unix-style pipes, generalized for use over a network.

Each socket has its own address on the network. A web server, for instance, would have an specific **address** (`www.ptf.com`), accessible by a specific **port** (80) with a specific **protocol** (TCP) on a specific network (the Internet).

The standard Perl distribution contains two primary modules for dealing with sockets. `Socket` is a low-level interface; `IO::Socket` is a high-level "wrapper" for `Socket`. We will use `IO::Socket` for most of our examples.

A socket is accessed through a filehandle. Like any other filehandle, you can read from it (e.g., `$foo = <SOCKET>;`) and print to it using the normal indirect object syntax (e.g., `print SOCKET "some data";`).

`IO::Socket`, however, returns a reference to a socket handle. As discussed in Chapter 9, *Curious Constructions*, references to handles do not need to be dereferenced. So, the returned reference can be substituted for `SOCKET`, as:

```
$foo = <$socket>;
print $socket "some data";
```

Here's an example of how to get the current time from a remote machine. Many Internet servers provide the current time via port 13; here we try to connect to the `daytime` port of a web server, which `IO::Socket::INET` resolves to port `13`.

The `new()` method accepts a hash containing the address of the machine, the port to connect to, and the protocol. It then creates a socket and connects to the remote socket.

Most Internet communication uses CRLF (carriage return/line feed) for line termination, but some uses just CR or LF. So, after we read from the server, we convert any CRLFs or LFs to CRs, then display the results.

```perl
#!perl -w
use IO::Socket;
my($sock, $line, $cr, $lf, $crlf);

$cr = "\015";
$lf = "\012";
$/ = $crlf = "$cr$lf";

$sock = IO::Socket::INET->new(
  PeerAddr => 'daytime.clock.org',
  PeerPort => 'daytime(13)',
  Proto    => 'tcp'
) or die($@);

while (defined($line = <$sock>)) {
  $line =~ s/$cr?$lf/$cr/g;
  print $line;
}
```

Displays:

```
Thu Dec 25 21:08:10 1997
```

Of course, we can also write to the filehandle. A slightly fancier script could communicate with a web server, using the standard HTTP port (80). After connecting, we print a request to the web server for a specified page (GET /macperl/), tell the server what protocol we are using (HTTP/1.0), then finish the request with two CRLFs. Finally, we read from the server, converting any CRLFs or LFs to CRs, and display the results, as before.

```perl
...
  PeerAddr => 'www.ptf.com',
  PeerPort => 'http(80)',
...
print $sock "GET /macperl/ HTTP/1.0$crlf$crlf";
...
```

It is good to know how to do all this, and even better to know the workings of the socket(), bind(), and connect() functions that IO::Socket hides from your view. In most cases, however, you will not have to work this hard. Here is an easier way ...

libnet

libnet is the common name for a group of Perl modules that support Internet networking. It includes modules for FTP (file transfer), POP3 (receiving email), SMTP (sending email), NNTP (accessing USENET news), etc. These modules are included with the MacPerl standard distribution. For information on updates, see the MacPerl Pages (`www.ptf.com/macperl`).

Let's revisit the code we used above to get the current time. We can do the same thing much more simply with the `Net::Time` module.

```perl
#!perl
use Net::Time qw(inet_daytime);
my($time);

$time = inet_daytime('daytime.clock.org');
$time =~ s/[\015\012]//g;
print "$time\n";
```

Displays:

```
Thu Dec 25 21:08:10 1997
```

One of the most important parts of libnet for MacPerl users, however, is the `Net::SMTP` module. Perl programmers often send Internet mail (usually using the SMTP protocol), using a Unix program called **sendmail**. MacPerl users, sadly, do not have that luxury. No problem; they can use Perl!

The libnet modules have extra Mac OS magic when used with MacPerl. The Internet Config host settings are automatically used as the defaults in the configuration module `Net::Config`. Subsequently, instead of specifying an SMTP host in the `new()` method, we let Internet Config supply that for us. If Internet Config is not set up, the SMTP host must be supplied.[3]

```perl
#!perl
use strict;
use Net::SMTP;
use Mac::InternetConfig;
my($smtp, $email, @emails, $subject, $message);
```

---

[3] Also consider supplying other options to the `new()` constructor, including the connection timeout.

```
$smtp    = Net::SMTP->new();
$email   = $InternetConfig{kICEmail()}; # my address
@emails  = 'friend@some.host.com';
$subject = "Subject: My test message\n\n";
$message = <<EOM;
MacPerl sent this message.  Nifty, eh?
EOM

$smtp->mail($email)         or warn('failure');
$smtp->to(@emails)          or warn('failure');
$smtp->data()               or warn('failure');
$smtp->datasend($subject)   or warn('failure');
$smtp->datasend($message)   or warn('failure');
$smtp->dataend()            or warn('failure');
$smtp->quit()               or warn('failure');
```

The mail has now been sent, as long as none of the methods failed. See the documentation of each module for the usage details. Also, remember that you can use Internet Config for many of the default hosts.

You can also use the Mailtools modules, on the CD-ROM, for creating, manipulating, and sending mail. Customized versions for MacPerl are usually available at the MacPerl Pages. But Mailtools is not just for dealing with individual messages; it can also be used for manipulating a mailbox such as Eudora's. If you use Eudora, this script will get the first message from your In box and display it:

```
#!perl
use Mail::Internet;
use Mail::Util qw(read_mbox);
use Mac::Files;
my($sysf, @msgs, $mail);

$sysf = FindFolder(kOnSystemDisk(),
  kSystemFolderType());
@msgs = read_mbox("$sysf:Eudora Folder:In");
$mail = Mail::Internet->new($msgs[0]);
printf("From: %s", $mail->head->get("From:"));
printf("To: %s\n", $mail->head->get("To:"));
print @{$mail->body};
```

LWP

LWP is the class of the **libwww-perl** modules, used for doing various web-related functions. It is commonly used to fetch pages on the web and to manipulate their data; it is included with the MacPerl distribution.

The LWP::Simple module retrieves a WWW page. Revisiting our second example under *Sockets* above, the following script does basically the same thing, except it does not return the HTTP headers, which you probably do not want anyway, and it converts the line endings automatically.

```perl
#!perl -w
use LWP::Simple;

getprint('http://www.ptf.com/macperl/');
```

The getprint() method gets the URL and prints the result, handling all the details. LWP has a lot more to offer; see its documentation …

AppleTalk

Because MacPerl runs on Macintosh computers, we should be (and are!) able to use the native protocol, AppleTalk, as our socket protocol. Even if an Internet-style (TCP/IP, etc.) network is available, AppleTalk might be preferable in some situations. For instance, AppleTalk does not care if the numerical address of your computer changes!

The AppleTalk protocols and functions are provided the same way as they are for Internet protocols, through the Socket module. Again, we make our calls via IO::Socket, which inherits from Socket. Versions of MacPerl prior to 5.1.6r4 do not recognize the subclass IO::Socket::APPLETALK, you may need to upgrade to a more recent version.

The script below runs on two Macs that reside on the same AppleTalk network.[4] AppleTalk does not connect to ports; instead, it uses **services**. Each service has a **name**, a **type**, and a **zone**. These three characteristics must form a unique address on the network. By default, the new() constructor

---

[4] It can also run on one Mac, if you have two versions of MacPerl (or the app and the MPW tool), one running the client, and one running the server.

will set the Type to match the Object (name). The zone will default to *, the default AppleTalk zone. These should be adjusted as necessary.

The only difference between the two calls to new() is that the server calls the Listen parameter. The server then does a while loop around the accept() method, eventually closing the handle to the client.

Both sides of the connection are using Mac OS line termination, so we do not have to worry about checking or changing the line termination characters.

```perl
#!perl -w
use strict;
use IO::Socket;
my($answer, $client, $line, $server, $sock);

$answer = MacPerl::Answer(
  'Who are you?', 'Client', 'Server'
);

if ($answer) {
  $sock = IO::Socket::APPLETALK->new(
    Object  => 'MyAppleTalkSocket'
  ) or die('Cannot start client');
  print $line while (defined($line = <$sock>));

} else {
  $server = IO::Socket::APPLETALK->new(
    Object  => 'MyAppleTalkSocket',
    Listen  => 1,
  ) or die('Cannot start server');

  printf("[Server at %s accepting clients]\n",
    join '.', sockaddr_atlk(getsockname($server))
  );

  while ($client = $server->accept()) {
    print $client "Connect!\n";
    print "Connect!\n";
    close($client);
  }
}
```

Debugging

Without a doubt, you will run into problems when working with sockets and network programming. But, because these facilities do their work "behind the scenes", it can be difficult to determine what is going wrong.

> **Hint:** Always check return values. Most methods and functions return undef or () for failure, so it is easy to check if something fails (see the Net::SMTP example above), so be sure to do so!

You can't see what a socket is doing in a direct manner (as you could with a text file or a window). Fortunately, **OTSessionWatcher** (included on the CD-ROM) solves this problem. It prints an ASCII or binary representation of the traffic that is going through OpenTransport TCP/IP (used by most Macs for Internet networking). Using OTSessionWatcher, you can see what data is being sent and received, as it is happening, and what is going wrong.

There are other similar methods you can employ in your own scripts, if you don't wish to use OTSessionWatcher or if you are not using OpenTransport for your program. Every time you send or receive data from a socket, you can echo it to a file or to the MacPerl window:

```
print $sock  "some data\015\012";
print STDOUT "some data\015\012";
while (defined($line = <$sock>)) {
  print FILE   $line;
  print STDOUT $line;
}
```

This is not as nice as using OTSessionWatcher, which shows the raw bits of data as they are passing through, but it can be of a big help. If the data you are transmitting is binary, by the way, you may wish to format it and print it in a more easily comprehensible (e.g., application-specific) form.

> **Note:** The number one problem area in Internet socket programming, especially in MacPerl, is in line termination. Make sure that your program does exactly what you mean when you tell it to print a line ending of any kind. Use the octal escape sequences \012 and \015 (instead of \r and \n) to increase clarity and portability.

Chapter 18:

- *AppleScript*
- *Other OSA Languages*
- *Apple Events*
- *An Apple Event Example*

AppleScript, Etc.

The purpose of Newspeak was not only to provide a medium of expression for the world-view and mental habits proper to the devotees of Ingsoc, but to make all other modes of thought impossible.

– George Orwell, *The Principles of Newspeak*

One of the main purposes of scripting languages is to talk to other programs or processes. On Unix systems, this is often called **IPC** (interprocess communication); Apple calls it **IAC**[1] (interapplication communication). IAC lets two programs share data, which typically includes a command, list, string, number, Boolean, or file alias.

There are several components to the IAC architecture in Mac OS. The one we will deal with here is **Apple Events**. Apple Events are a popular, high-level form of IAC; most Mac OS applications have Apple Event capabilities built in, so that they can communicate directly with each other.

Apple's proprietary scripting language, AppleScript, also speaks Apple Events. In fact, when an application is commonly referred to as "AppleScriptable", that really means that it is scriptable with Apple Events. Thus, AppleScript is just one language that can "speak" Apple Events.

Many Mac OS scripting languages are called **OSA** (Open Scripting Architecture) languages. These languages can be embedded into applications with a special component protocol; normally, these languages all speak Apple Events. AppleScript is the most popular of the OSA languages.

---

[1] A complete *Inside Macintosh* book is devoted to IAC, most of it relating to Apple Events. Obviously, we cannot cover all of Apple Events here in this book, but we attempt to provide enough information to use Apple Events effectively with MacPerl.

AppleScript

AppleScript is a very powerful tool. With various extensions,[2] it can be enabled to perform almost any function (e.g., handling regular expressions). It is particularly good at providing access to system resources (e.g., users and groups, audio CD information, or monitor resolution and depth[3]).

Calling AppleScript from MacPerl

The simplest way to do AppleScript-based IAC from MacPerl is through the function `MacPerl::DoAppleScript()`. The function is very simple; it takes a single argument (the complete text of an AppleScript) and returns a textual representation of whatever the AppleScript returns.[4]

The following simple example opens the startup volume in the Finder.

```
$vol = MacPerl::MakePath((MacPerl::Volumes())[0]);
$script = <<EOS;
tell application "Finder"
  open item "$vol"
end tell
EOS

print MacPerl::DoAppleScript($script)
  or die("Could not run script\n");
```

Displays:

```
startup disk of Application "Finder"
```

Using AppleScript from MacPerl is quite slow , however.[5] Like Perl scripts, AppleScripts must be (pre-)compiled before execution. To eliminate start-up delays, AppleScripts are normally saved in a compiled format.

---

[2] Called **OSAX**s (or OSAXen), these are stored in the Scripting Additions folder, which is either in the System Folder or the Extensions folder.

[3] MacPerl can use an installed OSAX too, via Apple Events, using the Finder as the target application.

[4] The AppleScript language will not be explained; the authors have neither the space nor the inclination.

[5] You can speed up AppleScript calls from MacPerl using `Mac::OSA`.

AppleScripts that are created by MacPerl scripts cannot take full advantage of this optimization, however, because the AppleScript code is kept in text format. So, time must be taken to compile the AppleScript before it can be run, adding a significant amount of start-up delay.

Calling MacPerl from AppleScript

Communication can also go the other way, originating with an AppleScript rather than MacPerl. In this case, the MacPerl script responds by means of the `MacPerl::Reply()` function as described in Chapter 12, *The MacPerl Package*. The script below could be executed from within Apple's **Script Editor** or a compatible AppleScript editor.[6]

```
tell application "MacPerl"
  return ¬
    "Days until the year 2000: " & (Do Script "
      use Time::Local;
      $d1 = timelocal(0, 0, 0, 1, 0, 100);
      $d2 = ($d1 - time()) / 60 / 60 / 24;
      MacPerl::Reply(int($d2))
  ")
end tell
```

Displays (on April 1, 1998):

```
"Days until the year 2000: 640"
```

A MacPerl script invoked by the `Do Script` command can do pretty much anything that a regular MacPerl script can do. If you need to use double quotes in the MacPerl script, simply escape them (e.g., `\"text\"`).

You can also embed AppleScript values into your Do Script event. We can't do it as easily as we did with MacPerl's DoAppleScript function, which evaluates the Perl variables before passing the string to the function, but we can use concatenation in AppleScript to accomplish the same thing.

```
set mytext to "just another MacPerl hacker"
tell application "MacPerl"
  return Do Script ¬
```

---

[6] To "break" and continue a long line of AppleScript code across more than one line, end each unfininished partial line of AppleScript code with the continuation character, ¬, (formed by the sequence option-return in Script Editor).

```
    "MacPerl::Reply('" & mytext & "')"
  end tell
```

Returns:

```
  "just another MacPerl hacker"
```

Lists

Often, you might need a list of elements returned from MacPerl to Apple-Script. The simplest way to do this is with delimited text that is joined by MacPerl and split up by AppleScript.

```
tell application "MacPerl"
  set myResult to Do Script ¬
    "MacPerl::Reply(join ('|', ('a'..'g')))"
end tell

set AppleScript's text item delimiters to "|"
set myList to text items of myResult
set AppleScript's text item delimiters to ""
return myList
```

Returns an AppleScript list:

```
  {"a", "b", "c", "d", "e", "f", "g"}
```

Or, going the other way, you might need an AppleScript list converted to a MacPerl array. This can also be done with delimiters; in this example, we use Text::ParseWords. We remove the brackets with a regex before passing the text to quotewords(), which uses ', ' as its delimiter.

```
use Text::ParseWords;
$script = <<EOS;
  set myList to {"a", "b", "c", "d", "e", "f", "g"}
  return myList
EOS
($result = MacPerl::DoAppleScript($script))
  =~ s/^\{(.*)\}$/$1/;
@array = quotewords(', ', 0, $result);
print join(' ', @array);
```

Returns:

a b c d e f g

Other OSA Languages

AppleScript may be the most popular of the OSA languages (largely because it is included with every MacOS distribution) but it is not the only OSA language. Other OSA-compliant languages are also available.

Frontier

Frontier is described by Userland as an automated Content Management System, built around an object database, an integrated scripting language, and an object-oriented website framework. The scripting language, User-Talk, has a more "algebraic" syntax than AppleScript uses. That is, where AppleScript's syntax tends to use English-like words such as `tell`, Frontier uses functions, parentheses, and argument lists.

```
#!perl -w
use Mac::OSA;
use Mac::Components;
use Mac::AppleEvents;
my($vol, $co, $script, $result);

$vol    = MacPerl::MakePath((MacPerl::Volumes())[0]);
$co     = OpenDefaultComponent
           (kOSAComponentType(), 'LAND');
$script = new AEDesc('TEXT', <<EOS);
return appleEvent
  (Finder.id, 'aevt', 'odoc', '----', alias("$vol"))
EOS
$result = OSADoScript($co, $script, 0, 'TEXT', 0);

print AEPrint($result);
AEDisposeDesc($script);
AEDisposeDesc($result);
```

Displays:

```
"startupDisk"
```

The Frontier application needs to be running before UserTalk can be called from MacPerl. The `Mac::OSA` module does most of the work here, and can be used in a similar manner with any OSA language, like AppleScript.

Apple Events

In our examples, a MacPerl script calls an AppleScript (or UserTalk script) or an AppleScript calls a MacPerl script. In either case, Apple Events are used to effect the interaction. The Apple Events themselves are well disguised, however, by the programming interface. Although you are free to use this interface in ignorance of the underlying structure, we suggest that you accompany us on a brief overview tour of Apple Event structure.

Apple Events have two major components: attributes and parameters. **Attributes** are the portions of the event that define how it is to be used. **Parameters** are contained in data structures similar to Perl's hashes, with a **keyword** as the key and some data as the value of that key. Parameter keywords are always composed of exactly four (eight-bit) characters.

Attributes

An attribute is composed primarily of an **event ID** and an **event class** (**suite**). Also given as attributes are such items as the **target application** for the event (specified by its **creator ID**).

An event ID is like the name of a function in Perl; an event must be defined in the program in order to use it. We cannot define arbitrary events for another application; we can only use the events that application has provided. These events all belong to some event class, or suite, much as functions in Perl all belong to a particular class or package.

```
tell application "Finder"
  open item "$vol"
end tell
```

To open an item, as we did in our earlier example, we would use the event ID `odoc`, which is in the class `aevt`. The target application is the Mac OS Finder, which has `MACS` as its creator ID. For example:

```
%ae = (
  target => 'MACS',          # creator ID
  class  => 'aevt',          # event class
  id     => 'odoc',          # event ID
...
);
```

Parameters

Parameters often describe information about an application's built-in **classes**[7] and **properties** of those classes. For instance, an application might have a window class; the name of the window and its position and size on the screen would be properties of that class.

A parameter might also be a simpler type of data, such as a string or file alias. Each parameter is named by a unique **keyword** and has some data assigned to it, like a Perl hash. Data is normally in the form of a **record** or a **list**, analogous to Perl scalars and arrays. Often, the most important data in an event is passed through the **direct object** parameter; the direct object parameter, for instance, has the special keyword '----'.

Any self-contained part of an Apple Event is a **descriptor**. This includes entire events with attributes and parameters, a standalone parameter, a record, or a list.

An Apple Event Example

Once we have our attributes and parameters, we can build an AppleEvent using the AEBuildAppleEvent() function which is part of the Mac:: AppleEvents package. The event that is returned from that function can then be sent via the AESend() function. The AEPrint() function can be used to print out text representations of events and descriptors.

The example below uses AEBuildAppleEvent() to do exactly the same thing our first example did through the AppleScript interface (opening the startup volume in the Finder). It's a lot more complicated than the previous version, however (although it runs much faster). Don't wory too much about the syntax of the example; it's largely here to show you that TMTOWTDI.

We set up a hash (%ae) to store our attributes and parameters for use in the AEBuildAppleEvent() function. Our build function takes all parameters as one argument, with additional arguments to the function if the parameters call for them, much like sprintf() in Perl. We make the value of $ae {'params'} an anonymous hash, so we can add as many values as necessary. In this case, the TEXT(@) notation calls for an additional argument.

---

[7] These are not the same as the event class. They are similar in concept to Perl classes.

In this example, there is only one named parameter sent to this event: the direct object parameter. The direct object parameter is passed an Apple Event **object specifier record**, which is a type of descriptor record.

We're not going to get into the nitty gritty details of how this all works here; that discussion is beyond the scope of this book. Suffice it to say that the example below is identical in functionality to the first example we gave in this chapter. Here goes!

```perl
#!perl -w
use Mac::AppleEvents;
my(%ae, $vol, $event, $reply);

$vol = MacPerl::MakePath((MacPerl::Volumes())[0]);
%ae = (
  target => 'MACS',          # creator ID
  class  => 'aevt',          # event class
  id     => 'odoc',          # event ID
  params => [
    "'----':obj " .          # direct object keyword
    "{want:type(cobj), " .   # 4-char class ID
    "from:null(), " .        # object's container
    "form:enum(name), " .    # form of object data
    "seld:TEXT(\@)}",        # actual object data
    $vol                     # the startup volume
  ]
);

# now build the event
$event   = AEBuildAppleEvent(
  $ae{'class'},              # event class
  $ae{'id'},                 # event ID
  'sign',                    # appl. signature
  $ae{'target'},             # creator ID
  0, 0,                      # end of this part
  @{$ae{'params'}}           # parameter list
) or die($^E);
$reply = AESend($event, kAEWaitReply) or die($^E);
print AEPrint($event), "\n";
print AEPrint($reply), "\n";
AEDisposeDesc($event);
AEDisposeDesc($reply);
```

When run, this displays:

```
aevt\odoc{'----':obj {want:type(cobj),
   from:'null'(), form:name, seld:"HD:"},
   &inte:cans, &timo:3600}
aevt\ansr{'----':obj {want:type(prop),
   from:'null'(), form:prop, seld:type(sdsk)}}
```

Pretty complex, isn't it?

If you're interested in learning more about Apple Event structure, and in building Apple Events in this fashion, we recommend:

- `macperlcat.pod`, on the CD-ROM

- *Inside Macintosh*, especially *Interapplication Communication*

- the various useful utilities such as AETE converter, on the CD-ROM

Part IV
Reference

Enough is as good as a feast.

– John Heywood, *Proverbs*, I.II

Chapter 19:

Operators

"That's not a regular rule; you invented it just now."
"It's the oldest rule in the book," said the King.
Then it ought to be number One," said Alice.

– Lewis Carroll, *Alice's Adventures in Wonderland*

This chapter provides a brief reference guide to the Perl (symbolic) operators and escape sequences. Perl has several dozen operators, far exceeding the counts of most modern programming languages. Actually, if you count the "named operators", such as `sleep`, there are over a hundred! For reasons of laziness,[1] however, we have chosen to treat Perl's named operators as if they were functions; you can find them in the next chapter (along with the control flow modifiers).

Nonetheless, the combinatorial complexity produced by Perl's wealth of even symbolic operators can be very confusing. In particular, it can make it difficult to read code that was written by other (ahem), less-restrained programmers. Fear not; if the Perl interpreter can figure this out, so can you!

Precedence And Associativity

Perl's operator precedence and associativity rules allow the interpreter to determine the order in which expressions should be evaluated. The rules actually work quite well; in most cases, if a programmer naively writes an

---

[1] One of the cardinal virtues in Perl!

expression, Perl will do what he expects. On the other hand, it's the little exceptions that make life so very interesting.

Consequently, you would be well-advised to add a few sets of parentheses when writing complex expressions. That way, neither you nor the poor guy who has to maintain your code will have to remember all of Perl's twenty-four (24!) levels of precedence and (corresponding) associativity rules.

Even so, you will occasionally encounter a piece of Perl code that doesn't use parentheses, so you will want to have a quick reference on Perl's operator precedence and associativity rules. Let's start with the official table, adapted slightly from the Perl manual pages:

Operator(s)	Associativity
Terms, list operators (leftward)	left
->	left
++ --	none
**	right
! ~ \ and unary + and -	right
=~ !~	left
* / % x	left
+ - .	left
<< >>	left
Named unary operators	none
< > <= >= lt gt le ge	none
== != <=> eq ne cmp	none
&	left
| ^	left
&&	left
.. ...	none
?:	right
= += -= *= etc.	right
, =>	left
List operators (rightward)	none
not	right
and	left
or xor	left

In general, if you find yourself confronted by some overly "cute" code (e.g., code that relies on obscure precedence or associativity interactions), your best strategy is to add parentheses until the order of operations is self-evident. Be careful to follow the precedence and associativity rules, however, lest you break the code you are trying to understand!

Precedence

Operators that are higher in the table have higher precedence; that is, they are interpreted before those with lower precedence. As you might expect, the multiply (*) and divide (/) operators have higher precedence than the add (+) and substract (−) operators. So, the expression:

```
$a * $x + $b
```

is interpreted as meaning:

```
($a * $x) + $b
```

After that, however, things get a bit more challenging. How, for instance, should the following expression be parsed?

```
$i ++ / 27 >= $j -- << 3
```

 Well, looking at the table, we see that the increment (++) and decrement (−−) operators have the highest precedence of any operators used in the expression. So, we can rewrite the expression as:

```
($i++) / 27 >= ($j--) << 3
```

The division (/) operator comes next in the table, giving us:

```
(($i++) / 27) >= ($j--) << 3
```

Finally, we get to the left-shift (<<) operator:

```
(($i++) / 27) >= (($j--) << 3)
```

Although the intent of the expression may still be unclear (and should be clarified by a comment!), the specific order of evaluation is not. By "steam-cleaning" imported code as you work on it, you can make life easier for yourself and successive maintainers.

Associativity

Associativity only comes into play when operators of equal precedence are combined in an expression. The Associativity column in the table indicates whether given operators are left, right, or non-associative. Again, by judicious use of parentheses, you can avoid worrying about associativity at all. But, if you get stuck with some ugly code, here are some hints at parsing it:

```
$a - $b + $c - $d
```

Because the add (+) and subtract (–) operators are left associative, the expression groups from left to right:

```
(($a - $b) + $c) - $d
```

Right associativity works in an analogous manner; this expression:

```
$a ** $b ** $c ** $d
```

evaulates as:

```
$a ** ($b ** ($c ** $d))
```

Some operators are not associative at all. Thus, when these operators are used, no particular grouping order is defined. Fortunately, as in this string concatenation example, the grouping order generally doesn't matter:

```
$a . $b . $c
```

Arithmetic Operators

The arithmetic operators are used when working with numeric expressions. These operators all operate in floating point mode, with one exception. Modulus operations are done in integer mode.

+	addition	$a + 1
–	subtraction	$a – 2
*	multiplication	2 * 2
/	division	355 / 113
=	assignment	$pi = 3.14159
**	exponentiation	10 ** 3
%	modulus (integer remainder)	$y % 5

String Operators

x	repeat by	'o' x 5
.	concatenate with	'butter' . 'fly'

Assignment Operators

By mixing the various arithmetic operators with the assignment operator, we get a collection of "shortcut" assignment operators.

=	"assignment"	`$pi = 3.14159`
+=	"increment by"	`$x += 2    # $x = $x + 2`
-=	"decrement by"	`$y -= 2    # $y = $y - 2`
*=	"multiply by"	`$w *= 7    # $w = $w * 7`
/=	"divide by"	`$v /= 2    # $v = $v / 2`
%=	"modulo by"	`$u %= 5    # $u = $u % 5`
**=	"raise to the power"	`$t **= 7   # $t = $t ** 7`
++	"autoincrement"	`$s++       # $s = $s + 1`
--	"autodecrement"	`$r--       # $r = $r - 1`

Comparison Operators

There are two types of comparison operators. Numeric comparison operators work only on numbers and look like mathematical symbols.

<	less than	`2 < 3`
>	greater than	`4 > 3`
<=	less than or equal to	`$i <= 0`
>=	greater than or equal to	`$x >= 10`
!=	not equal to	`5 != 7`
==	equal to (equality)	`2 == 2`
<=>	signed comparison	

String comparison operators work only on strings; their names are alphabetic strings as well (e.g., `cmp`). When comparing strings, remember that Perl is case sensitive.

lt	less than	`'three' lt 'two'`
gt	greater than	`'three' gt 'four'`
le	less than or equal to	`'a' le 'a'`
ge	greater than or equal to	`'b' ge 'a'`
ne	not equal to	`'ONE' ne 'one'`
eq	equal to	`'one' eq 'one'`
cmp	signed comparison	

Logical Operators

Boolean, or logical, operators evaluate from left to right, determining the truth of a statement in as few operations as possible. Consider this

```
if (($a == 1) && ($b < 2))
```

If $a is not 1, there is no point in evaluating the remainder of the expression, so Perl doesn't. These operators return the last value evaluated (not simply 1 or 0). The alphabetic versions (e.g., and, or) have lower precedence than their symbolic counterparts and are more mnemonic. They were created to be used in statements such as

```
open(IN, $file) or die;
```

The negation operators (! and not) return 1 if their operand is false; otherwise they return the null string. The xor, exclusive OR, operator has no direct counterpart. For an xor operation to evaluate as true, *exactly one* of the two operands evaluated must be true. Consequently, both operands will always be evaluated.

!	"logical NOT"	negate the truth of the expression
&&	"logical AND"	both operands must be true
||	"logical OR"	one or both operands may be true
not	"logical NOT"	negate the truth of the expression
and	"logical AND"	both operands must be true
or	"logical OR"	one or both operands may be true
xor	"logical XOR"	exactly one operand must be true

Bitwise logical operators perform their operations on the bits of the string (or number). These operators work on either string or numeric expressions, but work differently on each. If both operands are strings (or numbers), they are treated as strings (or numbers). However, if one operand is a string and the other is a number, the string will be converted to a number.

~	"bitwise NOT"	~1	# 4294967294
&	"bitwise AND"	5 & 3	# 1
|	"bitwise OR"	5 | 3	# 7
^	"bitwise XOR"	5 ^ 3	# 6

Bitwise negation produces the 1's complement of the input, evaluated as a 32-bit wide integer. That is, it turns all of the 1's into 0's and vice versa.

The first example above may thus be explained as follows:

Thirty-two bit binary value	Decimal value
00000000 00000000 00000000 00000001	1
11111111 11111111 11111111 11111110	4294967294

Bit-Shift Operators

The bit-shift operators return the value of the left-hand argument shifted (left or right) by the number of bits specified by the right-hand operator.

<<	left shift	3 << 1	# 12
>>	right shift	6 >> 1	# 3

Binding (Matching) Operators

The binding operators **bind** a scalar expression to a pattern **match**, a **substitution**, or a **translation**. The return value of !~ is the logical negation of =~, i.e., the pattern didn't match (!~ is unlikely to be meaningful in a substitution or translation).

=~	matches	$str =~ m/pat*/
!~	does not match	$str !~ m/pat*/

Reference / Dereference Operators

The backslash, ****, serves as a reference operator. This use of \ should not be confused with the \ used in creating escape sequences (described later in this chapter). As a reference operator, \ creates a reference to the argument that follows. If used on a list of items, it will return a list of references to each element of the input list.

The arrow operator, **->**, is the dereference operator; if the argument on the right hand side is an array or hash subscript, the argument on the left hand side is a reference to an array or hash. Otherwise, the right hand argument must be a method name (or scalar variable containing a method name); the left hand argument must either be an object or a class (package) name.

\	reference	*STDOUT
->	dereference (arrow)	$array->[1]

The ***** in the first example, *STDOUT, is used to prefix a **typeglob**; typeglobs are useful for passing or storing filehandles.

Range Operators

In list context, the range operator returns a list of all values between the left and right arguments, inclusive. For example, the following code fragment sets a loop from 1 to 10 by 1.

```
foreach $ndx (1..10) { print("$ndx\n"); }
```

In scalar context, the range operator returns true or false, flip-flopping based on the values of its operands. The return value remains false as long as the left argument remains false (the right argument is not evaluated). If the left argument becomes true, .. returns true and then remains true (not evaluating the left argument) until the right argument becomes true. After that, it becomes false again.[2]

The .. operator can test the right argument and become false again immediately. If this is not the behavior you want, use the ... operator instead; it does not test the right hand argument until the next evaluation. Otherwise, the two are identical.

```
..      range (flip-flop)          1..10
...     range (flip-flop)          /^Date/ ... /^$/
```

Comma Operator

In scalar context, the comma operator, **,**, evaluates its left hand argument, discarding the value, then evaluates the right hand argument and returns that value. You might wonder how this could be useful.

The following example (without annotation) can be found in *Programming Perl*, chapter 2. It parses **switches** (i.e., input arguments which begin with a dash, -).[3]

```
while ($_ = $ARGV[0], /^-/) {
    shift;
    last if /^--$/;
```

---

[2] Think of it as waiting to cross a street. Look to the left until it is safe to cross, then look to the right until it is safe to cross, then look back to the left.

[3] Note that while it is trivial to pass arguments of this type to the MPW perl tool, it is considerably more difficult when using the MacPerl application. However, the point of this example is to discuss the comma operator, not parsing arguments, *per se*.

Note that this code takes advantage of various defaults; the following is equivalent but more verbose

```
while ($_ = $ARGV[0], $_ =~ /^-/) {
    shift(@ARGV);
    last if ($_ =~ /^--$/);
```

But how do we explain the multiple arguments to `while` (and the comma)? Recall the explanation of the comma operator above. It first evaluates the left hand argument, the expression `$_ = $ARGV[0]`, which it discards (ignores). However, the expression *is evaluated*. The comma then causes evaluation of the right hand argument (the pattern match) and returns the result of this evaluation. Because the left side was evaluated, `$_` can be used in the right hand expression. Entry into the loop depends upon whether the (recently set) value of `$_` matches `/^-/`.

In list context, the comma operator is only a simple list argument separator; it doesn't throw anything away! The somewhat fancier **=>** is a synonym for the comma; it looks prettier when separating key / value pairs in hash definitions. It also happens, conveniently, to force the argument on its left to be interpreted as a string.

,	"comma"	`$x = ($a = 2, 3); @a = (1, 2);`
=>	"argument pairs"	`%h = (a => 'red');`

Conditional Operator

The ?: operator implements a very terse if-then-else style conditional, without taking up a lot of space; it can readily be embedded within other expressions. If the argument to the left of the ? evaluates to true, then the expression in the middle is evaluated and returned; otherwise, the right hand expression (to the right of the `:`) is evaluated and returned.

?:	conditional	`# $a = ($b > 3) ? 1 : 0;`

File Test Operators

The file test operators are unary operators. Each takes one argument (a filename or a filehandle) and tests an attribute of the associated file. Each returns 1 if the test holds true, 0 if false.

Many of these operators are meaningless (and therefore not implemented) on Mac OS, or have somewhat different meanings in MacPerl. In the descriptions below, the following typography conventions apply:

*   **Bold** indicates that the operator works unchanged in MacPerl.

*   ***Bold-Italic*** indicates that the operator is not available or is significantly different in MacPerl; we may have included information on workarounds, etc.

*   *Italic* indicates that the operator is not available in MacPerl.

File Mode (Permission)

-g	*-o*	**-r**	*-u*	**-w**	***-x***
-k	*-O*	**-R**		**-W**	***-X***

File Type

-b	*-c*	**-f**	*-p*	**-t**
-B	**-d**	**-l**	***-S***	***-T***

Existence and Size

-e	**-s**	**-z**

Age

-A	**-C**	**-M**

File Test Synopses

```
-? FILEHANDLE
-? EXPR
-?
```

All file test operators share the same syntax. We will not repeat it below. If no argument is given, tests $_ (unless specified).

-A

This test is treated by MacPerl as a synonym for the -M test. Under Unix, it returns the time since the file was last accessed.

-b

This test is not supported by MacPerl (returns a null string). Under Unix, it returns true if the argument is a "block special" file (buffered device).

- B

> File is a binary file. This test may mis-classify Macintosh text files containing many 8-bit ("option") characters. This is the opposite of -T.

-c

> This test is not supported by MacPerl (returns a null string). Under Unix, it returns true if the argument is a "character special" file (raw / un-buffered device).

- C

> Age of file in days since the file was created (as shown by Get Info), where 0 is the time the script started running. A file that was created after the current script started would have a negative age. Under Unix, the "creation date" refers to the most recent change to the inode.

- d

> File is a directory (folder).

- e

> File exists.

- f

> File is a regular file.

-g

> This test is not supported by MacPerl (returns a null string). Under Unix, it returns a true value if the argument has the "setgid" bit set.

-k

> This test is not supported by MacPerl (returns a null string). Under Unix, it returns a true value if the argument has the "sticky" bit set.

- l

> File is a symbolic link (alias).

- M

> Age of file in days since last modification (as shown by Get Info), where 0 is the time the script started running. A file that was modified after the current script started would have a negative age.

-o

> This test is not supported by MacPerl (returns 1). Under Unix, it returns a true value if the argument is owned by the user's effective uid.

-O

> This test is not supported by MacPerl (returns 1). Under Unix, it returns a true value if the argument is owned by the user's real uid.

-p

> This test is not supported by MacPerl (returns 1). Under Unix, it returns a true value if the argument is a named pipe (FIFO).

-r, -R

> File is readable. Under Unix, this applies to the effective (-r) or the real (-R) uid/gid. Under Mac OS, these tests have only a very limited meaning ; -R is indistinguishable from -r.

- s

> File exists and has non-zero size. Returns size of the file in bytes (as shown by Get Info).

- S

> File is a socket.

- t

> Filehandle is open to a terminal window. If no argument is specified, tests STDIN.

- T

> File is a text file. This test may mis-classify Mac text files containing many 8-bit ("option") characters. This is the opposite of -B.

-u

> This test is not supported by MacPerl (returns 1). Under Unix, it returns a true value if the argument has the "setuid" bit set.

-w, - W

> File is writeable. Under Unix, this applies to the effective (-w) or the real (-W) uid/gid. Under Mac OS, these tests have only a very limited meaning ; -W is indistinguishable from -w.

-x, -X

> File is executable. Under Unix, this applies to the effective (-x) or the real (-X) uid/gid. Under Mac OS, these tests have only a very limited meaning ; -X is indistinguishable from -x.

- z

> File exists and has zero size.

Quoting

Perl provides the customary quoting characters which we have discussed previously:

`'...'`	single quotes; literal, with no interpolation
`"..."`	double quotes; literal, with interpolation of $, @, and \
`` `...` ``	backquotes; command evaluation[4]
`(...)`	word list (comma separated)
`${...}`	a single identifier within the braces is treated as if in `'...'`
`<<EOF`	start of a here document; interpolated unless `'EOF'`

You may also choose instead to use the "generic" versions:

`q/.../`	literal; equivalent to `'...'` for each member
`qq/.../`	literal; equivalent to `"..."` for each member
`qx/.../`	command evaluation; equivalent to `` `...` `` (caveats included :-)
`qw/.../`	word list; equivalent to `(...)`, without the commas!

Everything between the delimiting / characters is considered to be quoted, as if each element had been quoted in the "conventional" manner. However, you are able to enclose the "conventional" quote marks within the quoted material without resorting to using \ to escape their special meaning.

```
$message = q/Don't type that!/;
$error = qq/The file "myfile" could not be found/;
@days = qw/Monday Wednesday Friday/;
```

Note that, as with pattern matching, the / is only a typical delimiter; any non-alphanumeric (non-whitespace) character may be used as the delimiter. In particular, if you choose a bracketing character as the starting delimiter (e.g. (, [, {, or <), the ending delimiter will be the matching

---

[4] With ToolServer; otherwise, only a few specific commands are implemented.

bracket. Embedding of delimiters is possible; embedded delimiters must match in pairs.

```
$date_str = q{Date: 02/28/98};
@days = qw(Monday Wednesday Friday);
```

The matching, `m//`, substitution, `s///`, and translation, `tr///`, operators can be considered as quoting methods. However, because these have rather "function-like" capabilities, we have chosen to postpone their discussion to the next chapter, *Reserved Words*.

Escape Sequences

The escape sequences are not, technically speaking, operators. They do not act upon their arguments (in fact, they have no arguments). However, they look as much like "line noise" as everything we have discussed so far in this chapter, and we could think of no better place to list them. So here they are. Each of these can be used to match a particular character, or character class, in a regular expression pattern. The first group can also be used in `print` statements.

`\`	"escape" character
`\a`	alarm (bell)
`\f`	formfeed
`\r`	return[5]
`\n`	newline[6]
`\t`	horizontal tab
`\b`	backspace[7]
`\0n`	match an octal number n[8]
`\d`	match any digit [0-9]
`\D`	match any nondigit

---

[5] On Unix systems (\015); generates a linefeed under MacPerl (\012).

[6] Generates a linefeed under Unix (\012); generates a carriage return (\015) under MacPerl.

[7] Note that \b has different meanings depending upon where it is used. In a character class or double-quoted string it represents a backspace. In parts of a regular expression, however, it represents a word boundary.

[8] A backslashed two- or three-digit octal number matches the character with that octal (ASCII) value. For example, \015 matches the **carriage return** character, **^M**.

\w	match any "word" character (letter, digit, or underscore)
\s	match any whitespace character (e.g., tab, space, newline)
\b	match at a word boundary

Regular Expressions

The Regular Expression operators are used in defining patterns. Do not confuse them with the other Perl operators which use the same characters!

[ ]	describe a character class[9]
( )	parenthesize for grouping
{n,m}	must match no fewer than *n* but no more than *m* times
{n,}	must match no fewer than *n* times
{n}	must match exactly *n* times
*	match 0 or more times; equivalent to {0,}
+	must match 1 or more times; equivalent to {1,}
?	must match exactly 0 or 1 times; equivalent to {0,1}
^	anchor a pattern to the beginning of the line
$	anchor a pattern to the end of the line
.	match any (single) character[10]
|	provide a choice of alternative matches

Switches

Perl **switches** (also called **options** or **flags**) may be specified on the command line or as part of the #! line that begins a script. While Perl recognizes nearly two dozen switches, not all of these are supported or have the same meaning under MacPerl as under Perl for Unix. Because of the way in which the #! line is emulated in MacPerl, many switches are supported from the command line only (MPW perl tool) and cannot be used in the #! line.

Several switches take (possibly optional) arguments. Optional arguments are shown within brackets, [ ]. Descriptive argument strings are given in *italics*. Be sure to use the name of a real module, command, etc., in place of the generic argument string!

---

[9] A **character class** is a set of characters, where the pattern may match any of the set. For example, the regular expression class [0123456789] describes the set of digits from 0 through 9, inclusive. For series classes, a dash, –, may be used to represent missing but assumed members (e.g., [0-9] also represents the same set of digits).

[10] Except \n unless you use the /s modifier on your pattern.

-0[*octal*]

> Specify the input record separator (in octal). Default is null, 0. Use 00 to specify a blank line as the record separator (i.e., #!perl -000). Equivalent to setting the $/ variable.

-a

> Autosplit mode with -n or -p (implicitly splits $_ into @F, splitting on spaces.). See also -F .

-c

> Check syntax only (but run BEGIN and END blocks). Equivalent to selecting Syntax Check from the MacPerl application Scripts menu.

-d[:*module*]

> Run script under the Perl debugger, optionally specifying a debugging *module*. Equivalent to selecting Perl Debugger in the MacPerl application Scripts menu.

-D[*number/list*]

> Set debugging flags (argument is a bit mask or flags). This only works if you have recompiled MacPerl with the -DDEBUGGING flag set. Unrelated to the Perl debugger.

-e '*commands*'

> Specify the complete script (usually one line) as the argument. MPW perl tool only; unsupported in #!perl line. If more than one Perl statement is included, escape any embedded returns with ∂ (option-d).

-F/*pattern*/

> Specify the *pattern* for autosplitting (-a). The //'s are optional.

-h

> Print help information (all possible switches and brief explanations).

-i[*extension*]

> Edit files processed by <> **in place** (i.e., the output will be placed back into the input file).[11] If *extension* is supplied, a backup copy of the

---

[11] In actuality, the input file is renamed and a new output file is created with the name of the original input file.

original file will be made, with `extension` added to the filename. Otherwise, the original input file is replaced.

`-Idirectory`

Specify a library `directory` to add to `@INC`, telling Perl where to search for modules (may be used more than once).

`-l[octal]`

Enable automatic line ending processing (`print` statements no longer require `\n`), optionally specifying the output record separator in octal. Default is the current value of the input record separator (i.e., newline unless modified). Turns on automatic `chomping` if used with `-n` or `-p`.

`-Mmodule`
`-mmodule`

Execute `use` *module*... before executing script.

`-M-module`
`-m-module`

Execute `no` *module*... before executing script.

`-n`

Assume a `while (<>) { ... }` style loop around script, automatically iterating over all input files. Use of `-p` overrides `-n`.

`-p`

Assume a loop like `-n` but also print each line. Use of `-p` overrides `-n`.

`-P`

Unsupported in MacPerl. Under Unix, runs the script through the C preprocessor before compilation.

`-s`

Enables rudimentary parsing for switches followng the script name on the command line. MPW `perl` tool only; meaningless in MacPerl app.

`-S`

Search for the script using `PATH` environment variable. MPW `perl` tool only; unsupported in MacPerl app. Used to make MPW Perl scripts directly executable by MPW shell, as

```
Perl -Sx "{0}" {Parameters};
```

-T

> Turn on taint checking. MPW command line only; unsupported in
> #!perl line. Select Taint Checks in the MacPerl application Scripts
> menu to get the same result.

-u

> Unsupported under MacPerl.[12] Under Unix, this option "dumps core"
> (i.e., saves the state of the executable program in a file named **core**)
> after parsing the script.

-U

> Allow unsafe operations such as unlinking a directory.

-v

> Print version number and patchlevel of Perl program.

-V[:*variable*]

> Print configuration information for Perl program. If *variable* is
> specified, print the value of that configuration variable. MPW
> command line only; unsupported in #!perl line.[13]

-w

> Turn on warnings for compilation of script.

-x[*directory*]

> Extract a Perl script from within other text. Skip past (ignore) any text
> before the #!perl line and perhaps change the current directory to the
> named *directory*. MPW perl tool only; unsupported in MacPerl app.
> Used to make MPW Perl scripts directly executable by MPW shell, as

```
Perl -Sx "{0}" {Parameters};
```

---

[12] Some versions of MacPerl will abort and terminate, leaving the application in an
unreliable state. The next invocation of a MacPerl script could crash. **Do not try this
switch.**

[13] However, if you need this information in the MacPerl app, you can use the One
Liner menu item to execute the command line, perl -V.

Chapter 20:

- *Alphabetical List*
- *Categories*
- *Synopses*

Reserved   Words

"When I use a word," Humpty Dumpty said in a rather scornful tone,
"it means just what I choose it to mean – neither more nor less."

– Lewis Carroll, Through the Looking Glass

This chapter provides a "Quick Reference" to Perl's "reserved words" or commands. These include the built-in functions and things that can be thought of as functions (the "named operators") as well as the control flow modifiers. The non-word symbolic operators, escape characters, and such can be found in the preceding chapter.

The chapter is organized into the following sections:

- An alphabetical list of all reserved words. The list includes all of the functions, named operators, and control flow modifiers which are available without your specifically use ing or require ing a module or library. The list also includes the "backquoted commands" which have been specifically implemented for MacPerl. Look here if you know the name of command you want to find.

- A table of all reserved words, organized by category. Look here if you know what you want to do, but aren't sure of the command's name.

- Detailed synopses for a chosen subset of these reserved words, organized alphabetically by name. The synopses include brief information on usage as well as occasional Mac OS-specific notes. Synopses are provided only for a subset of the commands listed in the first two sections.

Space considerations (and the desire not to reproduce what may be better found elsewhere) prevent us from including detailed information on every available Perl function! We hope this reference will serve as a memory aid for functions you already know about, and a sufficient hint for those which are new to you.

In particular cases, we have provided more detailed information. We have chosen to detail those functions which exist *only* in MacPerl, as well as those which exhibit *different behavior* under MacPerl.

In addition, we have provided synopses for those Perl functions which we feel are most useful and relevant to a wide range of Perl programming tasks. In particular, we have included many of the functions which were used in the examples in Part II of this book.

For explanations of the rest of the built-in functions and more information (including code examples) on those covered here, please see the online documentation ("Built-in functions" aka perlfunc.pod) and/or a good Perl reference book (e.g., *Programming Perl*). We also refer you to Parts II and III of this book.

For more information on the Mac OS Interface functions module, as well as details on the Macintosh Toolbox modules (which are not built in), see Chapters 12 and 13 and the online documentation (Macintosh specific features and Macintosh Toolbox Modules).

In each section, all names are given in `Courier` font; in addition, we have used the following typographical conventions to convey additional information:

- **Bold** indicates that we have included usage notes, etc. in the synopses.

- ***Bold-Italic*** indicates that this function is not supported by MacPerl or is only partially supported in MacPerl (as compared to Unix Perl); we have included information on differences, workarounds, etc., in the synopses.

- *Italic* indicates that the function is not available in MacPerl.

- `Plain Courier` text indicates that there are no noticeable differences between the way this command works under MacPerl as compared to Unix Perl. We refer you to the online documentation for specific details on usage, etc.

Alphabetical List

abs, accept, alarm, **Answer**, **Ask**, atan2

bind, *binmode*, bless

caller, **chdir**, *chmod*, **chomp**, **Choose**, chop, *chown*, chr, *chroot*, **close**, **closedir**, connect, **continue**, cos, crypt

dbmclose, **dbmopen**, **defined**, delete, **die**, **Directory**, do, **DoAppleScript**, *dump*

each, **else**, **elsif**, *endgrent*, *endhostent*, *endnetent*, *endprotoent*, *endpwent*, **eof**, eval, *exec*, exists, exit, exp

FAccess, fcntl, fileno, find, *flock*, **for**, **foreach**, *fork*, format, formline

getc, **GetFileInfo**, *getgrent*, *getgrgid*, *getgrnam*, gethostbyaddr, gethostbyname, gethostent, *getlogin*, *getnetbyaddr*, *getnetbyname*, getnetent, getpeername, *getpgrp*, *getppid*, *getpriority*, getprotobyname, getprotobynumber, *getprotoent*, getpwent, getpwnam, getpwuid, *getservbyaddr*, *getservbyname*, *getservbyport*, *getservent*, getsockname, *getsockopt*, **glob**, gmtime, **goto**, grep

hex, **hostname**

if, import, **index**, int, ioctl

join

keys, *kill*

last, lc, lcfirst, **length**, *link*, listen, **LoadExternals**, local, **localtime**, log, lstat

m//, **MakeFSSpec**, **MakePath**, map, **mkdir**, *msgctl*, *msgget*, *msgrcv*, *msgsnd*, **my**

next, no

oct, **open**, **opendir**, ord

pack, package, **Pick**, *pipe*, pop, pos, **print**, **printf**, push, **pwd**

q//, qq//, **Quit**, quotemeta, qw//, qx//

rand, read, **readdir**, readlink, recv, **redo**, ref, **rename**, **Reply**, require, reset, **return**, reverse, rewinddir, rindex, **rmdir** *s///*, **scalar**, seek, seekdir, select, *semctl*, *semget*, *semop*, send, **SetFileInfo**, *setgrent*, sethostent, *setnetent*, *setpgrp*, *setpriority*, *setprotoent*, *setpwent*, *setservent*, *setsockopt*, **shift**, *shmctl*, *shmget*, *shmread*, *shmwrite*, shutdown, sin, **sleep**, socket, *socketpair*, **sort**, splice, **split**, **sprintf**, sqrt, srand, **stat**, **stty**, study, **sub**, **substr**, **symlink**, *syscall*, sysopen, sysread, *system*, syswrite

tell, telldir, tie, tied, **time**, *times*, **tr///**, truncate

uc, ucfirst, *umask*, undef, **unless**, **unlink**, **until**, unpack, **unshift**, untie, **use**, *utime*

values, vec, **Volumes**

wait, *waitpid*, **wantarray**, **warn**, **while**, write

y///

Categories

The built-in functions are categorized below by type (e.g., Data Manipulation, Input/Output, Networking, etc.) and subtype (e.g. Numeric, Lists, etc.). Some functions may be listed in more than one category.

Data Manipulation – Numeric

abs	exp	rand	srand
atan2	int	sin	
cos	log	sqrt	

Data Manipulation – Conversion

chr	oct	pack	vec
hex	ord	unpack	

Data Manipulation – Lists (any)

grep	map	**scalar**	**split**
join	reverse	**sort**	unpack

Data Manipulation – Lists (@array)

pop	**shift**	**unshift**
push	splice	

Data Manipulation – Lists (%hash)

delete	exists	**values**
each	keys	

Data Manipulation – Time

gmtime	**localtime**	**time**	*times*

Data Manipulation – Strings and Patterns

chomp	**length**	quotemeta	**tr///**
chop	**m//**	reverse	uc
crypt	pos	rindex	ucfirst
eval	q//	**s///**	**y///**
index	qq//	**split**	
lc	qw//	**sprintf**	
lcfirst	qx//	**substr**	

Functions, Modules, and Classes

bless	**my**	require	tied
caller	no	**return**	untie
import	package	**sub**	**use**
local	ref	tie	**wantarray**

Group/User data

endgrent	*getgrgid*	*getpwnam*	*setpwent*
endpwent	*getgrnam*	*getpwuid*	
getgrent	*getpwent*	*setgrent*	

Input/Output – File System

chmod	lstat	**rmdir**	**unlink**
chown	**mkdir**	***stat***	***utime***
glob	readlink	**symlink**	
link	**rename**	truncate	

Input/Output – File

binmode	fileno	**open**	select
close	*flock*	*pipe*	sysopen
dbmclose	format	**print**	sysread
dbmopen	formline	**printf**	syswrite
eof	**getc**	read	tell
fcntl	ioctl	seek	write

Input/Output – Directory

closedir	**readdir**	seekdir
opendir	rewinddir	telldir

Mac OS Interface

Answer	**GetFileInfo**	**Quit**
Ask	**LoadExternals**	**Reply**
Choose	**MakeFSSpec**	**SetFileInfo**
DoAppleScript	**MakePath**	**Volumes**
FAccess	Pick	

Miscellaneous

defined	eval	ref	**sort**
do	find	reset	study
dump	formline	scalar	undef

Network Protocols

endprotoent	*getprotobynumber*	*setprotoent*
getprotobyname	*getprotoent*	

Networking – Sockets

accept	*getnetbyname*	recv
bind	*getnetent*	send
Choose	getpeername	sethostent
connect	*getservbyaddr*	*setnetent*
endhostent	*getservbyname*	*setservent*
endnetent	*getservbyport*	*setsockopt*
gethostbyaddr	*getservent*	shutdown
gethostbyname	getsockname	socket
gethostent	*getsockopt*	*socketpair*
getnetbyaddr	listen	

Networking – System V

msgctl	*msgsnd*	*semop*	*shmread*
msgget	*semctl*	*shmctl*	*shmwrite*
msgrcv	*semget*	*shmget*	

Process management

alarm	*fork*	*setpgrp*	*wait*
chdir	*getlogin*	*setpriority*	*waitpid*
chroot	*getpgrp*	**sleep**	**warn**

die	*getppid*	*syscall*
exec	*getpriority*	***system***
exit	*kill*	*umask*

Control Flow Modifiers

The control flow modifiers include commands for selection (conditional evaluation), repetition (looping), and movement within a block.[1]

continue	foreach	next	while
else	goto	redo	
elsif	if	unless	
for	last	until	

Inline execution (`backquoted commands`)

MacPerl has a limited capability to handle constructs like `command`, if you have ToolServer (and MPW). Additionally, whether you have ToolServer or not, a few commands are specifically implemented (emulated, really) by MacPerl. Each is described below as if it were a function. Remember that these commands use backquotes, not parentheses!

These commands may not be portable to platforms other than Mac OS. `pwd` and `hostname` should be available under Unix Perl. Unix systems have the stty command, but its options vary; read the manual. `Directory` and `glob` should be assumed to be non-portable.

`Directory`	**`hostname`**	**`stty raw`**
`glob`	**`pwd`**	**`stty sane`**

Synopses

Answer

```
MacPerl::Answer(PROMPT)
MacPerl::Answer(PROMPT, BUTTON1, BUTTON2, BUTTON3)
```

Puts up a dialog box with a message (PROMPT) and a choice of 1, 2, or 3 buttons for the user to click.

---

[1] goto is an "actual" function.

Ask

```
MacPerl::Ask(PROMPT, DEFAULT)
MacPerl::Ask(PROMPT)
```

Asks the user for a string. Returns undef if the dialog is cancelled.

chdir

```
chdir(EXPR)
```

Changes the working directory to EXPR, if possible.

chmod

```
chmod(EXPR, FILE)
chmod(EXPR, LIST)
```

This function has limited meaning under MacPerl. Disabling write permission is mapped to locking a file (or a list of files). For example:

```
chmod(0444, 'foo');        #   lock the file
chmod(0666, 'foo');        # unlock the file
```

chomp

```
chomp(VARIABLE)
chomp(LIST)
chomp
```

Removes the line ending character (corresponding to the current value of $/; the default is \n). Returns the number of characters removed. If VARIABLE is omitted, it chomps $_. If you chomp a list, each element is chomped.

Choose

```
MacPerl::Choose(DOMAIN, TYPE, PROMPT, CONSTRAINT,
                FLAGS, DEFAULT)
MacPerl::Choose(DOMAIN, TYPE, PROMPT, CONSTRAINT,
                FLAGS)
MacPerl::Choose(DOMAIN, TYPE, PROMPT, CONSTRAINT)
MacPerl::Choose(DOMAIN, TYPE, PROMPT)
```

Puts up a modal dialog, prompting the user to choose a network address. DOMAIN specifies the communication domain, as in socket(). TYPE is ignored by current domains. PROMPT is a message that will appear in the dialog. CONSTRAINT may be set to a packed value to restrict the types of acceptable addresses.

Choose was used primarily for networking and GUI purposes. However, the Socket module and various Mac Toolbox modules are now recommended for these uses.

close

```
close(FILEHANDLE)
```

Closes the file associated with FILEHANDLE.

closedir

```
closedir(DIRHANDLE)
```

Closes the directory (folder) associated with DIRHANDLE.

continue

```
continue
```

Repetition control flow modifier. See: while.

dbmclose

```
dbmclose(HASH)
```

Breaks the binding between a DBM file and HASH.

dbmopen

```
dbmopen(HASH, DBNAME, MODE)
```

Binds one of various types of database (DB) file to HASH. DBNAME is the name of the database. On Unix systems, if the database does not exist, it is created with permissions as specified by MODE (modified by the umask). File permissions are unsupported in MacPerl. If you don't plan to port your script to Unix, just pick a reasonable value (e.g., 0666).

defined

```
defined(EXPR)
defined
```

Returns a Boolean value telling whether EXPR has a value other than the undefined value undef. If EXPR is omitted, $_ is checked.

die

```
die(LIST)
die()
```

Prints the value of LIST to STDERR and exits with the current value of $! (errno). See also: warn.

Directory

```
`Directory`
```

Returns the current directory, followed by a newline. Same as `pwd`.

DoAppleScript

```
MacPerl::DoAppleScript(SCRIPT)
```

Executes an AppleScript script, SCRIPT. The AppleScript script code is usually presented as a string, if short, or within a here document.

each

```
each(HASH)
```

In list context, returns a two element array consisting of the key and value for the next element of HASH. In scalar context, returns only the key. See also: keys, values.

elsif

```
elsif (EXPR2) { ... }
```

Conditional control flow modifier. See: if for details.

else

```
else { ... }
```

Conditional control flow modifier. See: if, unless for details.

eof

```
eof(FILEHANDLE)
eof()
eof
```

The eof function returns true if the next read on FILEHANDLE will return end of file (or if FILEHANDLE is not open). Without an argument, eof returns the end of file status for the last file read.

Unlike many Perl functions, `eof` behaves differently if it is given an empty list as an argument, that is, `eof` and `eof()` may not produce the same result! Within a `while (<>)` loop, iterating across the files in `@ARGV`, `eof` without parentheses will test the status of *each* file. In contrast, `eof()` will only test the status of the *last* file in the list. In this case, `eof` without parentheses is equivalent to `eof(ARGV)`.

FAccess

```
MacPerl::FAccess(FILE, CMD, ARGS)
```

This function is only available when using the MacPerl MPW tool; it is not supported by the standalone application. `FAccess` manipulates various file information. To get the command constants, it is convenient to `require "FAccess.ph"`.

for

```
for (EXPR; CONDITION; EXPR2) { ... }
```

Repetition control flow modifier. Upon startup of a `for` loop, the initial state is set by `EXPR` and the truth of `CONDITION` is checked. If the condition is true, the block is executed. On the next and all subsequent iterations, `EXPR2` is evaluated and `CONDITION` is checked again. If `CONDITION` is still true, the block is evaluated again. The loop will continue, evaluating `EXPR2` each time, for as long as `CONDITION` ramains true. See also: `foreach`.

foreach

```
foreach SCALAR (LIST) { ... }
```

Repetition control flow modifier. A `foreach` loop is used to evaluate a block of code for each of a known list of scalars, typically the elements of an array or hash. Note that the loop variable, `SCALAR`, becomes a reference to the actual list element under consideration; modifying this variable will modify the original array or hash! See also: `for`.

Note: `for` and `foreach` are actually synonyms for the same command, and can be used interchangeably with the same syntax. Conventionally, however, they are most commonly used as we have shown.

getc

```
getc(FILEHANDLE)
getc()
```

Returns a string containing the next character (byte) read from FILE HANDLE. If no filehandle is specified, reads from STDIN. Returns a null string at end of file. See also: stty.

GetFileInfo

```
MacPerl::GetFileInfo(FILE)
```

In scalar context, returns the file type. In array context, returns (creator, type).

glob

```
glob(PATTERN)
<PATTERN>
`glob PATTERN`
```

Expands the glob PATTERN and returns a list of expanded file names. Only the "*" and "?" metacharacters are supported; Option-x is an (MPW-style) alternative to "*". For example, the glob pattern <*.pl> will match all files in the current directory whose names end in .pl.

goto

```
goto LABEL
goto EXPR
goto &SUB
```

A goto statement jumps to the specified location in a program and resumes execution at that point. Typically, the first form is used; goto jumps to the statement labeled LABEL. If an expression, EXPR, is given, this provides a label name whose scope is resolved dynamically.

The last form, goto &SUB, substitutes a call to subroutine SUB for the currently running subroutine. This is typically used by AUTOLOAD and not by mere mortal Perl programs.

hostname

```
`hostname`
```

Returns the name of the current Macintosh (if TCP/IP is running).

if

```
if (EXPR)      { ... }
elsif (EXPR2) { ... }
else           { ... }
```

Conditional control flow modifier. An `if` statement evaluates an expression, `EXPR`. If true, the following block of code is executed. If false, an `elsif` statement, if present, will be evaluated, testing `EXPR2` expression for truth, and so on.

Any number of `elsif` statements may be included; each is evaluated only if all preceding **conditions** were false. When any condition is true, that block is executed; any succeeding conditions are ignored.

An `else` statement may occur at the very end, to "catch" a condition that evaluated false through all preceding tests. See also: `unless`.

index

```
index(STRING, SUBSTRING, POSITION)
index(STRING, SUBSTRING)
```

Returns the position of the first occurrence of `SUBSTRING` in `STRING` at or after `POSITION`. If `POSITION` is omitted, starts searching from the beginning of the string.

keys

```
keys(HASH)
```

Returns an array consisting of all the keys of the named hash. See also: `each`, `values`.

last

```
last
```

Control flow modifier, repetition. The `last` statement forces a loop to end prematurely, skipping to the end of the execution block as if this were the last iteration (e.g., as if the test condition had returned false). If present, a `continue` block will *not* be evaluated. See also: `continue`, `for`, `next`, `redo`, `while`.

length

```
length(EXPR)
length()
```

Returns the length in characters of EXPR, or of $_ if EXPR is omitted.

LoadExternals

```
MacPerl::LoadExternals(LIBFILE)
```

Loads XCMD and XFCN extensions contained in file LIBFILE, which is searched along the same path as it would be for a `require`. The extensions are made accessible in the current package, unless they contain an explicit package name.

localtime

```
localtime(EXPR)
localtime()
```

Converts a time as returned by `time()` into a 9-element array with the time adjusted for the local time zone. If EXPR is omitted, uses the current time. The array returned is typically used as:

```
($sec, $min, $hour, $mday, $mon, $year, $wday,
  $yday, $isdst) = localtime(time);
```

All array elements are returned are numeric; $mon has the range 0..11; $wday has the range 0..6 with Sunday as day 0. $year is the number of years since 1900; that is, in the year 2000, $year will have the value 100 (No Y2K problem!).

m//

```
m/PATTERN/gimosx
/PATTERN/gimosx
```

Search a string for a pattern match and return true or false. Options are:

g	Global (i.e., replace all occurrences).
i	Case-insensitive pattern matching.
m	Treat the string as multiple lines.
o	Compile PATTERN only once.
s	Treat string as single line.
x	Use extended regular expressions, allowing blanks and comments.

MakeFSSpec

`MacPerl::MakeFSSpec(PATH)`

Encodes a path name into a string (volume #, directory #, File name) which is guaranteed to be unique for every file. Don't store this encoding between runs of MacPerl!

MakePath

`MacPerl::MakePath(FSSPEC)`

Implements the inverse of `MacPerl::MakeFSSpec()` (i.e., turns an encoding into a path name).

mkdir

`mkdir(DIRNAME, MODE)`

Creates the directory (folder) specified by `DIRNAME`. On Unix systems, the directory permissions are specified by `MODE` (as modified by the umask). Directory permissions are unsupported in MacPerl. If you don't plan to port your script to Unix, pick a reasonable value (e.g., `0755`).

my

`my(EXPR)`

Declares the listed variables to be private (lexically local) to the enclosing block or subroutine. If more than one value is listed, the list *must* be placed in parentheses.

next

`next`

Control flow modifier, repetition. The `next` statement forces a loop to immediately begin the next iteration, skipping the remainder of the execution block. If present, a `continue` block will be evaluated before the condition is tested, as if the loop had reached the end of this iteration normally. See also: `continue`, `for`, `last`, `redo`, `while`.

open

`open(FILEHANDLE, EXPR)`
`open(FILEHANDLE)`

Opens a file named by `EXPR`, associating it with `FILEHANDLE`.

If EXPR is omitted, the scalar variable of the same name as FILEHANDLE contains the filename. Insert extra characters (e.g., **>**) before the filename (EXPR) to control the access mode.

<   open for reading (default, may be omitted)
>   open for writing
>>   open for appending

On Unix systems, EXPR may begin or end with a pipe symbol, |, in which case it is interpreted as a command. This feature is not supported by MacPerl unless you are using ToolServer with MPW.

opendir

```
opendir(DIRHANDLE, EXPR)
```

Opens a directory named by EXPR, associating it with DIRHANDLE.

Pick

```
MacPerl::Pick(PROMPT, VALUES)
```

PROMPTs the user to pick a choice from a list of choices (VALUES). Returns undef if the dialog is cancelled.

print

```
print FILEHANDLE (LIST)
print (LIST)
print
```

Prints a string or a comma-separated list of strings. If FILEHANDLE is omitted, prints to the standard output (or to the last selected output channel). If LIST is omitted, prints $_.

printf

```
printf FILEHANDLE (FORMAT, LIST)
printf(FORMAT, LIST)
```

Prints a formatted string or a comma-separated list of strings. If FILE HANDLE is omitted, prints to the standard output (or the last selected output channel). Format specifiers include:

%s   a string
%c   a single character (specified by the given number)
%d   a (signed) integer (in decimal)

%f	a floating-point number (fixed decimal notation)
%e	an exponential floating-point number (scientific notation)
%g	a floating-point number, in %e or %f notation
%u	an unsigned integer, in decimal
%o	an unsigned integer, in octal
%x	an unsigned integer, in hexadecimal
%%	a (literal) percent sign

pwd

`pwd`

Print Working Directory. `pwd` returns the name of the current directory, followed by a newline. See also: `Directory`

Quit

MacPerl::Quit(LEVEL)

Controls MacPerl "Quit" functionality. If LEVEL is 0, don't quit after ending the script. If 1, quit if running under a runtime version; if 2, always quit. If LEVEL is 3, quit if this was the first script to be run since starting MacPerl.

readdir

readdir(DIRHANDLE)

Returns the next directory entry (filename, folder name, or alias) for the directory associated with DIRHANDLE. If used in a list context, returns an array containing all the rest of the entries in the directory.

redo

redo

Repetition control flow modifier. Restarts the current loop block without evaluating the condition. If present, the continue block is not executed. See also: continue, for, last, next, while.

rename

rename(OLDNAME, NEWNAME)

Changes the name of a directory (folder) or file. Returns 1 if successful, otherwise 0. This function does not work across file system (volume) boundaries, nor will it rename a volume.

Reply

```
MacPerl::Reply(ANSWER)
```

Replies to current DoScript request. Useful when calling Perl scripts from other applications.

return

```
return(EXPR)
return()
```

Returns from a subroutine with the value of the given EXPR. If EXPR is omitted, returns an empty list in list context, an undefined value in scalar context, or nothing in void context.

rmdir

```
rmdir(DIRNAME)
rmdir()
```

Deletes the directory specified by DIRNAME if it contains no files. Returns 1 upon success; otherwise it returns 0 and sets $! (errno). If DIRNAME is omitted, uses $_.

s///

```
s/PATTERN/REPLACEMENT/egimosx
```

Searches a string for a PATTERN, and if found, replaces that pattern with REPLACEMENT, returning the number of substitutions made. Options include those for m// as well as:

e   Evaluate the right side as an expression.

scalar

```
scalar(EXPR)
```

Returns the value of EXPR, interpreted in a scalar context.

SetFileInfo

```
MacPerl::SetFileInfo(CREATOR,TYPE,FILE...)
```

Sets the file TYPE and CREATOR IDs of the FILE(s).

shift

```
shift(ARRAY)
shift()
```

Shifts off the front (zeroeth) value and returns it, shortening the array by 1 and moving everything down. If ARRAY is omitted, shifts @ARGV (in the main program) or @_ (in a subroutine). See also: unshift.

sleep

```
sleep(EXPR)
sleep()
```

Causes the script to sleep for EXPR seconds (or forever, if EXPR is omitted).

sort

```
sort(LIST)
sort SUBNAME (LIST)
sort {BLOCK} (LIST)
```

Sorts LIST and returns the sorted list value. By default, sorts in standard string comparison order (undefined values, null strings, and ASCII character codes, in that order). This is a case-sensitive comparison!

If SUBNAME is specified, it gives the name of a subroutine to use in determining how to sort the list. In place of a SUBNAME, you can provide a BLOCK of code as in-line sort specification.

split

```
split(/PATTERN/, EXPR, LIMIT)
split(/PATTERN/, EXPR)
split(/PATTERN/)
split()
```

Splits a string into an array of substrings, returning the array. If LIMIT is specified and is non-negative, splits into no more than that many fields (but possibly fewer). If LIMIT is unspecified, trailing null fields are stripped. If EXPR is omitted, splits the $_ string. If PATTERN is omitted, splits on whitespace (after skipping any leading whitespace). If LIMIT is negative, it is treated as arbitrarily large.

sprintf

```
sprintf(FORMAT, LIST)
```

Like `printf()`, but returns a string , rather than printing it.

stat

```
stat(FILEHANDLE)
stat(EXPR)
stat()
```

Returns a 13-element array giving the status information for a file, either associated with a FILEHANDLE, or named by EXPR. If no argument is given, returns status of $_. Returns a null list if the stat fails. Several of the returned items are not defined identically to the Unix version. Items which would be meaningless under Mac OS are set to "reasonable" values to enhance portability.

The array returned is typically used as:

```
($dev, $ino, $mode, $nlink, $uid, $gid, $rdev, $size,
 $atime, $mtime, $ctime, $blksize, $blocks)
    = stat($filename);
```

where each element has the following meaning under Mac OS:

$dev	value reference number (vRefNum)
$ino	File/Directory ID (fileID/dirID)
$mode	file mode (see below)
$nlink	number of links (meaningless; set to 1)
$uid	numeric user ID (meaningless; set to 0)
$gid	numeric group ID (meaningless; set to 0)
$rdev	device identifier (meaningless; set to null)
$size	total size of file, in bytes
$atime	access time (meaningless; set to same value as $mtime)
$mtime	last modify time in seconds since 00:00:00 January 1, 1904
$ctime	file creation time in seconds since 00:00:00 January 1, 1904
$blksize	allocation block size
$blocks	number of blocks required to hold data (see below)

MacPerl guarantees that the $dev and/or the $ino field will differ if two different entities are stated. The file mode is 0777 for directories and files of type APPL/appe. It is 0666 for documents, except for locked ones, which are 0444. $blocks may be calculated as:

```
$blocks = int(($size + $blksize-1) / $blksize);
```

stty

```
`stty raw`
`stty sane`
```

Supported in the standalone MacPerl application. `stty raw` sets the MacPerl console (output) window to "raw" mode, i.e., it turns off echoing and interpretation of characters. In raw mode, a Perl program sees all characters entered, including backspace or delete characters and RETURN as if they were part of the input! This is useful for routines that ask for a secret password or request the user to "press any key".

`stty sane` restores normal mode. The same functionality is also available as `stty -sane` and `stty -raw` if you prefer thinking in those terms. In the code below, getc() reads a single character from standard input; getc() returns null at end of file. With `stty raw`, "no key pressed yet" will be interpreted as EOF. We use while to force the script to wait until a key is pressed.

```
print 'press any key to continue ';
`stty raw`;
$char = getc() while ($char eq '');
`stty sane`;
print 'Thank you';
```

sub

```
sub NAME {BLOCK}
sub NAME
sub {BLOCK}
```

Provides a subroutine definition or declaration. If BLOCK is omitted, this is a declaration only; be sure to define the subroutine eventually. If NAME is omitted, defines an anonymous subroutine.

substr

```
substr(EXPR, OFFSET, LENGTH)
substr(EXPR, OFFSET)
```

Extracts a substring out of EXPR and returns it.

The first character is at `OFFSET`; if `OFFSET` is negative, `substr` starts that far from the end of the string. `LENGTH`, if given, is the maximum length of the substring; otherwise, everything from `OFFSET` to the end of the string is returned.

symlink

symlink(FILENAME, NEWFILE)

Creates a new filename symbolically linked to `FILENAME`. Returns 1 if successful, otherwise 0. Under Mac OS, `symlink()` creates an *alias*.

Note: Mac OS aliases are not identical to Unix symbolic links. If an aliased file is renamed, the alias will reconfigure to point to the new name. Aliases are absolute (referenced to the root of a volume) and are tied to particular devices. If moved, they will continue to point to the original device (e.g., a shared volume or removable media).

system

system(LIST)

Asks the operating system to execute the commands in `LIST` and waits for the process to complete and return before continuing with the current program. The `system` function is commonly used under Unix, but it is not directly supported by MacPerl. It can be used with the MacPerl MPW Tool (in a limited fashion) if you have ToolServer installed.

tr//

tr/PATTERN/REPLACEMENT/cds

Translate all occurrences of the characters found in the `PATTERN` with the corresponding character in the `REPLACEMENT` and return the number of translations made. Options are:

c   Complement the pattern (match characters not in `PATTERN`)
d   Delete any characters found (and not replaced)
s   Squash/squeeze repetitions of replaced characters

time

time()

Returns the number of non-leap seconds since the system's "epoch".

Under Mac OS, the epoch is `00:00:00` local time, January 1, 1904. On Unix systems, the epoch is `00:00:00` UTC, January 1, 1970.[2]

times

```
times()
```

Returns a four-element array. Under Mac OS, only the first element returned (user time) is non-zero. The array returned is typically used as:

```
($user, $system, $cuser, $csystem) = times();
```

unless

```
unless (EXPR) { ... }
else          { ... }
```

Conditional control flow modifier. An `unless` statement evaluates an expression, `EXPR`. If false, the following block of code is executed. There is no "`elsunless`" clause. See also: `if`.

unlink

```
unlink(LIST)
unlink()
```

Deletes a list of files. Returns the number of files successfully deleted. If `LIST` is omitted, uses `$_`.

unshift

```
unshift(ARRAY, LIST)
```

Prepends `LIST` to the front of `ARRAY`, returning the new number of elements in the array. See also: `shift`.

until

```
until (EXPR) { ... }
```

Repetition control flow modifier. Repeatedly executes a block of code as long as `EXPR` is false. See also: `next`, `last`, `redo`, `while`.

---

[2] UTC, Coordinated Universal Time, is the new time standard. See `www.boulder`
`.nist.gov/timefreq/faq/q5.htm` for the history of the choice of acronym.

use

```
use MODULE
use MODULE LIST
```

Includes the named `MODULE` into your program, loading it into memory and importing any subroutines and variables included in that module. The `MODULE` name must not be quoted. If a `LIST` is given, only the elements of that list are added to the current namespace.

utime

```
utime(ATIME, MTIME, LIST)
```

Under Unix, changes the access and modification times (`ATIME` and `MTIME`) on each file in `LIST`. Under Mac OS, only `MTIME` is updated (use the same values for both times). The time values must be *numeric*. To get the current time value, use `time()`.

values

```
values(HASH)
```

Returns an array consisting of all the values of the named hash. See also: `each`, `keys`.

Volumes

```
MacPerl::Volumes()
```

In scalar context, returns the filesystem specification (FSSPEC) of the startup volume. In list context, returns FSSPECs of all volumes.

wantarray

```
wantarray()
```

Returns true if the currently executing subroutine was called in list context. Returns false if the call was made in scalar context.

warn

```
warn(LIST)
```

Prints the value of `LIST` to `STDERR` but does not exit. See also: `die`.

while

```
while (EXPR) { ... }
continue      { ... }
```

Repetition control flow modifier. A while statement repeatedly executes a block of code as long as EXPR is true. An optional continue statement may follow the block, to be executed every time the while block is continued, either by finishing ("falling off") or by an explicit command. See also: next, last, redo, until.

y//

```
y/PATTERN/REPLACEMENT/cds
```

Synonym for tr///. See tr/// for details.

Chapter 21:

- *Data Structures*
- *Format*
- *Input/Output*
- *Operating Environment*
- *Package Management*
- *Perl Interpreter*
- *Process Management*
- *Regular Expression*

Special Variables

Computer languages follow the extended Sapir-Whorf hypothesis, which states that because the Eskimos had 900 words for snow, they decided to move north.

– Dave Griffith

Perl has several dozen built-in "special" variables. Most of these are seldom used and thus impossible to remember. Complicating the situation further, these variables may have long ($INPUT_LINE_NUMBER), medium ($NR), or short ($.) names.[1]

Although the short names are quick to type, they have virtually no mnemonic value (What is $., anyway?). Worse, because they aren't alphabetical, they are difficult to look up in a printed index. So, we recommend that you use the medium or long names unless this begins to seem *very* tedious.

Perl supports the short (non-alphabetic) names by default. To use the English (i.e., medium or long) names, include this command at the start of your Perl script:

```
use English;
```

Note: Due to an implementation problem, use of the English.pm module causes Perl to act as if a "MATCH" variable has been used,

---

[1] The medium length names are borrowed, in general, from C and awk usage under the Unix operating system. Many of the short names are borrowed from sh, the Unix "Bourne shell".

slowing down any use of regular expressions in the script. Sigh. So, if you need the last bit of speed from your scripts, you may wish to avoid use of this module (until the bug is fixed :-).

Each entry begins with the applicable names, followed by a a summary of the variable's scope (e.g., global), access limitations (r-o or r/w), default value, and a short description. If the scope is given as global, you will need to localize the variable with `my()` or `local()` if you want to work with a more private copy in the current code block.

The access limitation designation, "r-o" (read-only) or r/w (read/write), is more prescriptive than descriptive: you may be able to write to a read-only variable, but we make no guarantees as to the results (nor do we recommend that you try it!).

Data Structures

These variables allow programs to affect the default behavior of certain operations related to data structures.

$LIST_SEPARATOR   (none)   **$ "**
    global, r/w, " " – character used to separate list elements when interpolated into a double-quoted string

$SUBSCRIPT_SEPARATOR   **$SUBSEP**   **$;**
    global, r/w, "\034" – character used to separate subscripts in (old) multi-dimensional array emulation

Format

Formats are a tool for creating printed reports, often in a page-oriented manner. The "output channel specific" variables below are relevant to specific filehandles. Thus, you must `select` the appropriate filehandle before you can use any of them.

With the exception of $ACCUMULATOR, all of the variables in this section can be set by a method whose name is the lower-case version of the variable name. For instance, these three commands are equivalent:

```
$FORMAT_FORMFEED = "\f";

format_formfeed HANDLE "\f";

HANDLE->format_formfeed("\f");
```

Formats are very useful for some tasks, but are excessively complicated for most output formatting jobs. Unless you need top-of-form processing or other format-specific features, consider using `print` or `printf`.

$ACCUMULATOR   (none)   **$^A**
    global, r-o, none – current value of the write accumulator

$FORMAT_FORMFEED   (none)   **$^L**
    global, r/w, `"\f"` – string to be output to force a formfeed

$FORMAT_LINE_BREAK_CHARACTERS   (none)   **$:**
    global, r/w, `" \n-"` – set of characters after which the line may be broken

$FORMAT_LINES_LEFT   (none)   **$-**
    output channel specific, r-o, none – number of printable lines left in the output page

$FORMAT_LINES_PER_PAGE   (none)   **$=**
    output channel specific, r/w, 60 – number of printable lines in the output page

$FORMAT_NAME   (none)   **$~**
    output channel specific, r-o, none – name of the current format

$FORMAT_PAGE_NUMBER   (none)   **$%**
    output channel specific, r-o, none – number of the current output page

$FORMAT_TOP_NAME   (none)   **$^**
    output channel specific, r-o, none – name of the current top-of-form format

Input/Output

(none)   **ARGV**   (none)
    global, r-o, none – filehandle that successively refers to files named in the command line (<> is shorthand for <ARGV>)

(none)   **DATA**   (none)
    global, r-o, system-dependent – filehandle for data encapsulated in a script file

(none)   **STDERR**   (none)
    global, r-o, system-dependent – filehandle for the "standard error" (output) stream

(none)   **STDIN**   (none)
   global, r-o, system-dependent – filehandle for the "standard input"
   stream

(none)   **STDOUT**   (none)
   global, r-o, system-dependent – filehandle for the "standard
   output" stream

(none)   (none)   _
   global, r-o, system-dependent – filehandle for data retrieved by a
   file, lstat, or test call

(none)   **@F**   (none)
   global within main, r-o, none – fields from the last input line, if
   autosplit (-a) mode is on

(none)   **$ARG**   **$_**
   global, r/w, none – default unspecified variable; used for I/O,
   pattern-matching, and miscellaneous other operations

(none)   **$ARGV**   (none)
   global, r-o, none – name of the file being read by <ARGV> or <>

$INPLACE_EDIT   (none)   **$^I**
   global, r-o, undefined – extension (if any) used for backup copies of
   files that are being edited "inplace" (see the -i command line
   flag); may be unset to disable inplace editing

$INPUT_LINE_NUMBER   **$NR**   **$.**
   global, r-o, none – number of the current input line

$INPUT_RECORD_SEPARATOR   **$RS**   **$/**
   global, r/w, "\n" – character used to separate input records

$LIST_SEPARATOR   (none)   **$"**
   global, r/w, " " – character used to separate list elements when
   interpolated into a double-quoted string

(none)   **$OFMT**   **$#**
   global, r/w, "%.14g" (approximately) – controls the format used
   by print in formatting numeric values; deprecated, use printf
   instead

$OUTPUT_AUTOFLUSH   (none)   **$|**

output channel specific, r/w, 0 – if non-zero, forces output to be
"unbuffered" (written immediately)

$OUTPUT_FIELD_SEPARATOR   **$OFS**   **$,**
global, r/w, " " – character used by print to separate fields

$OUTPUT_RECORD_SEPARATOR   **$ORS**   **$**
global, r/w, " " – character used by print to separate records

Operating Environment

These variables allow a Perl script to research (and occasionally modify)
the environment under which it is running.

(none)   **@ARGV**   (none)
global, r-o, none – the script's command-line arguments

(none)   **@INC**   (none)
global, r-o, none – names of files that have been included (e.g., by
do or require)

(none)   **%INC**   (none)
global, r-o, none – path information ("requested file" -> "full path
name") for files that have been included (e.g., by do or require)

(none)   **%ENV**   (none)
global, r-o, none – environment variables ("name" -> "value")

(none)   **%SIG**   (none)
global, r/w, none – used to set signal handlers ("signal name" ->
"handler name")

$BASETIME   (none)   **$^T**
global, r-o, none – starting time for the script's execution (in seconds
since the "epoch"); note that the Mac and Unix epochs differ!

$EXECUTABLE_NAME   (none)   **$^X**
global, r-o, none – name of the Perl interpreter, as invoked

$EXTENDED_OS_ERROR   (none)   **$^E**
global, r-o, none – (possibly) more descriptive error information
than $ERRNO; used for information on Toolbox modules

$OS_ERROR   **$ERRNO**   **$!**

global, r-o, none – value of the system `errno` variable (if evaluated numerically) or the corresponding system error message (if evaluated as a string)

$OSNAME   (none)   **$^O**
global, r-o, none – intended operating system for this port of the Perl interpreter

$PROGRAM_NAME   (none)   **$0**
global, r-o, none – name of the file containing the current Perl script

Package Management

These variables are used to support Perl's "package" facility.

@EXPORT   (none)   (none)
lexical, r/w, none – names of symbols that are exported by default from this package (try to use $EXPORT_OK, instead!)

@EXPORT_FAIL   (none)   (none)
lexical, r/w, none – names of symbols that cannot be exported from this package

@EXPORT_OK   (none)   (none)
lexical, r/w, none – names of symbols that are exported upon request from this package

%EXPORT_TAGS   (none)   (none)
lexical, r/w, none – sets of symbols that are exported upon request from this package

@ISA   (none)   (none)
lexical, r/w, empty – names of this package's base classes

%OVERLOAD   (none)   (none)
lexical, r/w, none – (was) used to overload a package's operators; now subsumed by the `overload` pragma

Perl Interpreter

These variables reflect (and occasionally control) the operation of the Perl interpreter. Naive programmers beware!

(none)   (none)   **$[**
global, r/w, 0 – index of the first element in an array

(none)   (none)   **$^M**
   global, r/w, none – arcane way to allocate memory in emergencies

(none)   (none)   **$^H**
   global, r-o, none – arcane compiler hints related to use of pragmas

$DEBUGGING   (none)   **$^D**
   global, r/w, 0 – numeric value of the debugging flags (see the -D
   command line flag)

$EVAL_ERROR   (none)   **$@**
   global, r-o, none – syntax error message from the preceding eval

$PERL_VERSION   (none)   **$]**
   global, r-o, none – version.patchlevel (e.g., 5.00401)

$PERLDB   (none)   **$^P**
   global, r-o, none – Perl interpreter's internal debugger flag

$WARNING   (none)   **$^W**
   global, r-o, 0 – value of the warning switch (boolean)

Process Management

These variables are, in general, only relevant on systems that support Unix-style process management. MacPerl does not currently do this.

$CHILD_ERROR   (none)   **$?**
   global, r-o, none – status returned by last sub-process

$EFFECTIVE_GROUP_ID   **$EGID**   **$)**
   global, r-o, none – effective group ID (EGID) of the current process

$EFFECTIVE_USER_ID   **$EUID**   **$>**
   global, r-o, none – effective user ID (EUID) of the current process

$PROCESS_ID   **$PID**   **$$**
   global, r-o, none – process ID (PID) of the current process

$REAL_USER_ID   **$UID**   **$<**
   global, r-o, none – real user ID (UID) of the current process

$REAL_GROUP_ID   **$GID**   **$(**
   global, r-o, none – real group ID (GID) of the current process

$SYSTEM_FD_MAX   (none)   **$^F**

global, r-o, 2 – maximum system file descriptor (largest file
descriptor passed to execed processes)

Regular Expression

These (read-only) variables are set by regular expression operations. The
variables $[1-9] are the most generally useful, containing text matched by
the corresponding set of parentheses in the preceding regular expression.

Each of these variables, except for $*, has a local value in the current
block, i.e., they are dynamically scoped. They do not need to be localized
with local() or my().

> **Note:** Use of the $MATCH ($&), $PREMATCH ($`), or $POSTMATCH ($`)
> variables anywhere in a Perl script will cause perl to save copies of the
> input strings to all regular expressions (in case they might be needed
> later). This can cause affected scripts to run substantially slower than
> they otherwise might! In short, don't use these variables casually.

(none)   (none)   **$[1-9]**
    dynamic, r-o, none – text found by this set of parentheses

$LAST_PAREN_MATCH   (none)   **$+**
    dynamic, r-o, none – text found by the last matching set of
    parentheses

$MATCH   (none)   **$&**
    dynamic, r-o, none – text found by the last successful pattern match

$MULTILINE_MATCHING   (none)   **$***
    global, r/w, 0 – set to 1 to allow multi-line matching within strings;
    deprecated, use /m and/or /s, instead

$PREMATCH   (none)   **$`**
    dynamic, r-o, none – string preceding the text found by the last
    successful pattern match

$POSTMATCH   (none)   **$'**
    dynamic, r-o, none – string following the text found by the last
    successful pattern match

Chapter 22:

- *What Is MPW?*
- *Using Perl With MPW*
- *Install The MPW Tool*
- *Examine The Folder*
- *Complete The Installation*
- *Try Out The MPW Tool*
- *Special Features Of The MPW Tool*

MPW Perl

Even workhouses have their aristocracy

– English proverb

This chapter describes the installation of the MacPerl MPW tool, then provides a brief "get acquainted" walkthrough. It also describes any peculiarities of using Perl under MPW which are not present in the MacPerl stand-alone application. If you already have a working copy of MPW Perl on your disk, you may want to skip this chapter. Or, you may wish to read the section on features and differences, in case you might see something new.

What Is MPW?

MPW, the Macintosh Programmer's Workshop, is Apple's command line interpreter for the Macintosh. It has been popular with Macintosh developers for years, but has only recently become available to the general public. The MPW program is referred to as the MPW shell.

MPW includes a built-in text editor with (its own interpretation of) regular expression processing, a procedure for writing scripts in the MPW command language, environment variables, and a set of MPW "tools" (specialized commands, written in languages such as C). MPW Perl is one such tool.

MPW uses windows, known as worksheets, which are always mapped to files; writing to any open worksheet is treated exactly as writing to a TEXT file. Unlike other shell-based environments, such as Unix, the MPW shell *is* the editor; the MPW editor is the shell. Commands are executed by selecting the text to be executed in any open worksheet and pressing ENTER on the keyboard.

Note that ENTER and RETURN are distinct in MPW. MPW treats RETURN the same way any text editor or word processor would; it's just a way to get to the next line. In fact, each MPW Worksheet is simply a text editor window. That is, until you select one or more lines of text and press ENTER. Then, *voila!*, MPW is also a command line processor (a **shell**).[1] For those who don't like to reach so far (or don't have an ENTER key), cmd-RETURN is synonymous with ENTER.

MPW's interaction mode, which draws heavily from both Smalltalk and Unix, can be a little disconcerting at first. You'll soon get used to the power and flexibility of the MPW editor, however. Let's say that you're typing along, editing a Perl script, and you can't remember the exact name of a file you want to open. Simply execute (with ENTER) the `files` command (right there in the middle of your editor session), then select and delete the extraneous filenames, leaving only the name you wanted. The filenames are even pre-quoted by MPW, as necessary, to protect spaces!

When MPW is acting like an editor, you will see the words MPW Shell in a little box in the upper left corner of the window's toolbar. When MPW is executing a program, the contents of this box will change to display the name of the active program (e.g., Perl). If the current Worksheet window ever seems to be ignoring you, check the contents of this "current process" box; chances are, the MPW shell is busy running a program.

The MPW editor is programmer oriented, with provisions for highlighting reserved words for various languages (Perl included), automatic indenting after a return, and selection of blocked code by double clicking on a delimiter. If you select the text of a filename, an item in the File menu reads "open selection" and will open that file. You can even add menu items to execute your own scripts!

Until recently, MPW was available only to Apple's registered developers. Now, however, it can be downloaded freely from Apple's Developer World site, `devworld.apple.com` (under Developer Tools), or by direct FTP from `ftp://ftp.apple.com` by following the path:

```
/devworld/Tool_Chest/Core_Mac_OS_Tools/MPW_etc.
```

---

[1] If you're only executing one line, you don't actually have to select it. Just make sure that the text insertion character, |, is positioned on the appropriate line.

Using Perl With MPW

When you use MPW with Perl, you'll be using the MPW `perl` tool, not the MacPerl standalone application. MPW tools are binary executables which work only from the MPW command line. If you try to double-click an MPW tool in the Finder, you will simply launch MPW. MPW tools have the type MPST and the creator 'MPS ' (note the trailing space!).

Tools are invoked with an MPW command which starts with the name of the tool (e.g., `perl`). The name of the tool may be specified as a full pathname, a relative pathname, or simply by the tool's name, in which case MPW will search for the tool in the directories listed in the global variable {Commands}. The command line can also include additional arguments which are separated by spaces.

> **Note:** Because Macintosh filenames may also contain spaces, some quoting may be needed. Macintosh filenames may also contain quote characters, so the quoting can get fancy.

A file which contains MPW commands is called a script. Scripts are always of type TEXT. A script can be executed by giving its filename on the MPW command line. Arguments can be passed and the script can contain looping commands, including recursive invocations of itself.

You can create scripts using the MPW editor or create them with another editor and run them under MPW. MPW Perl scripts may contain only Perl code, or a combination of other MPW shell commands and Perl code (in which case they are shell scripts, not Perl scripts). In the latter case, the scripts can only be executed by MPW, not by the standalone MacPerl app.

If you write an MPW Perl script, it is likely that you will also write an MPW script to invoke it. In many cases, you may find that an MPW script can handle system-level tasks more directly than can a MacPerl script. Doing the top-level script in Perl or in MPW is a personal preference.

Perl scripts must be saved as text and run from the MPW command line using the `perl` tool. You can't save them as droplets or Runtime programs, and you can't pass arguments from the MPW command line to standalone MacPerl droplets or Runtime versions.

Features

MPW provides a very good code editor. The editor displays Perl reserved words in a highlighted color (reserved words in a comment are also highlighted; sigh). Double-clicking on a variety of bracketing characters (e.g., } {] [ ) ( ) selects the text all the way down (or up) to the matching bracket.

MPW handles file name generation quite well. Unfortunately, MPW's filename generation and regular expressions use yet another new set of symbols. The "option" characters of the Macintosh keyboard are used for characters such as the escape character, ∂, and the "wild card" character, $\approx$. It can be a challenge to keep the regular expressions for Perl and MPW separate.

The MPW commando interface for formatting an MPW command or the call to a tool is pretty good. It would be possible to create a commando resource for Perl, but not so easy for a finished Perl script.

The SET and EXPORT commands in MPW allow variable use. Values are taken to be text, except that simple arithmetic is allowed in looping constructs. Several variables are assigned by MPW itself. The { } construct is used in command lines to identify environment variables. {Worksheet} is the full pathname of the current worksheet window, which is always open. {Active} is the name of the active window.

When MPW is started up, several variables are set in a script named MPW: Startup. You can and should set up your own variables (e.g., to point to regularly used MacPerl items). Depending on your MPW version (see the main Startup script), you may be able to create files named UserStartup•xxx, or place items in the Startup Items folder for execution.

> **Note:** Exported variables only apply to the MPW environment and will disappear when MPW is quit. If you're familiar with accessing CGI variables as exported environment variables in Unix, this won't work on the Macintosh!

Install The MPW Tool

If you have downloaded a recent copy of the MPW tool from an Internet FTP or WWW site, it will generally be compressed and encoded (e.g., with **StuffIt** (from Aladdin Systems) and **BinHex**). In this case, you will need to decode and uncompress the archive before continuing. StuffIt Expander, an expansion utility, is available on our CD-ROM, from many Macintosh archive sites, or from Aladdin Systems at www.aladdinsys.com.

The MPW tool on the enclosed CD-ROM has already been uncompressed and decoded into a double-clickable Installer application. As when installing the standalone application, you will need to launch the Installer and review the notes for any important last-minute notes, then choose the installation location.

> **Note:** Be sure to install the MPW tool on the same disk as the MacPerl application.The Installation process for the MPW tool has two parts. In Part 1, you will run the Installer application. The Installer will install the MPW tool, along with an MPW-based configuration script which you must then run (as Part 2) to complete the installation.

> If you have previously installed MPW and the MacPerl MPW tool, be sure to look these scripts over carefully before you execute them, to ensure that nothing they do will conflict with any startup scripts or configurations you have already put in place.

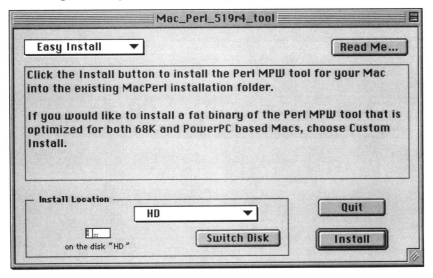

Steps to Install the MPW tool (Part 1)

1. Double-click the Installer application to start the installation. Be sure to review the instructions in the initial screen for any important last-minute notes. Print or save these notes, then click Continue.

2. Choose the same volume and folder where you installed the MacPerl app, then click Install. (The Read Me... button will take you back to the notes you reviewed in step 1.)

3. The Installer will install the MacPerl MPW tool along with an MPW-based configuration and install script which you must run to complete the installation.

4. When the Installer completes successfully, choose Quit. You do not need to restart your Macintosh.

Examine The Folder

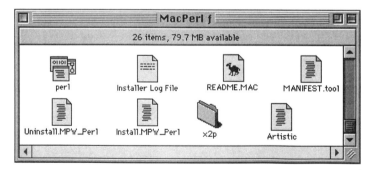

The MPW tool Installer places some new (MPW-specific) files into the MacPerl ƒ folder (created previously by the MacPerl app installation). Open the folder, if need be, and examine the contents again. (Scroll to the bottom if you don't see the new files right away).

Before you continue, take a look at the files that were installed:

- The **perl** tool is what you will be using when you run Perl under MPW.

- The README files, **README.MAC** and **README**, are identical to those installed with the same version of the MacPerl app. They contain release notes, information on known problems, special comments about the current release, etc. If you have not already done so, be sure to look at the README files. The Perl Artistic License is also duplicated here in the file **Artistic**.

- The **x2p** folder contains two related MPW programs that you may find useful when using MacPerl. **find2perl** is an MPW script that will convert an MPW `find` command to equivalent Perl code. **a2p** is an MPW tool for converting programs written in Awk to Perl.

- **Install.MPW_Perl** is an MPW script which we will use in a few moments to complete the installation process.

- **Uninstall.MPW_Perl** is an MPW script which you may run later, if you ever decide to uninstall the MacPerl MPW tool.

Complete The Installation

In order to complete the MPW tool installation, you will need to launch MPW, then run the Install.MPW_Perl script. The script will create a configuration file, which you may edit as needed. Run the script a second time, processing the configuration file and completing the installation process.

If you have not previously installed MPW, you must do so now before you can continue with the installation of the MacPerl tool. Also, if you do not yet know how to launch and run MPW, take some time to work with MPW before completing the installation of the MacPerl tool. Come back to this part of the chapter after you have learned more abut MPW.

Steps to Install the MacPerl MPW tool

1. Launch MPW.

2. Change the directory to the MacPerl *f* folder. Use the `directory` command or the Set Directory... menu item.

3. Execute the `Install.MPW_Perl` command. This will create and open a configuration file named `Config.MPW_Perl`.

4. Examine the configuration file and make any changes you require. Be sure to read the comments at the top of the file before making any modifications. The configuration file sets a number of useful variables. In most cases, the defalts should be acceptible. Save any changes.

5. Execute `Install.MPW_Perl` again. A set of commands will be printed in the MPW Shell worksheet window.

6. To complete the configuration step, select and execute (i.e., enter) the commands which are written to the worksheet window. These commands are set up as two parts. The first part installs the appropriate tools and scripts. The second part creates a startup file for Perl. If you have your own startup file, you may merge the contents of this part into it instead. You will probably want to execute this startup file, or quit and relaunch MPW, to make sure all the settings are in effect.

Try Out The MPW Tool

Locate the file, `myscript`, that you created with the MacPerl app. You may have to use the Set Directory ... menu item to navigate to the folder containing the script. If you no longer have this file, create and save a new MPW worksheet named `myscript`, containing the statement:

```
print 'hello';
```

Then, in your MPW shell window, enter the command:

```
perl myscript
```

You should see the result:

```
hello
```

Because we configured MPW in the previous step, MPW is able to find and run the `perl` tool.

Options, switches, and flags

Like many MPW tools, Perl may be run with any of several **options** (known also as **switches** or **flags**). Options begin with a dash, **-**, and usually consist of a single letter or a letter followed by a word, such as the name of a directory. Use the -h option to list all available options as well as an abbreviated usage statement for Perl.

```
perl -h
Usage: perl [switches] [--] [programfile] [arguments]
  -0[octal]  specify record separator ...
  -a         autosplit mode with -n or -p ...
```

One-liners

In your MPW shell window, enter the following command:

```
perl -e 'print "hello";'
```

You should see the same result printed to the window. The -e option tells perl to execute the following string as Perl code. The -e must immediately precede the string containing Perl commands; there may be no other Perl switches in between.

You can also use -e to execute a series of lines, i.e. a multi-line script, from the command line.

```
perl -e ' ∂
print("hello\n"); ∂
print("goodbye"); ∂
'
```

Be sure to include the ∂ escape character before the return on each line in the script or it will fail to execute. Also, be sure to select *all* of the lines before pressing ENTER.

Making your script executable

To make your script executable directly (i.e., allowing you to enter the command, myscript, rather than the command, perl myscript), add the following line of code just above your Perl code:

```
Perl -Sx "{0}" {"Parameters"}; Exit
```

Actually, oher MPW statements may come before or after the Perl -Sx "{0}" statement. Just make sure that there is an MPW Exit just before the perl code begins and that the first line of the perl portion is a `#!perl` statement.[2]

Special Features Of The MPW Tool

Because MPW is "command-line" oriented, MPW can pass command line switches (options) and values as well as filenames.

```
perl -lw myscript
```

In contrast, the standalone MacPerl application must have any command line switches specified inside the script, as:

```
#!perl -lw
```

Various shell variables can also be defined and will be expanded by MPW before passing a command line to Perl.

MPW scripts can be passed to ToolServer for execution in background or on a networked machine. In addition, the presence of ToolServer allows the `system()` function and backquoted commands to work under MacPerl.[3]

The MPW shell understands the concept of a working directory better than the Finder does. Using MPW, it's easy to set the current directory, then run a MacPerl script, instead of encoding the directory path into the script.

The MPW shell also understands about standard input, standard output, and standard error. These default to the MPW worksheet from which a command is entered but they can be changed by providing a filename, preceded by the appropriate **redirection** character, on the command line.

`>`	`myfile`	**output replaces contents of** `myfile`
`>>`	`myfile`	**output is appended to** `myfile`
`<`	`myfile`	**input is taken from** `myfile`
`≥`	`myfile`	**error output replaces contents of** `myfile`
`≥≥`	`myfile`	**error output is appended to** `myfile`

---

[2] Or `#!/usr/local/bin/perl` or whatever pathname is required if you intend to also run the script under Unix.

[3] If ToolServer is present, `system()` and backquotes will work under the standalone MacPerl app as well as the MacPerl MPW tool. However, you will still need MPW in order for ToolServer to have any (MPW) tools to serve!

The command line

The MacPerl tool has its own arguments so the command line is somewhat unusual:

```
"{perlpath}" [perl switches] "{script}" arg0 arg1 ...
```

where:

- `{perlpath}` is the path to the Perl tool; you may have set this up in your MPW:Startup file. The path may need to be quoted if there is any possibility of an intermediate directory name containing a space. If the tool has been installed in a folder on your standard path, you will only need to use the name `perl`.

- `[perl switches]` are optional command line flags such as `-e`, `-w`, or `-l`. Each must begin with a dash, `-`. If `-e` is used, it must be followed by a string containing Perl code to be executed.

- `{script}` is the path to your Perl source code. This name must not begin with a dash, even though `-` is otherwise legal in a filename. If you use the `-e` switch, the code may be placed "in line" within a quoted string.

- `arg0 arg1 ...` are the arguments to your Perl script after it starts executing. These could be filenames or variables which have been SET in preceding lines of an MPW script.

Note that the normal MPW, and Unix, convention is not followed for counting arguments. `Arg[0]` is the first argument, not the pathname of the Perl script, as you might expect. Consistent with other counting in Perl, the argument count is the cardinal of the last argument passed (one less than the number of arguments).

Reading Perl Help Files

The Mac port of Shuck is small and easily coexists with MPW (even on small Macs without virtual memory). A standalone Macintosh application can be launched from MPW by simply giving its path on the command line. The MPW installation script defines the variable `{MacPerl}` as the path to the **MacPerl** ƒ folder (the location of the `Shuck` application). Arguments on the command line specify files to be opened.

```
"{MacPerl}"Shuck "{MACPERL}"lib:Mac:Files.pm
```

The above command will execute the Shuck application and present the help information for Files.pm. Alternatively, you could type and select the text `Mac::Files`, then select the Perl Help item from the Find menu.[4]

If you prefer not to specify "`{MacPerl}`" every time (or if you did not run the installation script :-), you may place a copy (`duplicate`) of the Shuck application into your MPW Tools folder (or another location on your command **path**, e.g.:[5]

```
directory "{MPW}User Commands"
Duplicate -y "HD:MacPerl ƒ:Shuck" :Shuck
```

Or, just use the Finder to make an alias to Shuck in an appropriate folder. If you set the creator ID (signature) of all *.pm modules to that of Shuck, you will be able to invoke Shuck by double clicking any of them in the Finder.

```
directory "HD:MacPerl ƒ:lib:"
setfile ≈.pm -c Σuck
```

ToolServer and `system()`

ToolServer allows large processing jobs (e.g., compilations) to be split up among several networked Macs. A running instance of MPW can send an AppleEvent (i.e, the filename of an MPW script to be executed) to a Tool-Server application running on a remote machine. ToolServer then operates in background, returning an AppleEvent when it is finished.

With ToolServer installed, you can use Perl's `system()` function, as well as the command input (i.e., backtick) operator, to run MPW tools from inside MacPerl. For example, the following lines of MacPerl code will print a count of the lines and characters in the MPW Startup file .[6]

```
$file = '{MPW}Startup';
system("Count $file");
```

---

[4] This menu item is added by the perl startup file which was created when we did the configuration. It may not appear if you did not execute the startup file (or relaunch MPW) following the configuration step.

[5] Be sure to replace the name of the disk volume, e.g. HD, in these examples with the correct name for your system!

[6] This is not the most efficient way to do this particular exercise, of course; an MPW script would be much faster. The Perl code does, however, provide proof of concept.

ToolServer has its own startup script, which should be modified to define any aliases and environment variables that Perl will need. ToolServer also has its own unique creator ID, MPSX, which can be assigned to a script. Then, when a script is double clicked under the Finder, it will be sent to the Tool-Server application. The functionality is somewhat similar to a standalone MacPerl droplet.

A Framework for a "Combination" Script

The following example illustrates how a perl script can be embedded within a "regular" MPW shell script. Although the example itself doesn't do much of interest (although it does run), it provides a framework for a "combination" MPW shell and MacPerl script. Note that the perl portion of this example returns a non-zero exit status, which is caught and dealt with by the MPW shell portion.

```
set oExit    "{exit}"       # save the exit value
set exit 0                  # set to 0 so script won't
                            # abort after perl call

echo "# Do the pre-perl stuff here"

Perl -Sx "{0}"              # call the perl portion
set myStat "{Status}"       # save off the status

if ( "{myStat}" )
        echo "# Do the non-zero status stuff here"
Else
        echo "# Do the zero status stuff here"
End

set exit "{oExit}"          # restore the exit value
Exit {myStat}               # MPW shouldn't attempt to
                            # process past this point
-- it's perl from here on out

#!perl
print( "Start the perl script\n" );
print( "Do my perl processing\n" );
print( "Exit the script\n" );
exit 1;
```

Accessing Command Line Arguments

Internally, the arguments for a Perl script are provided in the array @ARGV. The variable $#ARGV provides the argument count (that is, the cardinal number assigned to the last argument). The contents of @ARGV may depend on whether you used `perl` to run your command or made a directly executable script. That is, arguments to the *script* become part of @ARGV, while arguments to *perl* do not.

The following example illustrates this behavior. Suppose you have a script, `myscript`, which contains the following loop:

```
foreach $arg (@ARGV) { print "$arg\n"; }
```

If you execute the script using `perl` as follows

```
perl -w myscript hello
```

it will print

```
hello
```

However, if you make the script directly executable by adding

```
Perl -Sx "{0}" {"Parameters"}; Exit
```

at the top, then execute it directly as

```
myscript -w hello
```

it will print

```
-w
hello
```

Returning a Value to MPW

An MPW script sometimes needs a result from a tool to indicate successful completion. The {Status} variable is normally set to zero to indicate a good result and to non-zero (perhaps a specific error code) to indicate failure.[7] Your MPW script can examine {Status} and cause itself to `exit` (if a non-zero value is detected) before it does something regrettable.

---

[7] This is the opposite of the way return values work within Perl, but is consistent with other shells and programs such as those found under Unix.

If an error occurs during compilation, Perl will return non-zero in {Status}. On normal completion of a script, {Status} will contain the value returned by exit(). If the script did not call exit(), the return value is assumed to be 0. Calling exit() with a string also results in {Status} being set to 0.

You may want to set the MPW variable, Exit, to 0 within any MPW script that calls or contains an embedded Perl script. This will prevent the MPW script from quitting if the Perl script returns a non-zero status.

Accessing MPW environment variables from within Perl

The special Perl hash %ENV stores environment variables.[8] This hash is filled from all existing environment variables in MPW at the time of execution of the Perl script. Thus, for instance, $ENV{Worksheet} is the full pathname of the MPW worksheet. Environment variable names are not case sensitive in MPW perl. Try:

```
perl -e 'foreach $key (keys(%ENV)) { ∂
  print("$key\t$ENV{$key}\n"); ∂
} '
```

MacPerl::FAccess

When called from the MPW perl tool, the MacPerl::FAccess function manipulates various file characteristics. To get the command constants, it's convenient to require "FAccess.ph". For details on MacPerl::FAccess, see the online help under Macintosh specific features.

---

[8] The MPW SET command can be used to set or (with no arguments) list these variables from the MPW command line.

Chapter 23:

- *What You Need*
- *Setting It Up*
- *Building MacPerl*
- *Building Extensions*

Building MacPerl And Extensions

> *I tell this tale, which is strictly true,*
> *Just by way of convincing you,*
> *How very little, since things were made,*
> *Things have altered in the building trade.*
>
> – Rudyard Kipling, *A Truthful Song*

MacPerl comes in **source code** form, so you can read the source code and, if you so desire, build the application and related files for yourself.

Perl's source code distribution is done for several reasons; primary among these are Perl's licensing terms and Perl's cultural terms, which encourage, in all cases, the distribution of source with any Perl binary. You might want to build the software yourself for any of several reasons:

- You come from a culture that does not trust precompiled software (unlikely if you are using Mac OS).

- You want to make changes to the source to suit your own needs.

- You want to make patches to submit to the main MacPerl distribution.

- You just want to see if you can do it.

Any of these reasons (or no reason at all) is sufficient; unlike typical Macintosh "freeware", MacPerl is freely redistributable in both source code and binary form. So, enjoy!

The MacPerl source code is not, for the most part, written in Perl; MacPerl itself, for instance, is written in C. So, whereas we use MacPerl to compile and run our Perl programs, we will need a C compiler to build MacPerl and any other C files.

If you do not have experience with C, you might not want to attempt this. Furthermore, unlike MacPerl itself, some of the libraries that are required to compile the MacPerl program are not free; in fact, they may seem quite expensive, depending on your resources and budget.

If you want to port extensions to MacPerl, you will need to set up the build process as described below; it is not necessary to actually build MacPerl in order to build extensions to it, but since you have to set up everything anyway, it couldn't hurt to try. Probably.

What You Need

The most important ingredient other than the source itself is **Metrowerks CodeWarrior**,[1] a popular programming development environment for Mac OS. The most recent version of MacPerl is geared toward CodeWarrior Pro 2, but it also uses some "obsolete" libraries and headers that are no longer bundled with CodeWarrior Pro 2. These must be gathered from older versions of CodeWarrior (e.g., CodeWarrior Gold 11).

The build process itself is done in MPW, which is discussed in Chapter 22, *MPW Perl*. You can use your own version of MPW if you like, but you will need to get the CodeWarrior MPW files installed. A special tool called **dmake** is used by MPW to do some of the building; it is available, along with other useful files, on our CD-ROM.

Setting It Up

These instructions are geared to the MacPerl 5.1.9r4 sources and assume that you have copies of CodeWarrior Pro 2 (CWPro2) and CodeWarrior Gold 11 (CW11). (The current reliance on the old libraries and headers is likely to be removed eventually; be careful if you're using a release later than Mac-Perl 5.1.9r4.) The instructions also assume that MPW has not already been installed.

1.   Install the following from the CWPro2 CD-ROM:

----

[1] See www.metrowerks.com. There is a free CodeWarrior Lite version of the program, but it is insufficient for our purposes.

- CodeWarrior MPW
- Metrowerks C/C++ for Mac OS Headers & Libs (for PPC and 68K)
- Metrowerks Standard Library (MSL C/C++)

You are, of course, free to install all of CodeWarrior, and this is actually recommended, but only the above are required.

2. Install the MacPerl application (if it is not installed already) and install the MacPerl sources.

3. Rename the Metrowerks MPW directory to MPW (MacPerl's makefiles require this). All of the directories mentioned below, except where noted, are specified relative to this directory.

4. Launch and configure MPW. Run the MPW script CW_Max_Dup_Update, which will copy relevant Metrowerks libraries to the MPW directories.

5. Install the MacPerl MPW tool (see Chapter 22, *MPW Perl*).

6. Install dmake. Take the files dmake and startup.mk and put them in the :MPW:Tools: folder. Put BuildProgram and BuildCommands in the :MPW: Scripts: folder (back up the existing versions, for safety's sake).

7. Find the obsolete libraries. On the CW11 CD-ROM, these are stored in a directory called (Obsolete ANSI Libraries). Run **copy_mw_libs.pl** (provided on the disc) to copy the libraries. It will prompt for the libs directory and the directory with the MPW Shell application.

   If you have the CW11 CD-ROM mounted, you have the option of copying directly from the CD-ROM. In this case, the script will also copy the files from step 8 below.

   This script makes new folders for the obsolete libraries:

:MPW:Libraries:OldMWPPCLibraries:	(for PPC libraries)
:MPW:Libraries:OldMW68KLibraries:	(for 68K libraries)
:MPW:Interfaces:OldMWCIncludes:	(for header files)

   The script then copies all the files from all the subfolders in the obsolete libraries folder into these folders.

8. Find the old runtime libraries. On the CW11 CD-ROM, they are stored in Metrowerks CodeWarrior:MacOS Support:Libraries:Runtime: (this step is performed automatically if the copy_mw_libs.pl script above is set to copy directly from the CW11 CD-ROM). Copy the following files to :MPW:Libraries:OldMW68KLibraries:

CPlusPlus.Lib	MPWRuntime.68K.Lib
MWCFM68KRuntime.Lib	ShLibRuntimeCFM68K.Lib

Copy the following files to :MPW:Libraries:OldMWPPCLibraries:

MWCRuntime.Lib	ShLibRuntime.Lib
MWMPWCRuntime.Lib	

9. Here is something that might take some hunting. Find NuToolLibs.o, version 3.4d8, created December 13, 1994. The file might be on some old MPW archive somewhere, but it is not on any recent CodeWarrior or MPW distribution. It is currently necessary for building, however. Once you find it, put it in :MPW:Libraries:CFM68KLibraries: (create the directory if it is not there).

10. In the MacPerl source distribution, the XL folder contains unresolved aliases. This needs to be fixed. Get the XL folder from the CD-ROM and copy those files into the folder in the source distribution.

11. In the MacPerl source distribution, the file Makefile.mk in the macperl folder needs some changes; it does not include all the needed directories. Copy the file Makefile.mk from the CD-ROM into the macperl folder in the source distribution.

12. Find InterfaceLib version 1.1.2 (it is on the CW11 CD). The newer version, 1.1.3, has some problems with CFM-68K. Go to :MPW:Interfaces& Libraries:Libraries: and replace version 1.1.3 of InterfaceLib in the MWPPCLibraries and MW68KLibraries folders with version 1.1.2.

13. Restart MPW.

Building MacPerl

If you followed all those directions precisely, there is a reasonable chance that the build process will go off without a hitch.

The general procedure for building is this: set the directory in MPW to your MacPerl_Src directory and execute the command:

```
BuildProgram build_perl
```

If all is well, this will run to its completion and you are finished. If so, congratulations! On the other hand, all might not go well, so here are some hints. Ignore compiler warnings. If compilation is prematurely terminated because of an error, remember that the error messages mean what they say (most of the time). Sometimes a library or header cannot be found; if so, find the file and put it where MPW is looking for it.

A good way to find a missing file is to use the Find File feature of Mac OS. Simply type in the name of the missing file; if files of different versions come up in your search, you will need to determine if the file wanted is old or new, and then determine which file you have is old and which is new.

Remember that the old files are in the Old* directories where we put the obsolete libraries and headers. New files are in the Interfaces&Libraries: subdirectories. The error message should report what directory it is looking in for the needed file.

If all else fails and you can't find your way home, ask the MacPerl mailing list. Also, our CD-ROM contains a large text file with the complete text of a MPW MacPerl build session, which may or may not help at all.

Installation

Some people prefer to use their MacPerl source directory as their main MacPerl directory. If you don't want to do this, you will probably have to copy all the newly built files by hand. This is not a difficult chore for someone who knows the MacPerl distribution well enough to build it. The applications are in :macperl:, along with some of the directories. The MPW perl tool and the lib and pod directories are in :perl:.

Building Extensions

As noted in earlier chapters, most CPAN-derived extensions do not work without modification under MacPerl. Extensions are usually written in C and XS and need to be ported and compiled as Mac OS shared libraries.

These shared libraries can only be used by the PowerPC and CFM68K versions of MacPerl. Non-CFM68K versions of MacPerl cannot load modules dynamically; for that, a module must be linked in statically during the build process. You can do this by adjusting the MacPerl makefiles to include those extra modules in the static build, but there is rarely a reason to do it, as most 68K Macs can handle the CFM68K version of MacPerl.

Some extensions need to be ported; that is, parts of the code need to be modified to work with MacPerl. Many extensions need no porting at all, compiling straight out of the box. For this runthrough, we'll write our own extension, a module called XPlusX.[2] It exports a function called x_plus_x(), which takes one numerical argument, adds it to itself, and prints the resulting value, rounded off to the nearest integer.

Here is the XS file, called XPlusX.xs:

```
#include "EXTERN.h"
#include "perl.h"
#include "XSUB.h"

MODULE = XPlusX   PACKAGE = XPlusX

void
x_plus_x(num)
  double num
  CODE:
    printf("%.0f\n", num + num);
```

Now, the module, XPlusX.pm:

```
package XPlusX;
require Exporter;
require DynaLoader;
@ISA = qw(Exporter DynaLoader);
@EXPORT = qw(x_plus_x);
$VERSION = '0.01';
bootstrap XPlusX $VERSION;
1;
```

---

[2] As you might imagine, we are not going to explain anything about XS itself, or writing modules. Please see perlmodlib, perlxs, perlxstut, ExtUtils::MakeMaker, h2xs, and *Advanced Perl Programming*.

And Makefile.PL:

```
use ExtUtils::MakeMaker;
WriteMakefile(
   'NAME'         => 'XPlusX',
   'VERSION_FROM' => 'XPlusX.pm',
   'XSPROTOARG'   => '-noprototypes'
);
```

We put all three of these files in the folder :MacPerl_src:perl:ext:XPlusX (creating the XPlusX folder). Then, the process is very similar to that used on Unix systems. But, instead of the Unix mantra:

```
perl Makefile.PL
make
make test
make install
```

We use:

```
perl Makefile.PL
BuildProgram all
BuildProgram install
```

Run each of those commands in succession. This will install the following files under :MacPerl_src:

:perl:lib:XPlusX.pm
:perl:lib:MacCFM68K:auto:XPlusX:XPlusX
:perl:lib:MacPPC:auto:XPlusX:XPlusX

If your source tree differs from the regular MacPerl tree, you will need to install these files in the appropriate place (e.g., the site_perl directory):

```
perl -x ":::PerlInstall" "-l" "{MACPERL}site_perl"
```

Now we can run the module and see what happens. Once the files are installed, you can run any test scripts that are provided.[3] We have not included test files with this module, however, so try this from MPW:

---

[3] Test files often fail because, possibly unlike the module they are written to test, they assume the presence of particular Unix filesystems.

```
perl -MXPlusX -we x_plus_x(2.4)
```

Or, try this from the application:

```
#!perl -w
use XPlusX;
x_plus_x(2.4);
```

Either of these should print 5. For fun, try other numbers, such as:

```
'2.24' . 9 x 13
'2.24' . 9 x 14
```

Part V

Resources

Knowledge is of two kinds.
We know a subject ourselves,
or we know where we can find information upon it.

– Samuel Johnson, 1775, in Boswell, *Life of Johnson* vol. ii

Chapter 24:

- *General*
- *Languages*
  - *Perl*
  - *AppleScript, Frontier*
  - *Miscellaneous*

- *Programming*
- *Networks, Etc.*
  - *Internet*
  - *World Wide Web*
  - *Security & Privacy*

Books, Etc.

Some books are to be tasted,
others are to be swallowed,
and some few to be chewed and digested;
that is, some books are to be read only in parts;
others to be read but not curiously;
and some few to be read wholly,
and with diligence and attention.
Some books also may be read by deputy,
and extracts made of them by others.

– Francis Bacon

The following listings are sorted into rough categories. Please be aware, however, that no such categorization scheme is perfect. Within the topical categories, the entries are coded and sorted by type, as:

Internet:

I:E	Email list
I:F	FTP (File Transfer Protocol) archive
I:U	Usenet group
I:W	WWW (World Wide Web) site

Publications:

P:B	Book
P:B,C	Book with one or more CD-ROMs
P:B,F	Book with one or more Floppy Disks
P:C	One or more CD-ROMs
P:M	Magazine

Within each type (e.g., Internet), the entries are alphanumerically sorted.

Note: We have placed flagged (>) comments below some of these resource entries. Although the absence of such a comment does not imply a negative evaluation, the presence of a flag generally indicates a very positive one...

General

Prime Time Freeware for UNIX Prime Time Freeware	P:B,C
Proceedings of the First Conference on Freely *Redistributable Software* Free Software Foundation FSF, 1996, ISBN 1-882114-47-7	P:B
The File Formats Handbook Günter Born Thomson Computer Press, 1995, ISBN 1-85032-117-5	P:B
The New Hacker's Dictionary, 3rd. Ed. Eric S. Raymond MIT Press, 1996, ISBN 0-262-68092-0	P:B

> Combines accurate definitions with delightful folklore

The UNIX Programming Environment Brian W. Kernighan, Rob Pike Prentice Hall, 1984, ISBN 0-13-937681-X	P:B
UNIX Review	P:M

http://www.unixreview.com/

> UNIX Review
> Miller Freeman
> 411 Borel Ave., #100
> San Mateo, CA 94402 USA

> +1 800 829-5475 (US only)
> +1 904 445-4662
> +1 904 446-2774 (fax)

UniForum http://www.uniforum.org/	I:W

UnixWorld online http://www.wcmh.com/uworld/	I:W
USENIX http://www.usenix.org/	I:W

Languages

Perl

comp.lang.perl.announce comp.lang.perl.misc comp.lang.perl.modules	I:U

> Very active discussion groups

Comprehensive Perl Archive Network (CPAN) http://www.perl.com/CPAN/	I:W

> The definitive online archive of Perl sources, etc.

Perl Language page http://language.perl.com/	I:W
Perl Reference page http://reference.perl.com/	I:W
The Perl Institute http://www.perl.org/	I:W

> The Perl Institute
> 2850 SW Cedar Hills Blvd., #62
> Beaverton, OR 97005-1354 USA

Advanced Perl Programming Sriram Srinivasan O'Reilly, 1997, ISBN 1-56592-220-4	P:B

> A wonderful book; covers many of the esoteric areas left blank
> by *Programming Perl*

Cross-Platform Perl Eric F. Johnson M&T, 1996, ISBN 1-55851-483-X	P:B,C

> Unix and Windows only

Discover Perl 5 Naba Barkakati IDG, 1997, ISBN 0-7645-3076-3	P:B,C
Effective Perl Programming: Joseph N. Hall, Randal L. Schwartz Addison-Wesley, 1997, ISBN 0-201-41975-0	P:B
Learning Perl, 2nd Ed. Randal L. Schwartz, Tom Christiansen O'Reilly, 1997, ISBN 1-56592-284-0	P:B

>   An excellent introductory work for readers who already know
     how to program in an algebraic language.

Learning Perl on Win32 Systems Randal L. Schwartz, et al O'Reilly, 1997, ISBN 1-56592-324-3	P:B
Perl: *The Programmer's Companion* Nigel Chapman Wiley, 1997, ISBN 0-471-97563-X	P:B
Perl 5 by Example David Medinets Que, 1996, ISBN 0-7897-0866-3	P:B
Perl 5 Complete Edward S. Peschko, et al McGraw-Hill, 1998, ISBN 0-07-913698-2	P:B
Perl 5 Desktop Reference Johan Vromans O'Reilly, 1996, ISBN 1-56592-187-9	P:B,C
Perl 5 for Dummies Paul Hoffman, Kathy Ivens IDG, 1997, ISBN 0-7645-0044-9	P:B,C
Perl 5 How-To: *The Definitive Perl Programming Problem-Solver,* 2nd Ed. Steven Asbury, et al Waite Group, 1997, ISBN 1-57169-118-9	P:B,C

Perl 5 Interactive Course   P:B,C
Jon Orwant
Waite Group, 1996, ISBN 1-57169-064-6

Perl 5 Quick Reference   P:B,C
Mícheál Ó Foghlú
Que, 1996, ISBN 0-7897-0888-4

Perl by Example   P:B
Ellie Quigley
Prentice Hall, 1994, ISBN 0-13-122839-0

Perl Resource Kit: P:B,C
Unix Edition
assorted authors (see below for details)
O'Reilly, 1997, ISBN 1-56592-370-7

> A stunning collection: four books and a disc; all on Perl! Includes:
> *Perl Module Reference*, Vols. 1 & 2 (Ellen Siever, David Futato)
> *Perl Utilities Guide* (Brian Jepson)
> *Programming with Perl Modules* (Nate Patwardhan, Clay Irving)

Programming Perl, 2nd Ed.   P:B
Larry Wall, et al
O'Reilly, 1996, ISBN 1-56592-149-6

> *The* reference book on Perl; readable, definitive, and quirky

Software Engineering With Perl: P:B,F
Toolsmithing for Better Software - Sooner
Carl Dichter, Mark Pease
Prentice Hall, 1995, ISBN 0-13-016965-X

Teach Yourself Perl 5 in 21 Days, 2nd Ed.   P:B,C
David Till
Sams, 1996, ISBN 0-672-30894-0

Teach Yourself Perl 5 for Windows NT in 21 Days   P:B,C
Tony Zhang, David Till
Sams, 1997, ISBN 0-672-31047-3

The Perl 5 Programmer's Reference   P:B,C
R. Allen Wyke, Luke Duncan
Ventana, 1997, ISBN 1-56604-750-1

The Perl Journal   P:M

> http://tpj.com
> perl-journal-subscriptions@perl.com

The Perl Journal
P.O. Box 54
Boston, MA 02101 USA

> Carries many informative articles on the philosophy and
> application of Perl

AppleScript, Frontier

AppleScript Finder Guide: P:B
English Dialect
Apple Computer
Addison-Wesley, 1994, ISBN 0-201-40736-1

AppleScript Language Guide   P:B
Apple Computer
Addison-Wesley, 1994, ISBN 0-201-40735-3

AppleScript Scripting Additions Guide   P:B
Apple Computer
Addison-Wesley, 1994, ISBN 0-201-40910-0

Applied Mac Scripting   P:B,C
Tom Trinko
MIS Press, 1995, ISBN 1-55828-330-7

Danny Goodman's AppleScript Handbook, 2nd Ed.   P:B,F
Danny Goodman
Random House, 1994, ISBN 0-679-7580602

Miscellaneous

The AWK Programming Language   P:B
Alfred V. Aho, et al
Addison-Wesley, 1988, ISBN 0-201-07981-X

> Readable and definitive

Mastering Regular Expressions Jeffrey E. F. Friedl O'Reilly, 1997, ISBN 1-56592-257-3	P:B

> Comprehensible, practical, and authoritative

Effective Awk Programming, 2nd Ed. Arnold D. Robbins SSC, 1997, ISBN 1-57831-000-8	P:B
PostScript by Example Henry McGilton, Mary Campione Addison-Wesley, 1992, ISBN 0-201-63228-4	P:B
Programming Python Mark Lutz O'Reilly, 1996, ISBN 1-56592-197-6	P:B,C

> Python is an interesting alternative to Perl. It is a powerful, interpreted, algebraic language.

sed & awk Dale Dougherty O'Reilly, 1990, ISBN 0-937175-59-5	P:B
The GNU Awk User's Guide Arnold D. Robbins FSF, 1996, ISBN 1-882114-26-4	P:B
UNIX Power Tools, 2nd Ed. · Jerry Peek, et al. O'Reilly, 1997, ISBN 1-56592-260-3	P:B

Programming

ftp://dev.apple.com/devworld /Technical_Documentation/Inside_Macintosh/	I:F
http://devworld.apple.com/dev/insidemac.shtml http://devworld.apple.com	I:W
Applying RCS and SCCS: *From Source Control to Project Control* Don Bolinger, Tan Bronson	P:B

O'Reilly, 1995, ISBN 1-56592-117-8

Frontier: P:B
The Definiţive Guide
Matt Neuburg
O'Reilly, 1998, ISBN 1-56592-383-9

Inside Macintosh/CD-ROM   P:C
Apple Computer
Addison-Wesley, 1994, ISBN 2-201-40674-8

> This is a gold mine of technical information on the Mac OS,
  Macintosh hardware, etc. You can even "try before you buy",
  using one of the online sources listed above.

Introduction to MPW   P:B
Apple Developer Press, 1995, ISBN 030-4057-B

MacTech Magazine   P:M
http://www.mactech.com

Metrowerks   I:W
http://www.metrowerks.com

MPW Command Reference   P:B
Apple Developer Press, 1993, ISBN 030-4058-A

Programmer's Guide to MPW:, Vol. 1   P:B
Exploring the Macintosh Programmer's Workshop
Mark Andrews
Addison-Wesley, 1991, ISBN 0-201-57011-4

> Out of print

Programmer's Guide to MPW:, Vol. 2   P:B
Masteringthe Macintosh Programmer's Workshop
Mark Andrews, Neil Rhodes
Addison-Wesley, 1992, ISBN 0-201-57012-2

> Out of print

The Official BBEdit Book   P:B,C
Bob LeVitus, Natanya Pitts
Ziff Davis, 1997, ISBN 1-56276-505-1

The Wiz Biz   P:B
Rick Cook
Baen Books, 1997, ISBN 0-671-87846-8

> "Q: How does a shanghaied computer geek conquer all the forces of darkness and win the love of the most beautiful witch in the world?
>
> A: By transforming himself from a demon programmer into a programmer of demons!"

Networks, Etc.

Internet

DNS & BIND   P:B
Paul Albitz, Cricket Liu
O'Reilly, 1992, ISBN 1-56592-010-4

Getting Connected: P:B
The Internet at 56K and Up
Kevin Dowd
O'Reilly, 1996, ISBN 1-56592-154-2

Managing Internet Information Services: P:B
World Wide Web, Gopher, FTP, and more
Cricket Liu, et al
O'Reilly, 1994, ISBN 1-56592-062-7

NetProfessional: P:M
Macintosh Solutions for the Internet

    http://www.netprolive.com
    subscribe@netprolive.com

    NetProfessional Magazine
    612 Howard St., 6th Floor
    San Francisco, CA 94105

Providing Internet Services Via the Mac OS   P:B,C
Carl Steadman, et al
Addison-Wesley, 1996, ISBN 0-201-48998-8

TCP/IP Network Administration   P:B
Craig Hunt
O'Reilly, 1992, ISBN 0-937175-82-X

World Wide Web

WebServer Magazine OnLine   I:W
http://webserver.cpg.com

60 Minute Guide to CGI Programming With Perl 5   P:B
Pobert Farrell
IDG, 1996, ISBN 1-56884-780-7

CGI Developer's Guide   P:B,C
Eugene Eric Kim
Sams, 1996, ISBN 1-57521-087-8

CGI Developer's Resource: P:B,C
Web Programming in Tcl and Perl
J. M. Ivler, Kamran Husain
Prentice Hall, 1997, ISBN 0-13-727751-2

CGI for Commerce: P:B,C
A Complete Web-Based Selling Solution
Gunther Biznieks, Selena Sol
M&T, 1997, ISBN 1-55851-559-3

The CGI /Perl Cookbook   P:B,C
Craig Patchett, Matthew Wright
Wiley, 1997, ISBN 0-471-16896-3

CGI Programming in C & Perl   P:B,C
Thomas Boutell
Addison-Wesley, 1996, ISBN 0-201-42219-0

CGI Programming on the World Wide Web   P:B
Shishir Gundavaram
O'Reilly, 1996, ISBN 1-56592-168-2

Creating Cool Web Pages With Perl   P:B,C
Jerry Muelver
IDG, 1996, ISBN 0-7645-3018-6

Developing CGI Applications With Perl   P:B
John Deep, Peter Holfelder
Wiley, 1996, ISBN 0-471-14158-5

How to Program CGI With Perl 5.0   P:B,C
Stephen Lines
Ziff Davis, 1997, ISBN 1-56276-460-8

How to Set Up and Maintain a World Wide Web Site, 2nd Ed. P:B
Lincoln D. Stein
Addison-Wesley, 1995, ISBN 0-201-63389-2

> A truly excellent book; wish we'd had it years ago!

HTML: P:B
The Definitive Guide, 2nd Ed.
Chuck Musciano, Bill Kennedy
O'Reilly, 1997, ISBN 1-56592-235-2

Information Architecture forthe World Wide Web   P:B
Louis Rosenfeld, Peter Morville
O'Reilly, 1998, ISBN 1-56592-282-4

Instant Web Scripts With CGI Perl   P:B,C
Selena Sol, Gunther Biznieks
M&T, 1996, ISBN 1-55851-490-2

Introduction to CGI/Perl: P:B
Getting Started With Web Scripts
Steven E. Brenner, Edwin Aoki
M&T, 1996, ISBN 1-55851-478-3

Special Edition Using Perl 5 forWeb Programming   P:B
David Harlan, et al
Que, 1996, ISBN 0-7897-0659-8

Web Client Programming with Perl   P:B
Clinton Wong
O'Reilly, 1996, ISBN 1-56592-214-X

Perl CGI Programming: P:B
No Experience Required
Erik Strom

Perl & CGI Programming Starter Kit   P:B,C
Simon & Schuster, 1996, ISBN 1-57521-078-9

Planning and Managing Web Sites On The Macintosh: P:B,C
The Complete Guide to WebSTAR and MacHTTP
Jon Wiederspan, Chuck Shotton
Addison-Wesley, 1996, ISBN 0-201-47957-5

Webmaster in a Nutshell   P:B
Stephen Spainhour, Valerie Quercia
O'Reilly, 1997, ISBN 1-56592-229-8
O'Reilly, 1997, ISBN 1-56592-305-7 (deluxe)

>   A very useful book for web site administrators; Chris says it's
       the most valuable book a Webmaster could have! The deluxe
       version contains several ORA books on CD-ROM.

Webmaster Macintosh: P:B,C
How to Build Your Own World Wide Web Server
Without Really Trying, 2e
Bob LeVitus, Jeff Evans
Academic Press, 1997, ISBN 0-12-445602-2

Teach Yourself CGI Programming With Perl 5 in a Week   P:B,C
Eric Herrmann
Sams, 1996, ISBN 1-57521-196-3

Web Programming Secrets with HTML, CGI, and Perl   P:B,F
Ed Tittel, et al
IDG, 1996, ISBN 1-56884-848-X

Web Server Technology: P:B
The Advanced Guide for World Wide Web Information Providers
Nancy J. Yeager, Robert E. McGrath
Morgan Kaufmann, 1996, ISBN 1-55860-376-X

World Wide Web Journal   P:M
World Wide Web Consortium
O'Reilly

Security & Privacy

Actually Useful Internet Security Techniques　　　　　P:B
Larry J. Hughes, Jr.
New Riders, 1996, ISBN 1-56205-508-9

Applied Cryptography:　　　　　P:B
Protocols, Algorithms, and Source Code in C, 2nd ed.
Bruce Schneier
Wiley, 1996, ISBN 0-471-11709-9

> The book the NSA really wishes you wouldn't buy.

Bandits on the Information Superhighway　　　　　P:B
Daniel J. Barrett
O'Reilly, 1996, ISBN 1-56592-156-9

Building Internet Firewalls　　　　　P:B
D. Brent Chapman, Elizabeth D. Zwicky
O'Reilly, 1995, ISBN 1-56592-124-0

> authoritative and readable

Computer Crime:　　　　　P:B
A Crimefighter's Handbook
David Icove, et al
O'Reilly, 1995, ISBN 1-56592-086-4

Computer Security Basics　　　　　P:B
Deborah Russell, G.T. Gangemi, Sr.
O'Reilly, 1991, ISBN 0-937175-71-4

Computers Under Attack:　　　　　P:B
Intruders, Worms, and Viruses
Peter J. Denning, Ed.
Addison-Wesley, 1990, ISB650-0

> An excellent collection of readable, insightful, and
> authoritative papers

Pretty Good Privacy　　　　　P:B
Simson Garfinkel
O'Reilly, 1994, ISBN 1-56592-098-8

Internet Cryptography   P:B
Richard E. Smith
Addison-Wesley, 1997, ISBN 0-201-92480-3

Practical UNIX & Internet Security, 2nd ed.   P:B
Simson Garfinkel, Gene Spafford
O'Reilly, 1996, ISBN 1-56592-148-8

The Electronic Privacy Papers: P:B
Documents on the Battle for Privacy
in the Age of Surveillance
Bruce Schneier, David Banisar
O'Reilly, 1996, ISBN 1-56592-148-8

Web Security & Commerce   P:B
Simson Garfinkel, Gene Spafford
O'Reilly, 1997, ISBN 1-56592-269-7

Chapter 25:
Contact Information

If I have seen farther than others,
it is because I was standing on the shoulder of giants.

– Isaac Newton

If I have not seen as far as others,
it is because giants were standing on my shoulders.

– Hal Abelson

In computer science, we stand on each other's feet.

– Brian K. Reid

Addison-Wesley

Addison-Wesley
Route 128
Reading, MA 01867 USA

http://www.aw.com/
+1 800 822-6339 (USA only)
+1 617 944-3700

Apple Computer

Apple Computer, Inc.
1 Infinite Loop
Cupertino, CA 95014 USA

http://www.apple.com/
+1 408 996-1010

Cambridge

Cambridge University Press
40 West 20th Street
New York, NY 10011-4211 USA

information@cup.org
http://www.cup.org/
+1 212 924-3900
+1 212 691-3239 Fax

Coriolis

Coriolis Group Books
7339 E. Acoma Dr., #7
Scottsdale, AZ 85260 USA

http://www.coriolis.com/
+1 800 410-0192 (USA only)
+1 602 483-0192

Free Software Foundation

See GNU Project

GNU Project

The GNU Project
59 Temple Place, Suite 330
Boston, MA 02111-1307 USA

gnu@prep.ai.mit.edu
ftp://prep.ai.mit.edu/pub/gnu/
http://www.gnu.ai.mit.edu/
+1 617 542-5942, -2652 Fax

IDG Books

IDG Books Worldwide, Inc.
919 E. Hillsdale Blvd., Suite 400
Foster City, CA 94404 USA

feedback@www.idgbooks.com
http://www.idgbooks.com/
+1 800 762-2974 (USA only)
+1 415 655-3000

International Data Group

See IDG Books

John Wiley & Sons

See Wiley

MIS Press

MIS Press
115 West 18th Street
New York, NY 10011 USA

mispress@interport.com
http://www.mispress.com/

MIT Press

MIT Press
55 Hayward Street
Cambridge, MA 02142 USA

mitpress-orders@mit.edu
http://mitpress.mit.edu/
+1 800 356-0343 (USA only)
+1 617 625-8569

Morgan Kaufman

Morgan Kaufmann Publishers Inc.
340 Pine St, 6th floor
San Francisco, CA 94104 USA

orders@mkp.com
http://www.mkp.com/
+1 415 392-2665
+1 415 982-2665 Fax

New Riders

New Riders Publishing

info@mcp.com

201 West 103rd St.
Indianapolis, IN 46290 USA

O'Reilly

O'Reilly & Associates
103A Morris Street
Sebastopol, CA 95472 USA

http://www.mcp.com/newriders/

nuts@oreilly.com
ftp://ftp.oreilly.com/
http://www.oreilly.com/
+1 800 998-9938 (USA only)
+1 707 829-0515, -0104 Fax

Osborne/McGraw-Hill

Osborne/McGraw-Hill
2600 Tenth Street, Sixth Floor
Berkeley, CA 94710 USA

http://www.osborne.com/
+1 800 227-0900

Prentice Hall

Prentice Hall
113 Sylvan Avenue, Rt. 9W
Englewood Cliffs, NJ 07632 USA

orders@prenhall.com
http://www.prenhall.com/
+1 800 947-7700 (USA only)
+1 201 592-2000

Prime Time Freeware

Prime Time Freeware
370 Altair Way, Suite 150
Sunnyvale, CA 94086 USA

info@ptf.com
http://www.ptf.com/
+1 408 433-9662, -0727 Fax

QUE

QUE Corporation
11711 N. College Ave.
Carmel, IN 46032 USA

info@mcp.com
http://www.mcp.com/que/
+1 317 573-2500, -2583 Fax
+1 800 428-5331

SAMS

Sams Publishing
201 West 103rd St.
Indianapolis, IN 46290 USA

info@mcp.com
http://www.mcp.com/sams/
+1 317 573-2500, -2583 Fax
+1 800 428-5331

Springer-Verlag

Springer-Verlag
175 5th Avenue
Attn: Computer Science
New York, NY 10010 USA

custserv@spint.compuserve.com
http://www.springer.de/
+1 800 SPRINGER (USA only)

Sybex

Sybex, Inc.
1151 Marina Village Parkway
Alameda, CA 94501 USA

info@sybex.com
http://www.sybex.com/
+1 510 523-8233, -6840 Fax

Thomson

Intl. Thomson Computer Press
20 Park Plaza, 14th Floor
Boston, MA USA

http://www.itp.de/

USENIX

The USENIX Association
2560 Ninth Street, Suite 215
Berkeley, CA 94710 USA

office@usenix.org
http://www.usenix.org/
+1 510 528-8649
+1 510 548-5738 Fax

Walnut Creek CDROM

Walnut Creek CDROM
4041 Pike Lane, Suite D
Concord, CA 94520 USA

orders@cdrom.com
ftp://ftp.cdrom.com/
http://www.cdrom.com/
+1 800 786-9907 (USA only)
+1 510 674-0821 Fax

Wiley

John Wiley & Sons, Inc.
605 Third Ave.
New York, NY 10158-0012 USA

info@qm.jwiley.com
http://www.wiley.com/
+1 212 850-6000, -6088 Fax

Ziff-Davis

Ziff-Davis Press
5903 Christie Ave.
Emeryville, CA 94608 USA

info@mcp.com
http://www.mcp.com/zdpress/
+1 800 688-0448 (USA only)

Who We Are ...

Vicki Brown (vlb@cfcl.com) has been using Unix (and variants thereof) for nearly 15 years; she began programming in awk and sh almost from the beginning. Vicki has also been working with Macs for 11 years, both in the employ of Apple Computer, and in her personal life. The Mac OS is her second favorite operating system and favorite user interface.

Vicki started using MacPerl in 1995, when she needed to crunch a large quantity of spreadsheet data. Resisting the idea of learning Excel macros, she leaped into MacPerl. She soon discovered that Perl allowed her to perform almost any programming task on the (shell-less, awk-less) Macintosh. Vicki lives in San Bruno, California with her spouse, Rich Morin, several cats, and many computers, including multiple Macintoshes.

Jerry Jager (jager@cfcl.com), of Jager Communications, solves various design issues for us. In particular, he designed this book's cover layout.

Rich Morin (rdm@ptf.com) has used scripting languages for 30 years, starting with Stanford's experimental Wylbur system. He does all of his serious programming in Perl these days, using both Macintosh and Unix systems.

Rich writes a monthly column (I/Opener) for SunExpert Magazine and has written many articles for other industry publications. In his spare time, he operates Prime Time Freeware (www.ptf.com) and provides laps for cats.

Chris Nandor (pudge@pobox.com) is the webmaster and head web developer for Peterson's, an educational publishing company in Princeton, NJ. A 1995 Journalism graduate of Biola University, Chris now telecommutes full-time from his home in Carver, MA.

Chris has been working with Macs for 10 years and MacPerl for two years. He has spent much of his time over the last year working with MacPerl and Apple Events and, in fact, has written an article on the subject for The Perl Journal (December, 1997).

Matthias Neeracher (neeri@iis.ee.ethz.ch) is a Perl hacker trapped in a graduate student's body. He began MacPerl in 1991, as a project to do on weekends while serving in the Swiss Army. To the great benefit of the MacPerl community, Matthias has continued work on the project to this day. He says that he never leaves home without a Swiss Army Knife.

Delight Prescott has always had a great love of Fantasy. She knows that there has to be a place where there is magic, and things are fun most of the time, and exciting the rest of the time, even if only in our imagination.

Delight has been painting and selling her fantasy art for over 20 years, and still loves what she does. In her work, inspired by the fabulous artists who illustrated fairy-tale books around the turn of the century, she continues to try and capture the magic and mischief of a made-up world. Delight's work may be seen at www.professional.org/delight/.

The artwork on the front cover, entitled "Escape", shows a young wizard escaping from a stormy, lightning-blasted sky. His refuge is the daytime universe, complete with a castle which could be taken from the tales of Scheherazade. It is a beautiful city of foreign intrigue, with pristine snow-covered alps in the background. It symbolizes an escape from something very unpleasant into an idyllic place.

The artwork on the back flap, entitled "Dragonlord", depicts a wizard who is completely comfortable with his dragon and firelizards. He is in total control and his dragons show both affection and ease around him.

Prime Time Freeware (info@ptf.com; www.ptf.com) publishes books and CD-ROMs that are related to freely redistributable software (freeware). PTF is always looking for product ideas; if you would like to see a product happen (or better, would like to work on one!), please let us know.

"Where shall I begin, please your Majesty?" he asked.
"Begin at the beginning." the King said, gravely,
"and go on till you come to the end: then stop."

Lewis Carroll, *Alice's Adventures in Wonderland*

Notes

Index